Preaching Peace in

Renaissance Italy

Sano di Pietro, "La Predica di San Bernardino nella Piazza di San Francesco" (Bernardino preaching in the Piazza of San Francesco). The painting is in the Museo dell'Opera del Duomo in Siena. Courtesy of Foto Lensiini.

Cynthia L. Polecritti

Preaching Peace in Renaissance Italy

Bernardino of Siena &

His Audience

The Catholic University of America Press
Washington, D.C.

Library of Congress Cataloging-in-Publication Data

Polecritti, Cynthia L., 1954–

　　Preaching peace in Renaissance Italy : Bernardino of Siena and his
audience / Cynthia Polecritti.

　　　　p.　cm.

　　Includes bibliographical references and index.

　　1. Bernardino, da Siena, Saint, 1380–1444.　2. Reconciliation—
Religious aspects—Catholic Church—History of doctrines.

3. Christian saints—Italy Biography.　I. Title.

BX4700.B55P65　2000

282'.092—dc21

[B]

99-36513

ISBN 0-8132-0960-9 (alk. paper)

For my grandparents, Anna Yanok Kostic (1908–1986) and Michael Kostic (1915–1991), and my sister, Jacqueline Moyer (1944–1990), with loving gratitude

Contents

Acknowledgments

This book could not have been completed without the long-term support of my friends, family, and students.

Many thanks, too, to those friends and colleagues at the University of California, Santa Cruz who read and commented on the manuscript: Jon Beecher, María Elena Diáz, Lisbeth Haas, Gail Hershatter, Peter Kenez, Buchanan Sharp, and Lynn Westerkamp. Daniel Bornstein, Thomas Cohen, Robert Davis, and several anonymous readers made valuable suggestions as the manuscript circulated for tenure and for publication.

The diligence of my student research assistants over the years—Rick Court, Donna-Renee Martin, Melody Moss, Hannah Schardt, and Tina Wirth—saved me much time in the library, and the support and concern of my graduate students Melody Moss and Tina Wirth have been much appreciated. Another former student, Molly Newman, worked on the bibliography while she was awaiting the birth of her son. The cheerful efficiency of Candace Freiwald, of Stevenson College, eased all the tasks associated with an ongoing project. I especially thank Cheryl Van De Veer of Santa Cruz's Document Publishing and Editing Center for her patience and precision as she readied the manuscript for publication. Her colleague Zoe Sodja also deserves thanks for her work on an earlier version during my tenure review.

Several institutions made this book possible. Research grants from the University of California, Berkeley enabled me to spend two irreplaceable years in Siena in 1982–84 when I was a graduate student, while subsequent grants from the Academic Senate at Santa Cruz provided financial support and course relief. Thanks to Siena's Museo dell'Opera del Duomo, Museo Civico, and Foto Lensini for permission to reproduce the photographs. I have spent many peaceful hours in Siena's Biblioteca Comunale degli Intronati, thanks to the helpfulness of its staff.

The ideas in this book were formulated during its first incarnation as a Ph.D. thesis at Berkeley, and I am especially indebted to the friends and colleagues I met as a graduate student. I was privileged to be trained at Berkeley in the late 1970s through the 1980s, when my peers and I were exposed to new methodologies but never abandoned the steady anchor of social history, even when our work moved in different directions. My dissertation was nurtured by the support of the Women's Medieval and Renaissance Thesis Group, whose members included Katherine Christensen, Jessica Coope, Suzanne Desan, Helen Ettlinger, Paula Findlen, Margaret Malamud, the late Mary Mansfield, Karin McHardy, Karen Scott, Elizabeth Sloane Haugen, Carol Staswick, Sharon Strocchia, and Vie-Vie Wang. Many years later, I still miss the intellectual companionship and lively conversation we enjoyed at our monthly dinner parties. Stephen Greenblatt, Virginia Hanger, Mike Hakkenberg, Mimi Kusch, and Steve Kusch also read the thesis, while countless discussions over the years with my friends Katherine Christensen, Steve Kusch, and Karen Scott were invaluable in shaping my approach to history.

Finally, my teachers at Berkeley provided models of scholarship: William Bouwsma for his intellectual rigor and attention to the larger, human issues within historiographical debates; Peter Brown for his insistence on a profound reading of the sources and a creative eclecticism in the use of anthropology, as well as his kind encouragement of this project. My greatest intellectual debt over the years has been to my mentor, Gene Brucker, whose generous support, professionalism, and deep love of Italy have been an inspiration to his students. *Mille grazie.*

Abbreviations

For the reader's convenience, I cite Bernardino's sermons by place preached, date, volume, and page. For example: Siena 1427, I, 95.

The published editions of the vernacular sermons are:

Le prediche volgari (Florence 1424). Ed. Ciro Cannarozzi. 2 vols. Pistoia: Pacinotti, 1934.

Le prediche volgari (Florence 1425). Ed. Ciro Cannarozzi. 3 vols. Florence: Libreria Editrice Fiorentina, 1940.

Le prediche volgari (Siena 1425). Ed. Ciro Cannarozzi. 2 vols. Florence: Rinaldi, 1958.

Prediche volgari sul Campo di Siena 1427. Ed. Carlo Delcorno. 2 vols. Milan: Rusconi, 1989.

OTHER ABBREVIATIONS ARE:

AFH	*Archivum franciscanum historicum*
Cateriniano-Bernardiniano	*Atti del simposio internazionale cateriniano-bernardiniano (Siena, 17–20 aprile 1980)*. Ed. Domenico Maffei and Paolo Nardi. Siena: Accademia Senese degli Intronati, 1982.
Siena Biblioteca	Biblioteca Comunale degli Intronati di Siena

Preaching Peace in
Renaissance Italy

Introduction

*P*ossibly the most seductive image in all of Sienese painting is the figure of Pax in Ambrogio Lorenzetti's "Allegory of Good Government." Unlike the stalwart postures of her more vigilant (and virginal) sisters on the right side of the fresco, her body reclines luxuriously on an embroidered cushion, one arm supporting her pretty head while the other negligently holds a branch of olives. Pax is magnificently at ease: transparent, clinging drapery defines the curve of breast and thigh, her knees are slightly apart, her forearms exposed. Most of the other allegorical figures stare directly at the viewer in a stern warning, but she gazes at the wall on the viewer's right, towards Lorenzetti's companion fresco of "Good Government in the City." Clearly she finds nothing to worry about in this ideal Siena where trade and festivity flourish. Pax has not a care in the world.[1]

1. Quentin Skinner, emphasizing prehumanist political ideology, characterizes Peace's repose as a kind of victory stance; see "Ambro-

The artist chose to portray Peace as a lovely and tantalizing woman whom everyone desires, but Pax was an elusive lady. Fifteen years after this fresco was painted, the government which commissioned it was overthrown by a bloody revolt.[2] *Buon governo*—that ideal of a benevolent commune presiding over peaceful and united citizens—was a state dreamed of by both poets and practical men. But the sweet dream of peace presented a melancholy dilemma for Italy in the later middle ages. Dante in rage could demand of her:

Cerca, misera, intorno dalle prode
le tue marine, e poi ti guarda in seno,
s'alcuna parte in te pace gode.

[Search, wretched one, round the shores
of thy seas, then look within thy bosom,
if any part of thee rejoice in peace . . .][3]

The answer could only be "No." And most of this agony was self-inflicted: for Dante, the greatest enemy was the one within, that civil strife which lacerated the peace of the cities. Among the most gruesome images in the Inferno are the Sowers of Discord, whose dismembered bodies and gaping wounds are signs of the divisions they had spawned in life.

Contemporaries and historians alike agree that many Italian cities were characterized by violence, both personal and political; vendetta

gio Lorenzetti: The Artist as Political Philosopher," Proceedings of the British Academy 72 (1986): 1–56. Earlier discussions of the political content of the Lorenzetti frescoes focus on Thomist-Aristotelian influences; for example, see Nicolai Rubinstein, "Political Ideas in Sienese Art: The Frescoes by Ambrogio Lorenzetti and Taddeo di Bartolo in the Palazzo Pubblico," Journal of the Warburg and Courtauld Institutes 21, no. 1–2 (1958): 179–207. For the underlying cultural content of the frescoes, see Loren Partridge and Randolph Starn, *Arts of Power: Three Halls of State in Italy, 1300–1600* (Berkeley and Los Angeles: University of California Press, 1992), 11–80.

2. William M. Bowsky, *A Medieval Italian Commune: Siena Under the Nine, 1287–1355* (Berkeley and Los Angeles: University of California Press, 1981), 299–306.

3. Dante, *Purgatorio*, trans. and commentary by John D. Sinclair (New York: Mentor, 1961), 84–85.

and faction can almost be seen as part of the geographical setting, a natural feature of the historical landscape. Communal governments, however, kept struggling to secure peace, their efforts ranging from confiscation and exile (these being, admittedly, yet another sign of factional conflict) to the establishment of official *pacieri*, or peacemakers. But there were also far more dramatic attempts to pacify community hatreds. Italy in the late Middle Ages witnessed a series of charismatic preachers who tried to reform society in one grand gesture. Fiery words delivered by holy men in the churches and piazze were often followed by emotional repentance and the kiss of peace in mass reconciliations that could lead to a real, though temporary, lull in urban tensions.

The relative sameness of these events, coupled with our knowledge that their effects were fleeting, explains why historians have seldom examined them closely. Jacques Heers dismissed them as "mystical rites which were in the last analysis inconsequential."[4] Surely this is an overhasty judgment. Aside from the fact that clerical peacemakers often collaborated with secular authorities, the very recurrence of these "mystical rites" over a long period of time suggests an importance that went beyond absolute "success" or "failure." The preachers were clearly speaking to deep-rooted impulses in their society, their call for peace one acceptable answer to Dante's search for the impossible. Not only does the reception of the preachers' message tell us much about popular devotion, but the structure of the peacemakings themselves reveals how Italians tried to control a tense social reality.

4. Jacques Heers, *Parties and Political Life in the Medieval West*, trans. David Nicholas (Amsterdam: North Holland Publishing Company, 1977), 205. A few historians, however, are beginning to take the phenomenom of religious peacemaking seriously: Augustine Thompson, O.P., examines thirteenth-century peacemakers in *Revival Preachers and Politics in Thirteenth-Century Italy: The Great Devotion of 1233* (Oxford: Oxford University Press, 1992), while Daniel Bornstein traces the evolution of the Bianchi penitential movement and its mission of social peace in *The Bianchi of 1399: Popular Devotion in Late Medieval Italy* (Ithaca, NY: Cornell University Press, 1993). Jennifer Selwyn provides an invaluable southern Italian perspective in her study of peacemaking Jesuits: "Planting Many Virtues There: Jesuit Popular Missions in the Viceroyalty of Naples, 1550–1700" (Ph.D. diss., University of California, Davis, 1997).

Preaching peacemakers still played a vigorous role as late as the fifteenth century. In fact, thanks to the Observant reform movement, Italy experienced a resurgence of popular preaching which rivaled the days of the earliest friars. City after city found these new holy men to be attractive partners in their attempts to quell social discord, and eagerly solicited their help. It is significant, then, that the greatest peacemaker of the Quattrocento also became its most representative saint.

On the evening of May 20, 1444, in a convent just outside the city of L'Aquila in the Abruzzi, the Franciscan preacher and holy man Bernardino Albizzeschi died. He died as he had lived, rejecting the world and its comforts, insisting like Francis of Assisi that his last bed be the ground itself. The odor of sanctity which surrounded the corpse was the first sign that here indeed lay the remains of a saint: although the body lay exposed for days, it emitted no foul smell. Miracles of healing took place immediately.

News of Bernardino's death spread rapidly throughout the Italian peninsula. Those places which had enjoyed a special relationship to the deceased, particularly his native town of Siena, had great cause to rejoice, since they believed they had a new advocate in Heaven. Memorial festivities were ordered by the Sienese government and an attempt was made to retrieve the body from L'Aquila, but the Aquilesi had no intention of surrendering their newly aquired holy flesh. The Sienese and other friends of Bernardino quickly exerted pressure for canonization. Just six years after his death, popular acclamation received the official seal of approval when Pope Nicholas V canonized the Sienese hero.[5]

5. For the miracles, see the accounts in the lives by Barnabò da Siena and Maffeo Vegio: *Acta Sanctorum*, Maii tomus V, die vigesima (Paris and Rome: V. Palme, 1866), 112–14 and 130–35. For the list of miracles in the canonization trials published by Celestino Piana, see "I processi di canonizzazione su la vita di S. Bernardino da Siena," *AFH* 44 (1951): 114–17. A. Liberati discusses the canonization proceedings in "Le vicende sulla canonizzazione di S. Bernardino," *Bullettino di Studi Bernardiniani* 2 (1936): 91–108; relevant documents are in "Le prime manifestazioni di devozione dopo la morte di S. Bernardino," *Bullettino Sanese di Storia Patria* 2 (1936): 149–61. Daniel Arasse analyzes the celebrations which took place after Bernardino's death in "Fervebat Pietate

This remarkably short waiting period between death and canonization marks Bernardino as a supremely successful saint whose reputation as a living holy man and subsequent cult were linked together almost seamlessly.[6] He thus belongs to that elite company of saints who
are fully acknowledged in their own time. Aside from a few dissenting
voices from rival clerics, there clearly was a happy consensus in 1450
among church officials, secular authorities, and devotees; behind
Bernardino's triumph must have stood an exceedingly satisfied clientele. From the suppliants healed at his tomb to the thousands of
tough mercantile elites who had once been stirred by his preaching,
Bernardino, alive or dead, provided something for almost everyone.

His biography, in fact, can serve as a pristine model of effortless
sainthood. The earliest hagiographers record no real inner struggle as
is so often found in the lives of charismatic figures, no sudden revulsion against a previous way of life. Unlike the carefree youth of Francis or the soul-searching of Ignatius Loyola, Bernardino's childhood
and early maturity were free of both self-indulgence and recriminations: he is portrayed as a *puer senex*, preternaturally wise and good.
Like his earlier compatriot Catherine of Siena, he was—or so claims
Leonardo Benvoglienti, who wrote a biography less than two years after Bernardino's death—an exceptionally religious child and adolescent whose quick intelligence and ascetic behavior were encouraged by
his guardians. As a young boy, he supposedly practiced charity by sav-
ing his own food as alms for the poor, stoned ardent homosexuals who
were attracted to his good looks, and enjoyed "preaching" to his
youthful companions. Even his birth date, September 8th, the Nativi-

---

Populus: Art, devotion, et societé autour de la glorification de S. Bernardin de Sienne,"
Mélanges de l'École Francaise de Rome (Moyen-Age et Temps Modernes) 89, no. 1 (1977): 189–233.

6. Peter Burke criticizes the methodology of those who deal with the sociology of
sainthood and forget to ask whether saints reveal the values of their own age or of that
in which they were canonized; "How to Be a Counter-Reformation Saint," in *The Historical Anthropology of Early Modern Italy: Essays on Perception and Communication* (Cambridge:
Cambridge University Press, 1987), 52. Bernardino's situation is a rare one—increas-
ingly so in the early modern period; he is one of the last of the great saints who was
quickly and fully appreciated on both the popular and the bureaucratic levels.

ty of the Virgin, augured his commitment to the Queen of Heaven
and her Son, while his one romance was a devotion to a portrait of
Mary painted on Siena's Porta Camollia. There seems to have been no
familial conflict over his decision to enter the clergy. The only meager
food for a psychohistorian is his upbringing by a solicitous group of
pious women.

Bernardino's sanctity was seemingly unruffled by any major *crise de
conscience.* His entrance into public life was instead an act of heroic
charity: just twenty years old, he spent months in Siena's Ospedale di
Santa Maria della Scala nursing plague victims in the scourge of 1400,
becoming seriously ill as a result. But if he experienced a dark night of
the soul neither his hagiographers nor his sermons tell us anything
about it. On the eve of manhood, his only psychological dilemma was
a brief moment of indecision about which religious order would suit
him best. Two years after his experience in the Ospedale, he formally
entered the Franciscan order.[7]

Bernardino chose to follow one of the strictest paths available to
him at the beginning of the Quattrocento. The Observants of the late
Trecento had played an important role in the revitalization of the
Franciscans. The Umbrian Paoluccio de' Trinci (d. 1390) and his followers had restored both austerity and spiritual idealism to an order
which had grown fat and complacent. When Gregory XI gave them
permission in 1373 to live in their own communities and to follow a
stricter version of the Rule, the Observants were able to revive the soul

---

7. The story of Bernardino's youth is told by Leonardo Benvoglienti, "Vie de Saint
Bernardin," ed. Francois Van Ortroy, *Analecta Bollandiana* 21 (1902): 53–80. An early and
detailed biography in Italian is Felice Alessio, *Storia di San Bernardino da Siena e del suo tempo* (Mondovi: Tipografia B. Graziano, 1899); in English, A. G. Ferrers-Howell, *San
Bernardino of Siena* (London: Methuen, 1913) is superior but, like Alessio's, tinged with
hagiography. The best introduction to Bernardino's life, including an overview of his
preaching, is still Iris Origo, *The World of San Bernardino* (New York: Harcourt, Brace,
and World, 1962). Franco Mormando provides a concise biography in his study of
Bernardino's preaching against witches, homosexuals, and Jews. See *The Preacher's
Demons: Bernardino of Siena and the Social Underworld of Early Renaissance Italy* (Chicago: University of Chicago Press, 1999), 29–38.

of their spiritual forebears, this time purged of heresy and committed to obedience as well as poverty. The renewed asceticism of the friars helped win back popular favor while their orthodoxy made them fierce soldiers against the remaining Fraticelli heretics. Although Observant fervor would gradually decline and the friars drift back into a more comfortable existence, for much of the fifteenth century they followed the pattern of Saint Francis, rejecting the world for themselves yet embracing it as preachers and social activists. Just as Francis had satisfied the needs of thirteenth-century city dwellers, so did the Observance do the same for the Quattrocento. What it ultimately gave to urban Italy were some of the greatest voices in the history of Catholic preaching. Many of the Quattrocento's most exciting preachers were reform Franciscans, especially Giovanni da Capestrano, Giacomo delle Marche, and Alberto da Sarteano. But the preaching of the Observants would find its greatest expression in Bernardino of Siena.[8]

In the process of becoming a preacher, Bernardino rose to a high position within the order. As the well-educated son of the noble Albizzeschi, he possessed both learning and tact, and eventually became the vicar of the Tuscan Observants (1414). If there was a real turning point in his adult life, however, it did not come until he was already thirty-seven years old. A novice's prophetic outcry instructed him to leave his convent in Fiesole and go to Lombardy to preach. In 1417 Bernardino thus began the most successful part of an already flourishing career. He attracted enormous crowds, first in the north and then in central Italy, his visits enlivened by great bonfires of vanities and often culminating in mass peacemakings. Aiding the celebrity preacher in his mission of peace and penitence was his propagation of the Holy Name of Jesus, symbolized in a concrete way by a tavoletta with the monogram YHS, designed by himself and dramatically displayed to

---

8. The early Observant movement is summarized by John Moorman, *A History of the Franciscan Order from Its Origins to the Year 1517* (Oxford: Clarendon Press, 1968); also see Arthur Fisher, "The Franciscan Observants in Quattrocento Tuscany" (Ph.D diss., University of California, Berkeley, 1978).

the audience at key points during his sermons. Bernardino hoped that the YHS, its golden letters and rays surrounded by a blue field, would become a substitute for factional emblems. A sure sign of its success in the public imagination was that rivals smelled idol worship and succeeded in getting Bernardino charged with heresy, first in 1426 and then again in 1431. In both cases, the solidly orthodox Bernardino was cleared by the pope.[9] Thanks to the YHS, which served as an emotional trigger for his listeners, and to his powerful preaching style, he continued to bring in the crowds.

Bernardino was constantly on the move during most of the 1420s and often thereafter, urging sinners throughout north and central Italy to abandon their vices and preaching against faction in the Franciscan spirit of *carità*. In addition to his preaching forays, he found the time to become one of the leaders of the Observance and the first person to serve as Vicar-General (1438–42). He also managed to write the many volumes of his Latin sermons and treatises at his home base of La Capriola in the peaceful Sienese hills. His busy life and the immense satisfactions it gave him compelled Bernardino to refuse the three bishoprics of Siena, Ferrara, and Urbino so that he could remain an active preacher. This intense commitment to preaching lasted until the end of his life when, very ill, he decided to evangelize southern Italy rather than die comfortably at La Capriola.[10] From one stage to another in Bernardino's life there was only an unmistakable progression from holy childhood to holy orders, from famous preacher to saint.

A widespread popular cult and the quick canonization guaranteed that the saint would soon outdistance memories of the man. Soon after his death there was a proliferation of hagiography, *laude*, and ser-

9. Ephrem Longpré, "S. Bernardin de Sienne e le nom de Jesus," *AFH* 29 (1936): 142–68, 443–77, and 30 (1937): 170–92 tells the story of the YHS controversy, with related documents.

10. He may have left Siena because he did not relish the inevitable demands which would be made on his corpse. Bernardino knew how the idolization process worked and, even during his lifetime, felt suffocated by individuals who pressed him for help after his preaching.

mons in his honor, and Saint Bernardino was comfortably enshrined in the Franciscan pantheon alongside Francis and Anthony of Padua as the epitome of asceticism and peace. In Siena, this image was supplemented by the ubiquitous pictures of a frail and toothless holy man painted by the local artist Sano di Pietro. Bernardino is in fact one of the earliest saints for whom we have some rough idea of his physiognomy, thanks to the many portraits by artists who had actually seen him, but his very individual features quickly became stylized into a type: the gaunt Observant with his readily identifiable symbol, the YHS tavoletta.[11] Within a few short years, the man was transformed into an icon.

Bernardino's success as a major saint who was venerated in many parts of Italy reveals much about the religious ideals of the Quattrocento, a time when cultural values were undergoing rapid change on several fronts. While a sharply individual personality emerged when he preached, his persona nonetheless fulfilled a series of conventions. His sainthood was "porous," with his life and his subsequent reputation absorbing many religious currents, both old and new. His brand of holiness was an adaptable one: the ascetic public image, embodied in his doleful portraits, placed him securely in the tradition of world-renouncing holy men, while his preaching on contemporary issues situated him in the sophisticated urban world. His learning and eloquence elicited praise from humanists at the same time as his crowd-pleasing tactics satisfied the average listener.[12] Skillfully donning the

11. The body which lies in the magnificent tomb in L'Aquila is recognizably Bernardino's; compare the refined features of the corpse with those of the nearby death mask (and with the Sienese portraits). For the saint in fifteenth-century art, see Daniel Arasse, "Saint Bernardin ressemblant: La Figure sous la portrait," *Cateriniano-Bernardiniano*, 311–32.

12. Vespasiano da Bisticci, the Florentine *cartolaio* and biographer, fondly remembered Bernardino's visits to his shop in a relaxed portrait of the preacher arguing with the humanist Giannozzo Manetti; see *Vite dei uomini illustri del secolo XV*, ed. Paola D'Ancona and Erhard Aeschlimann (Milan: Ulrico Hoepli, 1951), 139. Diana Webb has shown how Bernardino was a modern saint with great appeal to humanists like his biographer Maffeo Vegio; see "Eloquence and Education: A Humanist Approach to Hagiography," *Journal of Ecclesiastical History* 31, no. 1 (January 1980): 19–39.

robes of an inspired prophet when it suited him, he also gained respect as an administrator. It is noteworthy that the two most important male saints of the Quattrocento, Bernardino and Antoninus, were practical men who moved easily within the secular world; neither inhabited the margins, either socially or psychologically.[13] His flexibility is best seen in his preaching: he designed rituals which inspired dramatic displays of group piety, but his words always emphasized individual conversion. Even though he cunningly employed visual devices such as the YHS and the public bonfire, Bernardino, a century before Erasmus and Luther, directed his listeners' attention towards the Word. As he somewhat daringly advised, it was better to miss the Mass than the sermon.[14] In his view, attendance at sermons was crucial because it enabled the soul to free itself from the darkness of ignorance. Thus, in his emphasis upon an intensely personal faith and in his optimism about the power of education, Bernardino shared in the most progressive ideas of his time.

The very difficulty of neatly categorizing Bernardino is what makes him so valuable in understanding fifteenth-century religion. As his sermons show us again and again, the most striking aspect of belief in the Renaissance is its complexity, the ability to blend together what appear to the modern eye as conflicting belief systems.[15] Centuries of

13. Despite his emaciated appearance, few saints could be further from the extreme ascetics of the fourteenth century than the practical and straightforward Bernardino; contrast the Trecento figures profiled by Richard Kieckhefer in *Unquiet Souls: Fourteenth-Century Saints and Their Religious Milieu* (Chicago: University of Chicago Press, 1984). For Antoninus's thought and its social context, see Peter Francis Howard, *Beyond the Written Word: Preaching and Theology in the Florence of Archbishop Antoninus, 1427–1459* (Florence: L. S. Olschki, 1995).

14. Siena 1427, I, 149.

15. The best introduction to popular devotion in the Renaissance is now Bornstein's *The Bianchi of 1399*; see his astute comments on the relationship between "popular" and "orthodox," 3–7. The wide-ranging articles in *Christianity and the Renaissance: Image and Religious Imagination in the Quattrocento*, ed. Timothy Verdon and John Henderson (Syracuse, NY: Syracuse University Press, 1990), give a good idea of the varied religious experiences available to fifteenth-century Italians.

tradition are mixed, sometimes uneasily, with the new demands posed by a secular world. Although the model of the spectacularly ascetic saint was still valid, Bernardino and his fellow Observants became so popular because they were able to speak to contemporary needs even as they provided traditional reassurance.[16] This is illustrated by the most famous passage in all of Bernardino's sermons—the humorous description of his own venture into the solitary life. As a fervent young man, he decided to go into the "wilderness," attempting to make himself more "angel than man." Leaving Siena by the Porta Tufi, he heroically walked off into the countryside with the intention of subsisting only on wild herbs and thistles. But this angel's flesh proved weaker than the spirit; as Bernardino wryly told a Sienese audience in 1427, when he tried to eat a handful of thistles,

> I placed it in my mouth and began to chew . . . chewing, chewing . . . but it wouldn't go down![17]

It is a telling point. The extravagant heroism of the Desert Fathers was not to be his. The decision to wander in the "desert" was made in a confident assessment of his powers, but the solitary life would prove uncongenial to a man who would eventually seek salvation through his preaching of social community. Bernardino's chosen social space was not the desert but the piazza.

More importantly, the story shows the preacher's understanding of human limitations. Bernardino constantly advised his listeners to do

16. Catherine Fieschi of Genoa (1447–1510) would still attempt to fit the pattern of the self-denying ascetic, disciplining both her will and her natural revulsion by forcing herself to eat the lice of the desperately ill people she tended. On the other hand, her initial extreme fasting soon gave way to a somewhat more moderate regime and to the charitable impulse which would animate the rest of her life; see Kenneth Jorgensen, S.J., " 'Love Conquers All': The Conversion, Asceticism, and Altruism of St. Catherine of Genoa," *Renaissance Society and Culture: Essays in Honor of Eugene F. Rice, Jr.*, ed. John Monfasani and Ronald G. Musto (New York: Italica Press, 1991), 87–106.

17. ". . . messemela in bocca cominciai a masticarla . . . Mastica, mastica . . . , ella non poteva andare giù." The wry admission is told in its entirety in Siena 1427, II, 788–90.

what they could, even as he acknowledged their worries about salvation. This intimate glimpse into a personal "failure" was intended to reassure them that the path to goodness was not as strenuous as they feared. The rejection of the world implied in his vocation and strictly maintained in his own virginal body was thus always a qualified rejection. It is true that he made many converts to the Observance, but most of his preaching was designed to convince average people that salvation was also available to them. This means that although Bernardino could judiciously employ the threat of hellfire, he—like other successful preachers—was as concerned with this world as with the Judgment to come. On the other hand, he never stopped giving a fresh voice to time-honored beliefs. The magnificent peacemaking sermon which is the climax of his visit to Siena in 1427 is effective because it is a moving discourse on the impermanence of worldly happiness.

It was, in fact, the fragile balance between acceptance and rejection of this world which made Bernardino such an effective preacher for his time, and such an elusive figure today. For just when it seems as if we have captured the essential man beneath the flexible preacher, he slips out of our grasp. It comes as a shock, for example, to hear an Observant Franciscan routinely coupling spiritual and material rewards for good behavior, even if we remember that many in his audience saw their religion as a way to manipulate the divine for secular ends. A rigorist even within his own times, this apostle of *carità* ruthlessly demanded that homosexuals and witches be burned alive. And Bernardino avidly campaigned against what he regarded as "superstition," but could still tell hair-raising stories which partook of the same belief system he was supposedly fighting against. One of the most vivid examples is his tale of the blasphemer who calls on a devil, and who is then mauled and killed by a demon in the form of a winged griffin. The incident took place in 1414, Bernardino says, and he had it on good faith from the priest, Don Jacopo, to whom the dying man confessed.[18]

18. Siena 1425, I, 177–78.

Bernardino's inner paradoxes are nowhere more apparent than in his discussion of civil discord. It would seem that this, of all subjects, should have received straightforward treatment from the great peacemaker; indeed, most of his preaching on the themes of vendetta, faction, and forgiveness was a conventional, if fervent, restatement of Christian precepts. But Bernardino, so aware of the living audience before him, could make subtle adjustments which reflected what his listeners were willing to hear. His attitude towards vendetta, for example, was occasionally accepting. Even his conventionality shows how he could prudently stifle his customary bluntness in order to avoid giving offense; faction was discussed in a veiled way which ignored political specifics. Bernardino's preaching on civil discord was something of a tightrope walk where he clung to the thin line separating Christian idealism and social practice. On the other hand, he had a richly nuanced understanding of secular culture and its demands, particularly its pressures on men and its effects on women: his preaching on honor and the intense conflict between the public and private self spoke to tenaciously deep-rooted anxieties.

Even the contradictions and the straining points in the sermons reveal how Italians saw themselves, their God, and their relations with others. His vernacular sermons not only discussed the bonds of love and hatred, but every other social relation as well: from sex to familial ties, from the behavior of priests with their flocks to government and the treatment of criminals. Not least among these social relations was that between preacher and audience. It was the exchange which took place between them, whether articulated by Bernardino or unconsciously accepted, which molded his preaching and explains why his ideology was not always consistent with his goals.

It is the audience which must remain in the forefront of any discussion of Bernardino. In the conclusion to a study of religious visions which took place in Spain in July 1931, William Christian invites us to realize the importance of the receivers of cultural messages, religious and otherwise:

In the Basque visions and movements, general anxieties and hopes are answered by individuals with instructions said to come from God, but it seems clear that the cultural content enunciated is as much a consensual product of the followers and the wider society as of the leaders, the prophets, or the Saints. The audience, the Greek chorus, the hagiographer, the message takers and the message transmitters should be as much the focus of our attention as the charismatic figures on whom they are concentrating.[19]

The content of Bernardino's preaching and the events which took place during his sermons were shaped by the response of his listeners and by the larger culture in which both he and they were located.[20] He was never just a priest handing down stale Christian maxims, but a receptive orator who manipulated the dynamic between himself and an active crowd.

Thanks to his sermons, hundreds of which were recorded as he spoke, we can observe the reactions of his audience. These were remarkably varied, reminding us that the smooth consensus which emerged after his death camouflaged the difficulties he faced each time he stood at the pulpit. Despite his clear popularity, there was dissent as well as hostility and resistance. Candace Slater has found an analogous situation in the tales which surround a holy man in modern Spain, the local and uncanonized Fray Leon of Granada (d. 1956). Slater interviewed an array of people in Granada and discovered "counterlegends," stories that do not buy the standard line about Fray Leon. What emerges from the myriad shades of opinion among those

19. William A. Christian, Jr., "Tapping and Defining New Power: The First Month of Visions at Ezquioga, July 1931," *American Ethnologist* 14, no. 1 (February 1987), 163. Christian fully explores these visions and their political context in *Visionaries: The Spanish Republic and the Reign of Christ* (Berkeley and Los Angeles: University of California Press, 1996).

20. Daniel Lesnick has outlined a similar process occurring between fourteenth-century preachers and their Florentine audience in *Preaching in Medieval Florence: The Social World of Franciscan and Dominican Spirituality* (Athens, GA: University of Georgia Press, 1989).

who knew him personally and others who were too young, from the
stories of cynics and devotees alike, is a kind of "religious plural-
ism."[21] Public opinion in the fifteenth century was similarly nuanced,
with people having a wide range of attitudes towards even the uncon-
tested holy, such as Bernardino.[22] Not only did a variety of persons
come to his sermons, from widows to cloth cutters to humanists, but
there were surely dissonant voices and counterlegends which have been
lost. The great value of the recorded sermons is that they catch the
preacher in the act, where we see that his control of the audience,
beautifully adept for the most part, was more tenuous than either eyewitnesses or his own confident perceptions admit. When he *describes*
the act of sermon-giving, we see well-regulated listeners who behave as
they should; when we follow the undercurrents of what actually *happens*, a livelier picture emerges. It is clear that the placid consensus must
have been fragmented at times and that there were more reactions to
Bernardino than the records have left us. This is especially true in the
case of his peacemakings, where behind the idealized scenes of concord lay a tougher reality.

This study will explore the relationship between Bernardino and
his audience in their roles as peacemaker and pacified. In what ways

21. Candace Slater, *City Steeple, City Streets: Saints' Tales from Granada and a Changing
Spain* (Berkeley and Los Angeles: University of California Press, 1990). William Christian, in his early study *Person and God in a Spanish Valley* (New York: Seminar Press, 1972),
also found heterogeneity in the modern Spanish countryside: the individual testi-
monies he collected from a single village (see esp. 135–51) indicate the natural variation
in religious response that anthropologists find when they are dealing with living situations, even within traditional societies. Historians of religion and ritual, on the other
hand, sometimes ignore individual behavior in their attempt to discover a consensus
and what may well be a false "norm."

22. For a sensitive reading of the complex pressures which created "saints," see
Aviad Kleinberg, *Prophets in Their Own Country: Living Saints and the Making of Sainthood in the
Later Middle Ages* (Chicago: University of Chicago Press, 1992). Laura A. Smoller dis-
cusses the audience reaction to a great contemporary of Bernardino, in "Miracle,
Memory, and Meaning in the Canonization of Vincent Ferrer, 1453–1454," *Speculum* 73,
no. 2 (April 1998): 429–54.

did his listeners respond to his charismatic presence? What were they willing to hear about faction and vendetta? How did Bernardino persuade enemies to exchange the kiss of peace? What was the nature of the spiritual and psychological consolation he offered? The most important theme in Bernardino's peacemaking is his marriage of rhetoric and ritual, and the profound drama which emerges from their intersection with the soul. The surviving vernacular sermons permit us to follow, even if at an arduous distance, the conversion process itself. Bernardino's most famous sermons, delivered in Siena in 1427, are extraordinary not only because they are the most accurate renditions of the words of any medieval or Renaissance preacher, but because they were built around a peacemaking.[23] Besides being an opportunity to trace the way in which a great preacher moved souls, a close examination of Bernardino as peacemaker points to the many tensions which existed in a Christian culture permeated by an alternative set of values. Bernardino was not so much an elite cleric who tried to impose social control upon his listeners as a man who harboured many of their values even as he fought to change them. His sermons inevitably reveal the conflict between Christian preacher and the darker assumptions which he and his audience shared.

Yet on the surface, Bernardino and his listeners were most comfortable discussing social conflict in simple, dualistic terms. The preacher's narrative vignettes, which make him one of the great storytellers of his

23. The Siena 1427 sermons were recorded by a cloth cutter, Benedetto da maestro Bartolomeo, and Bernardino, pleased by his presence, would help him along. While we should avoid a naive reading of the text, to a certain extent the historian needs to rely on what she "hears": even more than the spontaneous interruptions and asides noted by Benedetto, the preacher's speech rhythms and sometimes awkward hesitations are convincing. However, Bernardino or his assistants might have helped Benedetto fill in gaps later. Despite the fact that these sermons are among the most important documents from the Quattrocento, historians have not analyzed them for their peacemaking content. Nor is Delcorno's excellent edition of the 1427 course matched by the other published editions of Bernardino's recorded sermons. See Franco Mormando's discussion of the *reportationes* and the problem of multiple recordings and extant manuscripts: *The Preacher's Demons*, 40–45.

age, and his mastery of visual description, serve a function far beyond entertainment. His vivid words and "painted" narratives tend to reduce complexity to images of light and darkness, creating an easily grasped moral choice and a possible conversion. Lorenzetti's frescoes, for example, provided him with fuel for his peacemaking sermons since they set up a striking opposition between Good and Evil (or War and Peace, as he incorrectly labelled them).[24] As he told a Sienese audience in 1425, he sometimes used images of their *"bellissima inventiva"* when he preached in other cities. He pleaded with his listeners to consider the straightforward alternatives of peace and discord:

> Turning towards Peace, I see merchandise circulating, I see dances, I see houses being mended, I see vineyards and fields being sowed and worked, I see girls getting married and people going on horseback to the baths, I see flocks of sheep, etc. And I see a man hanged in order to maintain holy justice . . .

But turning towards the opposite wall, the one of "The Allegory of Bad Government" which the lovely Pax so pointedly disdains:

> On the contrary, I don't see dancing, I don't see merchandise. Instead, I see men killing each other; houses aren't being prepared, but laid waste and burned. No one works the land, the vines are ripped up, no one sows. People aren't using the baths or other delights; I don't see them going outside. O men! O women! The dead man, the raped woman, no herds if not prey, men in treachery slaying one another! Justice is on the ground, her hands and feet tied, her scales broken. And everything man

---

24. John Larner says that Bernardino misread the frescoes, since they are not an allegory of "War and Peace," but of "Justice and the Common Good" (or, more schematically, of "Good and Bad Government"); *Culture and Society in Italy, 1290–1420* (New York: Scribner, 1971), 115–16. If so, this may have been a convenient misreading, since the preacher may not have wanted to emphasize "Bad Government" with Sienese officials seated in his audience. However, Jack M. Greenstein has argued that the frescoes do in fact represent "The Peaceful and the Wartorn Cities"; see "The Vision of Peace: Meaning and Representation in Ambrogio Lorenzetti's *Sala Della Pace* Cityscapes," *Art History* 2, no. 4 (December 1988): 492–510.

does he does with fear. And therefore the Apocalypse, in the 13th chapter, shows War figured as a beast who rises from the sea . . .[25]

Peace on the one hand, War on the other: Bernardino's dilemma was to persuade his listeners to make the obvious choice in their own lives. But the Beast of the Apocalypse lay within, and the intricate bonds of vendetta and faction cut too deep to be easily unloosed. Bernardino's sermons could only reflect the chasm in the minds of both preacher and audience between an imagined ideal and the social world. And yet it was the delicate interplay between them which brought about peace-makings in a society where honor, revenge, and prudent self-interest were the guiding values.

25. Siena 1425, II, 266. "Voltandomi a la pace, vego la mercanzie andare atorno; vego balli, vego racconciare le case; vego lavorare vigne e terre, seminare, andare a' bagni, a cavallo, vego andare le fanciulle a marito, vego le grege de le pecore etc. E vego impicato l'uomo per mantenere la santa giustizia. E per queste cose, ognuno sta in sante pace e concordia. Per lo contrario, voltandomi da l'altra parte, non vego mercanzie; non vego balli, anco vego uccidare altrui; non s'acconciano case, anco si guastano e ardono; non si lavora terre; le vigne si tagliano, non si semina, non s'usano e bagni nè altre cose dilettevoli, non vego se no' quando si va di fuore. O donne! O uomini! L'uomo morto, la donna sforzata, non armenti se none in preda; uomini a tradimento uccidare l'uno l'altro; la giustizia stare in terra, rotte le bilance, e lei legata, co' le mani e co' piei legati. E ogni cosa che altro fa, fa con paura. E però l'Apocalisse, decimoterzo capitolo, dimostra figurata la guerra in una bestia che esce del mare . . . "

CHAPTER ONE

The Preacher and the Crowd

"El predicatore conviene che sia come un ischermidore..."

Bernardino possessed a remarkably well-developed sense of himself as a preacher and of his listeners as active participants in the process of conversion. For him, the sermon was a decisive moment that suspended this world and provided the opportunity for a complete change from one's previous life.[1] It was, in fact, the very threshold of heaven. In 1427 he told the Sienese that their Campo, or main piazza, where he preached was a "half-paradise" surrounded by invisible presences, those

1. For the religious experience as a psychological threshold, see Victor Turner on liminality and *comunitas*, in *The Ritual Process: Structure and Anti-Structure* (Chicago: Aldine Publishing Co., 1969), 94–130, and, with Edith Turner, *Image and Pilgrimage in Christian Culture: Anthropological Perspectives* (New York: Columbia University Press, 1978).

angels from heaven eager to hear the word of God.[2] Since Bernardino shared with his audience a belief in the legitimate supernatural, there is no reason to think that these invisible spectators were anything but a reality for him. The image he cherished in his mind's eye was a holy trinity where good spirits, dutiful humans, and commanding preacher were all poised to do battle with the shadows that lay in wait. For just as there was a flock of guardian angels in attendance, so was there also a host of devils who hoped to divert their prey's attention from the sermon. This meant that constant vigilance was essential on the part of both preacher and audience.

For the most part, Bernardino felt that the enterprise was a success. The pious depictions of his preaching by the Sienese artists Sano di Pietro and Neroccio di Bartolommeo would have pleased him since they represented the sermon as he wanted it to be: the preacher in command of an orderly and attentive audience. But a *cassone* scene by Vecchietta offers an alternative viewpoint. It is a Renaissance fantasy in which the preacher is dwarfed by elaborate architecture with magnificent receding arches. The pulpit is covered with rich tapestries and heraldic trumpeters are stationed at Bernardino's right. If the setting departs from the more realistic scenes of Sano and Neroccio, Vecchietta's image is perhaps more accurate in its depiction of the audience. Instead of placid and monotonous rows of devout listeners, individuals are placed casually in the foreground, engaged in various conversations. The unmistakable impression is of a heterogeneous group with more on its mind than the tiny figure so far away.[3]

The reality of a Bernardino sermon fluctuated between this seemingly informal gathering and the intense absorption shown in the more conventional paintings. At times, the sermon became the liminal state idealized by the preacher, with people fervently responding to his words in behavior which was at once emotionally liberating and an ex-

2. Siena 1427, I, 128–29.

3. Neroccio's painting is in Siena's Palazzo Pubblico, Sano's two depictions in the Museo dell'Opera del Duomo. Vecchietta's *cassone* is in Liverpool; for a description, see Piero Misciatelli, "Cassoni Senesi," *La Diana* 4, no. 2 (1929): 117–26.

pression of civic unity. But at any point, the experience could be fragmented by skeptics, hecklers, and all those who attended sermons for other than pristine religious motives. This meant that sermon-giving always retained some element of the unpredictable and that the preacher had to respond accordingly. And most sermons functioned not just as religious event, but as entertainment; indeed, few fifteenth-century Italians would have distinguished between the two. Bernardino's audience could appreciate his preaching on many more levels than the historian who only has access to the dry manuscript page. The most memorable of his sermons ably combined the Word of God with extravagant visual display, and it is the latter which probably left the more striking impression on the average person. This means that what the historian "reads" is not necessarily what the audience "heard." Just as Michael Baxandall has shown us that it is essential to look at a fifteenth-century painting with the "cognitive style" of the Quattrocento, so must we try to listen to the sermons as they were actually preached.[4] The surviving vernacular sermons and several vivid eyewitness accounts can recreate, at least in a limited way, the experience of hearing Bernardino speak, the reactions of his listeners, and the atmosphere prevailing at his sermons.

I. The Preacher's Vocation

In a sermon to the Sienese in 1427, Bernardino mimicked a conversation that could have been taking place at that very moment:

> A fellow standing over there on the side is saying: "That one [i.e., Bernardino] sure is giving it to us hot! Hey, what good is it to talk so much?" Another man asks: "What good are so many sermons?" I'll answer you who asks "what good are so many sermons?"! What good is it to be saved? I'm telling you that there were never so many sermons necessary as now . . .[5]

4. Michael Baxandall, *Painting and Experience in Fifteenth-Century Italy* (Oxford: Oxford University Press, 1972), esp. 29–108.

5. Siena 1427, I, 170. "Uno sta colà da canto, e dice:—Costui ce la caccia molto calda. Doh, che bisogna tanto dire!—L'altro dice:—Che bisogna tante prediche!—

A scoffer's patience must have been tried during a preaching visit by Bernardino. In this particular instance, he had to endure forty-five days of sermons which sometimes lasted up to three hours at a time. An immense mental and physical effort was required of both speaker and listener, especially if they had to stand under a hot August sun. But in his tart reply to the restless, Bernardino felt no need for apologies: in these evil times the wicked needed all the sermons they could get.

And here was the man to give them. Bernardino had preached for years after becoming a priest in 1404, but the real beginning of his fame was when he went to Lombardy in 1417. For five years he traveled throughout the north, spreading God's Word, pacifying towns, preaching on the Name of Jesus, and becoming in the process a genuine religious celebrity. Meanwhile, the mental horizons of this Tuscan expanded greatly. As he confided to the Sienese, ten years ago he thought he knew something about the world but now he realized that it was nothing at all. By 1427 he could boast, "I've learned so much about the world that, I declare, it would seem very much indeed."[6] Never one to be falsely humble, he acknowledged here that the growth of his personality occurred simultaneously with his development as a preacher. It is this satisfaction which can be heard over and again in the sermons—the just pride of a man who has discovered himself in his work. Bernardino is not the best subject for psychological analysis, because he tended to be reticent about most aspects of his personality; he chose to say little, for example, about his asceticism or his mystical experiences. His "self" only emerged in the pulpit as a series of controlled revelations about his identity as a preacher. It was his great accomplishment as an orator which pleased him most and which would bring him to the Kingdom of Heaven. John of Capestrano, who knew him well as friend and colleague, quoted Bernardino as saying, "If I

Io rispondo, a te che dici 'che bisogna tante prediche?'—Che bisogna tanto camparti?—E dicoti che mai non bisognoro tanto le prediche, quanto bisognano ora."

6. Ibid., I, 497.

could not preach, I could not live" ("Si non debere[m] praedicare, non posse[m] vivere").[7]

Part of this satisfaction derived from the pure pleasure he felt in his craft. Just as a student is unable to learn without joy in his book, neither can the preacher succeed unless he delights in speaking. Bernardino clearly reveled in the gift of his tongue:

> God has given the instrument of the tongue only to Man—noble instrument! You come to hear the preacher and for two or three hours he delights you! God didn't give us a more beautiful instrument, a more blessed part . . .[8]

The pleasure was such that it even brought him good health when he preached. On one occasion he explained that he was unable to speak the day before because he felt "almost dead," and this morning he still felt the same way. But,

> now that I've come, I feel strong as a lion; I still felt weak as I was saying Mass, but now I feel as if I could joust.[9]

The self-fulfillment he obtained in the pulpit apparently satisfied all personal ambition. A common motif in paintings after his death is the presence of three bishops' mitres discarded at his feet. Each time he was offered one, the preacher was not even tempted to accept. The

7. "Sermo S. Iohannis de Capistrano, O.F.M ineditus de S. Bernardino Senensi O.F.M.," ed. Ferdinando Doelle, AFH 6 (1913), 76–90. Capestrano, following Benvoglienti's idealized biography of the adolescent Bernardino, described how the future saint knew his calling even in youth: "Infantulus autem bonae indolis ab ecclesia in domum rediens, parabat sibi altare et coram eo genuflectebat ad instar sacerdotiis, ostendens se divina celebrare, ita quod omnes, qui videbant, praenosticabat illum fore futurum sacerdotem. Similiter ea, quae audivit in sermone, pueris congregatis praedicavit," 85.

8. Florence 1424, I, 451. "Iddio à dato lo stromento della lingua all'uomo, gentile stromento! Venite a udire el predicatore, due o tre ore che vi diletta! Non ci à dato Iddio più bello stromento, membro benedetto . . ."

9. Siena 1427, II, 822. ". . . e ora so' fatto come uno lione, tanto mi sento gagliardo: che pure mentre ch'io dicevo la messa mi sentivo debile e ora mi sento per modo ch'io giostrarei."

administrative and pastoral duties of office would only inhibit him in his true calling. But his keen awareness of his gifts did not blind him to their limitations. Individuals persisted in trying to gain access to the busy man, harassing him for advice. Although he sometimes failed to escape—his lively tales of personal encounters attest to this—Bernardino was annoyed by the loss of time. On several occasions he literally begged his admirers not to bother him when he was off duty. The desired rhythm of his life was writing, giving, and then recovering from sermons.

The preaching vocation gave birth to a number of subsidiary roles, and Bernardino took pride in each persona. Although he tried to maintain an emotional distance from his flock, he was still infused with a heroic sense of mission. Christ had commanded his Apostles to spread the Gospel, and Saint Francis had told his followers to preach about "vices and virtues, and the pain and the glory."[10] Bernardino saw himself as a worthy descendant of both traditions. He was, however, closer to Paul than to the gentle Francis, his self-image pronouncedly masculine in fifteenth-century terms.[11] In a striking image, he depicted the preacher as a swordsman:

> It is fitting that the preacher be like a fencer who gives the point and the cut and the flat from the side, in front, behind . . .[12]

And a preacher's words could be like "little flames of fire" that sear those who listen.[13] Swordsman and flamethrower, Bernardino used his martial skills when he preached on the Apocalypse. He proclaimed that there was a direct correlation between God's judgment of an evil city and the absence of preachers. If no learned man preached there

10. Florence 1424, II, 1.

11. For more on Bernardino's "male" spirituality, see Richard Kieckhefer, "Holiness and the Culture of Devotion: Remarks on Some Late Medieval Male Saints," in *Images of Sainthood in Medieval Europe*, ed. Renate Blumenfeld-Kosinski and Timea Szell (Ithaca, NY: Cornell University Press, 1991), 288–305.

12. Florence 1424, II, 3. "El predicatore conviene che sia come uno ischermidore che dà di punta e di taglio e di piatto, dal lato e dinanzi e di rieto . . ."

13. Florence 1425, II, 429.

for ten years, it was a sure sign of disaster—the people would become "heretics and patarines and beasts."[14] His was a voice that needed to cry in the wilderness, for there would only be silence before the coming of the Antichrist.[15]

A good preacher, however, could combat the symptoms of an impending doom. For example, in the spring of 1425 Bernardino felt that the Florentines were in great spiritual danger, thanks to the lingering influence of Manfred of Vercelli, the controversial Dominican who had been in the city from May 1419 to October 1423. This professional rival aroused millenarian sentiments among the populace which disturbed the self-consciously orthodox Franciscan. Bernardino's sermons reveal a man on the defensive who was clearly the target of criticism from certain unnamed elements in the city; he angrily warned the Florentines not to believe preachers who spoke ill of others. But despite the criticisms which he endured, he maintained great confidence in his powers. Had Frate Bernardino been here, he boasted, *he* could have done something about the heresy.[16]

The preacher with the flaming sword was also a role that emerged when he denounced witches, sodomites, and partisans.[17] His merciless attitude towards these disrupters of social and religious order showed

14. Ibid., I, 78.

15. Siena 1427, I, 150.

16. Florence 1425, I, 227. For Manfred of Vercelli, see Roberto Rusconi, "Fonti e documenti su Manfred da Vercelli, O.P., e il suo movimento penitenziale," *Archivum Fratrum Praedicatorum* 47 (1977): 51–107, and *L'attesa della fine: Crisi della società, profezia ed Apocalisse in Ialia al tempo del grande scisma d'Occidente, 1378–1417* (Rome: Istituto Storico Italiano per il Medio Evo, 1979), 236–46; for a discussion of Bernardino's relationship to millenarianism, see 246–57, and Franco Mormando, "Signs of the Apocalypse in Late Medieval Italy: The Popular Preaching of Bernardino of Siena," *Medievalia et Humanistica: Studies in Medieval and Renaissance Culture*, 23, ed. Paul M. Clogan (Lanham, MD: Rowman and Littlefield, 1997), 95–122.

17. Unlike most of his Tuscan contemporaries, Bernardino associated witchcraft with heresy and advocated the stake. See the comprehensive discussions by Bernadette Paton, "'To the Fire! Let Us Burn a Little Incense to God': Bernardino, Preaching Friars, and Maleficio in Late Medieval Siena," in *No Gods Except Me: Orthodoxy and Religious Practice in Europe*, ed. Charles Zika (Melbourne: History Department, University of Melbourne, 1991), 7–36, and Mormando, *The Preacher's Demons*, 52–108 and 235–37.

no trace of the sweet friar eulogized after his canonization. But Bernardino was usually gentler with the ordinary mass of sinners. As he explained to the Florentines in 1424, he was admonishing them because he was moved by compassion: "I have come to you for this. God has sent me to preach to you about your errors and to show you the dangers you'll come to if you don't amend."[18] Compassion is the key to the fifteenth century's portrait of Bernardino as the *padre dolce*, which may help explain his wide popularity. Although he was capable of brutality when he savaged witches and homosexuals in his preaching, he could balance venom with a softer touch. He saw himself and was seen by his mainstream audience as a *padre penitenziale* whose listeners were his children. In fact, he thought of himself as a partner in child rearing alongside the fleshly parents, and he was particularly anxious that children be brought to the sermons. He believed that he had a generative function in the creation of their characters: the parents prepared the field and the preacher sowed the good seed. Eventually his words would reach fruition and the young people would grow into "good and angelic persons."[19]

Adult sinners, however, were notorious for their intractability. A recurring theme in the sermons is the difficulty of softening hardened hearts grown old and obstinate in sin. Yet repentance, stimulated by the preacher's words, was always possible. Perhaps the most striking image Bernardino had of himself is expressed towards the end of the Lenten sermons which he delivered in Florence in 1425. Lazarus, ill unto death, becomes a metaphor for the sinful Florentines: "Behold the populace of Florence which you love, Jesus: it is sick." The sisters Martha and Mary, standard representatives of the Active and Contemplative Lives, have hastened to Christ with this message. Bernardino blends the two women into a symbol for preachers who proclaim both the contemplative life that knows what is good and the active life that puts it into effect. And so the preached truth can heal the diseased soul:

18. Florence 1424, II, 24.
19. Ibid., I, 200, and Florence 1425, II, 325.

When a person is ill, he has a pounding pulse and useless limbs. Thus he who preaches the truth lightly touches the wrist and finds that the pulse climbs, thinking that it can leap into Paradise dressed and with shoes (i.e., at once). But when they (i.e., the sinful-infirm) hear the truth about their sins, they descend towards damnation; the pulse goes down towards the inferno. They ask: "Who can save himself when the path is so narrow?" [I say] that it is easier for those who are still alive than dead. I never reprehend you for your sins without dying of sadness that they so increase your infirmity. I never reprehend your sins without the hope that my words might cure them.[20]

The language in this tightly condensed passage is somewhat obscure, perhaps due to the recorder's inability to follow the argument. But the point Bernardino is trying to make here is indeed complicated. It is, in effect, a summary of the conversion process itself, from the unrealistic belief that one can leap to heaven in a single bound to the depressing realization of one's sins, which then plummets the soul to the depths. The preacher who has aroused these mixed emotions then assures the penitent that salvation—the cure—is in fact possible. Bernardino has shifted from the Martha-Mary imagery with which he began the discourse on Lazarus. She who warns—that is, the preacher—is now transformed into the doctor who, by touching the spiritual pulse with words of truth, can heal the ailing soul.[21]

20. Florence 1425, II, 60. "Quando la persona è inferma à 'l polso battaglioso e à le membra rotte. Così rettamente chi predica la verità ti tocca il polso e truovalo andare in su e in giù. Io veggo il polso del populo all'andare in su [pens]andosi di saltare in paradiso calzati e vestiti. [Essi] odono una verità de' loro peccati; vengono in [giù a dan]azione; l'andare il polso in giù verso il ninferno. [Dico]no: Chi si salverà a così istretta via? Più [facile è vivo] che morto. Io non vi riprendo mai de' [vostri peccati] che io non muoia di dolore pe' [vostri peccati che aumen]ntano le 'infermità, e che si medichino."

21. Was Bernardino aware of the antique and humanist tradition that believed in the power of healing words? See George W. McClure, "Healing Eloquence: Petrarch, Salutati, and the Physicians," *Journal of Medieval and Renaissance Studies* 15, no.12 (Fall 1985): 317–46; also see McClure's *Sorrow and Consolation in Italian Humanism* (Princeton: Princeton University Press, 1991), esp. 46–72. Bernardino's audience, though, may have been reminded of forbidden practices which mingled healing and magical formulas.

Given the nature of the Lazarus story, a third role is also implied, though not explicitly stated. The audience could scarcely forget that it was Christ who resurrected Lazarus. Bernardino was always careful to emphasize that he was merely the mouthpiece of the Word, but his confidence in the power of preaching consistently hints at a belief in his elevated spiritual status. It is likely that he wanted the Florentines to make a connection between Preacher and Christ so that they, discouraged sinners, might have stronger faith in the possibility of their resurrection. In fact, his preaching went even further. By saying that it was better to forgo Mass and hear the sermon, if a person could not manage both, it becomes clear that the Christ with whom he preferred to identify was the Truth-giver rather than He who offers the Sacrifice. Bernardino was always a preacher before he was a priest. He assumed that it was indeed possible for him to resurrect lost souls; his words of truth raised the pulse beat and thus inflamed the will towards the Good. Through the Word, then, the preacher was also a savior.

The exalted confidence he felt in his profession naturally extended to his personal fate. No Luther he, Bernardino was able to speak in calm assurance of his own salvation. He asked the Florentines: if God rewards those who give alms to men's miserable bodies, then what glory awaits the preachers and confessors who convert men's souls? A mere word could save thousands of people from Hell.[22] He even promised the Sienese that he would personally testify for them at the Last Judgment—that is, if they would mend their wicked ways.[23] Of course, the responsibility ultimately rested on the listeners, and so he was absolved of all blame if they refused to heed his words:

> If I'm believed, it will be good for me and good for you. But if I'm not believed, I'll have done my part, and you'll be harmed.[24]

22. Siena 1427, I, 171; Florence 1424, I, 93.
23. Siena 1427, I, 171–72.
24. Florence 1424, II, 23. "Se io sarò creduto arò fatto bene a me e bene a voi. Se non sarò creduto arò fatto el fatto mio e vo' v'arete el danno."

Whatever the results of his preaching, Bernardino's activity in the pulpit provided a satisfying outlet for his personal gifts. His proud awareness of the preacher's multiple callings—armed warrior against sin, Apostle of the Word, father, sower, doctor, savior—shows how indissolubly linked the man was to his vocation, his personal identity far different from the ascetic celebrated in the hagiography. Despite his simultaneous lives as administrator and devout Franciscan, Bernardino's truest personality was the public one, only fully realized before an audience. As he once exclaimed, "What happiness I sometimes feel inside when I preach!"[25]

II. Preaching Style

Bernardino's role transformations were possible only because he was a master of the tools of his craft. His supple oratory was as multifaceted as his self-presentation. He worked, however, within a standard medium which had been practiced for almost two centuries, and his techniques were those employed by most successful preachers. The framework of his sermons is firmly traditional, structured by the innumerable divisions and point-by-point arguments in which the Scholastics delighted. Briefly, a medieval sermon was a formal division and discussion of a Scriptural text, beginning with the *thema*, or biblical verse, and followed by the *prothema*, another passage which served as an introductory prayer (Bernardino, however, preferred to substitute for the *prothema* an invocation to the Virgin). The main body of the sermon consisted of an *introductio*, *divisiones*, and *dilationes*. The preacher then concluded with a brief *clausio*, or summary, and a prayer. This form is a somewhat dry and lifeless convention to modern ears, but it was undoubtedly a great help to both preacher and audience because of its clarity and frequent repetitions.[26]

25. Siena 1427, II, 1303.
26. A good introduction to medieval sermons is D. L. D'Avray, *The Preaching of the Friars: Sermons Diffused from Paris before 1300* (Oxford: Oxford University Press, 1985); a collection of articles on a range of medieval sermons is in *De Ore Domini: Preacher and*

Bernardino's mature preaching style was by no means a revolution against this traditional sermon but rather a subtle transformation of it. In the 1424 and 1425 sermons given in Florence, he began to change some of the smaller rules of the game. Both Carlo Delcorno and Grazia Fioravanti Melli have shown how Bernardino slowly replaced the usual *thema* from the day's Gospel with a Scriptural passage of his own choice; at first, he even felt the need to apologize for the substitution, explaining that another verse was sometimes more relevant to his listeners' needs.[27] This period of cautious innovation was complete by 1427 when he reached the height of his powers. In the Siena sermons of that year, he never abandoned the useful Scholastic framework but felt comfortable enough to take liberties when it suited his purpose.

the Word in the Middle Ages, ed. Thomas L. Amos, Eugene A. Green, and Beverly Mayne Kienzle (Kalamazoo, MI: Medieval Institute Publications, 1989). For Italian preaching, see the works (previously cited) by Howard, Lesnick, and Thompson; also see Carlo Delcorno, *La predicazione nell'età comunale* (Florence: Sansoni, 1974), and *Giordano da Pisa e l'antica predicazione volgare* (Florence: L. S. Olschki, 1975); Alfredo Galletti, *L'eloquenza dalle origini al XVI secolo* (Milan: Casa editrice dottor Francesco Vallardi, 1938); Ida Magli, *Gli uomini della penitenza: Lineamenti antropologici del medioevo Italiano* (Milan: Garzanti, 1977); Ottavia Niccoli, *Prophecy and People in Renaissance Italy* (Princeton: Princeton University Press, 1990), 89–120; Bernardo Nobile, "Romiti e vita religiosa nella cronachistica italiana fra '400 e '500," *Christianesimo nella storia: ricerche storiche esegetiche*, 5 (Bologna: 1985), 303–40; John O'Malley (on humanist-influenced preaching), *Praise and Blame in Renaissance Rome: Rhetoric, Doctrine, and Reform in the Sacred College* (Durham, NC: Duke University Press, 1979); Bernadette Paton, *Preaching Friars and the Civic Ethos: Siena, 1380–1480* (London: University of London, 1992); and for a collection of representative documents, Roberto Rusconi, *Predicazione e vita religiosa nella società Italiana* (Turin: Loescher, 1981). For northern Europe, see Robert W. Scribner, *Popular Culture and Popular Movements in Reformation Germany* (London: Hambledon Press, 1987), esp. "Oral Culture and the Diffusion of Reformation Ideas" and "Preachers and People in the German Towns," 49–69 and 123–43; Larissa Taylor, *Soldiers of Christ: Preaching in Late Medieval and Reformation France* (New York: Oxford University Press, 1992); and H. Leith Spencer, *English Preaching in the Late Middle Ages* (Oxford: Oxford University Press, 1993).

27. Grazia Fioravanti Melli, "Bernardino da Siena: I quaresimali Fiorentini del 1424–5," *Rassegna della Letteratura Italiana* 77, no. 3 (September–December 1973): 565–84; Delcorno, "L' 'ars praedicandi' di Bernardino da Siena," *Cateriniano-Bernardiniano*, 422–25; Zelina Zafarana, "Bernardino nella storia della predicazione," *Bernardino predicatore nella società del suo tempo: 9–12 ottobre 1975* (Todi: L'Accademia Tudertina, 1976), 53–55.

Clearly, he had come to realize that the spiritual lesson superseded an absolute adherence to the traditional form.

But the form was, at any rate, merely a wooden embroidery frame supporting Bernardino's material; it is the color and texture of the cloth which one remembers. His words, like those of other great preachers, seemed bright and immediate to his listeners because they confronted the problems of everyday life. The exemplum, or encapsulated story-cum-moral, was one of his primary devices. If the sermon's formal structure served as a guidepost for memory and understanding, then the exemplum provided both practical advice and entertainment.[28] Although the exemplum was a standard feature of late-medieval sermons, Bernardino effectively departed from tradition in his specific choice of tales. Delcorno has analyzed the preacher's use of exempla and has found that of the 756 stories in the surviving repertoire, more than half (411) are based on historical and personal accounts. Thus, although he had a rich corpus of religious tales to draw upon, Bernardino deliberately concentrated on other kinds of material. He used, for instance, only five stories of visions and nine accounts of Marian and Eucharistic miracles, although there is of course a natural abundance of exempla from Franciscan *leggende*. Delcorno has characterized this new emphasis on nonreligious tales as "the secularization of the exemplum."[29] It seems that by the early Quattrocento the needs of the audience had subtly shifted in favor of the "worldly."

Most of the tales are good illustrations of a particular moral point,

28. A summary of important exempla in use during the Middle Ages is in Frederic S. Tubach, *Index Exemplorum: A Handbook of Medieval Religious Tales* (Helsinki: Suomalainen Tiedeakatemia [Academia Scientiarum Fennica], 1969). A wide sampling of Bernardino's exempla, along with an examination of his other techniques, can be found in Franco Mormando, "The Vernacular Sermons of San Bernardino da Siena: A Literary Analysis" (Ph.D. diss., Harvard University, 1983).

29. Delcorno, "L' 'exemplum' nella predicazione di Bernardino da Siena," in *Bernardino predicatore*, 80. But the preacher's emphasis on "secular" exempla does not mean that he abandoned the miraculous. Some of his best tales occupy a space poised midway between "reality" and the supernatural; remember, for example, the story about the devil-griffin, Siena 1425, I, 177–78.

but others tend to develop a life of their own. The storyteller's absorption in his art could overwhelm the spiritual lesson. In one tale, Bernardino explains to the Sienese how the undecided soul wavers when it does not know good from evil. He describes a monkey near the church of San Cristoforo in Siena who steals a child from his cradle, carries it off to a rooftop, and keeps swaddling and unswaddling it; the frightened bystanders don't know whether to shoot the monkey, scream at it, or wait to see what will happen.[30] It is a vivid and ingenious example, but most listeners probably remembered more about the monkey's antics than about the soul's dilemma. In another story, a rich widow yearns to take a young husband but is afraid of the gossip which will surely ensue. She therefore orders a kinsman to flay (*scorticare*) a horse and gallop it through the streets for three days in succession. On the first day, the entire city scrambles to watch the spectacle. But on the second day fewer people are interested, and on the last no one even bothers to watch. The widow in great relief concludes that gossip is short-lived and that she can marry her young man after all.[31] This exemplum was intended to show that it does not matter what gossips say, but in retrospect all one really remembers is the striking image of the unfortunate horse. We can glimpse here one of the ways in which the preacher was temporarily willing to sacrifice the end for the means. Much of the pleasure of a Bernardino sermon was probably due to its meandering quality, its cheerful excursions into the earthy or the bizarre.[32]

The entertainment value of a particular tale could be inextricably linked to the moral lesson, sometimes in ways that are difficult for the

---

30. Siena 1425, II, 59.

31. See the version in Siena 1427, II, 144–45. The tale is not original to Bernardino; see Tubach, *Index Exemplorum*, 397.

32. Long before Bernardino's time, some critics noted that the moral point of the exemplum was being superseded by narrative. According to Marian Mulchahey, Passavanti, in the fourteenth century, complained that some of his fellow preachers were "jongleurs and storytellers and buffoons"; see "Dominican Education and the Dominican Ministry in the Thirteenth and Fourteenth Centuries: Fra Jacopo Passavanti and the Florentine Convent of Santa Maria Novella" (Ph.D. diss., University of Toronto, 1989), 359.

twentieth-century mind to comprehend. Quattrocento audiences had a taste for more gruesome entertainment than we can stomach, and Bernardino willingly indulged their appetite for brutality. In a sermon to the Florentines on "true friendship," he begins with a little story on what friendship is *not*. A young boy in Verona who heard Bernardino preach against sodomy resolved to break off his liaison with a soldier. The irate soldier thereupon killed his former catamite with "a little knife" and fled the city, while the martyred boy, Bernardino assures the Florentines, immediately ascended into heaven. Finally, justice prevailed, the murderer was returned to Verona, and his body was quartered and then distributed among the four divisions of the city. The details of this true story are related with a brutal economy of style, and the preacher clearly took a savage pleasure in the fate of the soldier, just as his listeners most certainly did.[33]

The marriage of instruction with pleasure is best displayed in Bernardino's quick, pithy metaphors, his ability to shape words into images which would be immediately accessible to a lay audience. They demonstrate a sharp observation of the everyday and a willingness to employ even the lowliest details of life. Sin is compared to the infectious filth of community outhouses. Confession is like the process of lifting stones from a house ruined by dampness: serpents and scorpions are hidden beneath but when you raise the stones the evil things scatter. And it is always necessary to make a full confession "just as the good housekeeper sweeps her home and throws out all the dirt without piling it into corners." The preacher could make the audience see everything from a well-bred lady greedily stuffing cherries into her mouth to a cockroach reposing on a pile of dung.[34]

The exemplum, too, could wander into vulgar territory, much to the amusement of the audience. Bernardino, in an attempt to warn his female listeners about vanity, wanted to show that habit determines taste. So he used the metaphor of a privy cleaner who passes out when

33. Florence 1425, III, 27.

34. Florence 1424, I, 8–9 for confession; Siena 1427, I, 582–83 for the lady and the cherries, one of Bernardino's most famous tales.

he is near some perfumed ladies; the unfortunate man can only be revived when someone holds a piece of dung beneath his nose. The audience seemed to enjoy the joke too much since Bernardino had to snap: "You laugh when you should cry!"[35] The preacher felt that elevated subjects should be explained in such a way that "you can almost touch them and feel them."[36] As a result, his sermons possessed an enormous range of tones, fluctuating between the apocalyptic and the humorous, the earthy and the sublime.

Since his subject matter embraced everything from the beauty of heaven to a woman who spat worms from her mouth, Bernardino needed an absolute command of his tongue, "that noble instrument." His was a flexible, humorous, colloquial language. The stories were often punctuated by exclamations ("Doh!," "Deh!") or animal sounds, especially in the 1427 sermons, where the recorder tried to include every interjection. And Bernardino had a keen understanding of the effect of single words. When speaking about the lines on a partisan's tombstone he grimly jokes that instead of "Rest in peace (*pace*), " they should read "Rest in pitch (*pece*)."[37]

We must always imagine Bernardino's words as they were spoken or we will miss their hypnotic effect. Listen to his repetition of words for emphasis:

> El diavolo ha messo tanto divisione tra voi, che se voi non vi guardate,
> per certo, io temo, temo, temo da qualche male.[38]

---

35. Siena 1425, II, 83. This earthy story was perhaps Bernardino's creative transformation of a moral tale similar to the one in the fourteenth-century "Fior di Virtù": an angel, traveling around in disguise with a hermit, comes across the stinking carcass of a horse and isn't bothered by the smell. Yet when he sees a beautiful and well-dressed woman in a garden, he holds his nose in disgust. The puzzled hermit asks him why he does so and the angel replies: "Perchè pute più a Dio la vanagloria che tutte le carogne del mondo." *Novelle Italiane: Dalle origini al Cinquecento*, ed. Goffredo Bellonci (Rome: Lucarini Editore, 1986), 20.

36. Florence 1425, I, 263.

37. Siena 1427, I, 342.

38. Ibid., II, 663.

[The devil has placed so much division among you, that, if you don't watch out, I fear, fear, fear some evil.]

or to the rhythmic intonations of his sentences:

. . . ogni volta che tu usi per modo che non possono generare figliuoli, sempre fa peccato. E quanto è peccato? Oh, è uno grandissimo peccato! O, è uno grandissimo peccatone![39]

[. . . each time that you do it in a way that won't generate children (i.e., practice sodomy), you commit a sin. And how much of a sin? Oh, it's a very big sin! Oh, it's an enormously big sin!]

All of these devices—the humorous or hair-raising stories, the animal imitations, the calculated effect of the Italian itself—amused the listeners and kept them coming to the sermons. But because Bernardino's real purpose was to change deep-rooted behavior, he needed to appeal to much more than his audience's desire to be entertained. His greatest secret in winning over a crowd, aside from the rituals which will be discussed below, was his effort to make a one-to-one contact with the individual. If you want to spread the good news of the sermon, he instructs the housewife, "talk it over with your little old mother who is sick and cannot come to hear."[40] Bernardino would unfailingly pick the most touching example; in this case, it was the widowed *nonna* of so many Tuscan homes.

Bernardino's technique of involving each person emotionally was akin to the methods used in Franciscan devotional literature. That popular fourteenth-century handbook known as *Meditations on the Life of Christ*, for example, described the agonies of the Crucifixion in an extremely detailed and personalized way so that the reader or listener would viscerally identify with the characters and scene.[41] It was an ap-

---

39. Ibid., I, 588.
40. Ibid., I, 195.
41. *Meditations on the Life of Christ: An Illustrated Manuscript of the Fourteenth Century*, ed. Isa Ragusa and Rosalie B. Green (Princeton: Princeton University Press, 1961). A good

peal to both imagination and sentiment, a way to first visualize and then internalize a message by playing on the heartstrings. Bernardino used a similar technique in his recounting of the sacrifice of Isaac, sparing no pathetic detail in his description of Abraham's sad journey with his son and of the boy's perfection:

> What perfection did that boy have? He possessed innocence, goodness, and obedience. It isn't said how old he was but the Doctors estimate that he was about twelve or thereabouts since he had a good understanding. It follows that he must have been very beautiful [*bello bello*]. God had made him in his own image, blond and curly-headed.[42]

The preacher hadn't forgotten that more than one parent in his audience had lost a beloved child with a fully developed personality—and who was *bello bello*.

Bernardino's ability to empathize, combined with his observation of detail and his talent for mimicry, were combined in the dialogue, a form which he made as vivid and colorful as the exemplum. He either duplicated conversations (real or imaginary) or constructed interior monologues of the perplexed soul debating with itself over some dilemma. He was especially alert to the tendency of people to deceive themselves and enjoyed using the dialogue to expose their false reasoning. In one example, he presents the addled reasoning of a young girl who has received a desperate note from a "suicidal" admirer:

> And the crazy girl will say: "Alas! I don't know what to do. If I don't consent and he kills himself, then I'll be the cause of his death; and if I do consent, this will be a very great sin; but murder is still a worse sin than any other." And she will say to herself: "I'd sooner content him than be

---

discussion of the imaginative process involved is in Lesnick, *Preaching in Medieval Florence*, 161–71.

42. Florence 1425, II, 243–44. "Che perfezione aveva quel figliuolo? Aveva innocenzia, santità, benignità, bonità, e obbedienzia. Non pone il tempo ch'egli avesse, ma stimasi pe' dottori che fusse d'anni dodici o circa, che aveva buono conoscimento. Per quello che seguita poi doveva essere bello bello; Iddio l'avea fatto a suo modo, ricciutello e biondo."

the cause of his death." And I say to you that you are a crazy fool! [*pazza-ccia*]. Get rid of this conscience of the devil! O, even if he kills himself, what is it to you? Now, are you so stupid that you believe that he'd kill himself? Don't believe it! Oh, even if he does kill himself, let him, since it's a shame that the evil fellow is alive! And make sure that you never consent to anyone, because you will be deceived. O crazy little women who get four sweet words and then suddenly think they are on top of the world! . . . and then afterwards people go around slandering them.[43]

To enter the intimate concerns of secular life often required an imaginative leap for the middle-aged preacher. Clearly, his personal encounters, whether taking place informally or during the sermon, sharpened his understanding of the layperson's world.

Bernardino also attempted to engage his listeners by addressing them as individuals during the course of the sermon and by placing them in a direct relationship with himself. His *"io"* could become self-revelatory when he wanted to make himself one with the *"tu"* or *"voi"* of his audience. At his most familiar, he would look over the gathering and begin with a personal remark:

Well! It seems to me that you are having a fine morning and I together with you, despite the pain in my side and in my kidneys. I'm feeling very robust [*gagliardo*] today.[44]

43. Siena 1425, I, 41. "E la pazza dirà in sè: 'Oimè! che io non so che mi fare. Se io non gli acconsento e costui s'uccida, io so' cagione che costui muoia; e se io gli acconsento, questo è grandissimo peccato; ma egli è pur peggio l'omicidio che niuno altro peccato.' E dirà in sè: 'Io voglio più tosto contentarlo, che essere cagione di questo omicidio.' E io ti dico che tu se' una pazzaccia! Leva via quella coscienza del diavolo! O, se ben s'uccidesse, che n'ài tu a fare? Mo, se' tu sì gran bestia che credi che s'uccidesse? Non tel dare a credare! O, se pur s'uccidesse, lassalo uccidare, però che 'l gattivo è peccato che viva. E fa' che mai non acconsenta a niuno, però che voi sete tutte ingannate da loro. O paze femminelle, che come ànno quattro parole dolci, subitto lo' pare essare in cima del monte, e poi vi vanno vituperando."

44. Siena 1427, II, 828. "Doh! E' mi pare a vedervi che voi aviate stamane la buona mattina, e io con voi insieme: al dispetto del mal del fianco e de la ranella, io mi sento molto bene gagliardo."

In the case of his fellow Sienese, this personal link of *"io"* and *"tu"* was especially pronounced. His preaching had a noticeable effect during the 1425 Siena sermons since the city's statutes were modified and a huge YHS emblem was placed above the main portal of the Palazzo Pubblico, where it remains to this day.[45] Bernardino must have felt a considerable amount of satisfaction by the time he reached the end of his visit. The beginning of one of his last sermons displays both his satisfaction and his tender use of a special relationship:

> I've been thinking, seeing how much time I've spent tiring myself out for you—I believe I've preached about forty sermons—that love and discretion are pressing me now . . . You and I, and I and you, we're tired. But what am I saying?! It doesn't tire me out to have you live like worthy Christians. And neither for you, I think; the labor has been a delight and will continue to be one for the next few days.[46]

Faces in the crowd were never abstract ones to Bernardino. *"Tu,"* whether a fellow Sienese or any soul to be saved, was an intimate friend.

Although he delighted in his oratorical skill, the preacher never became so involved in the music of his own voice that he failed to notice individual reactions. His eyes seem to have been constantly roving the audience in order to detect signs of restlessness or disagreement. Long sermons could put weary listeners to sleep and Bernardino was very quick to notice such lapses. Once he interrupted the sermon to reprimand two women who were dozing, "the one making a pillow of the other."[47] These kinds of asides are found throughout the 1427 Siena

45. The documents for the commission of the YHS emblem are in Gaetano Milanesi, ed. *Documenti per la storia dell'arte Senese* (Siena: Onorato Porri, 1854–56), II, 128–30.

46. Siena 1425, II, 254. "Io mi so' pensato, vedendo quanto tempo io so'affadigato in voi, che credo circa a quaranta prediche io v'ò fatte, che stringendomi la carità e discrezione, e considerando io non ò a stare con voi se no' tutta questa semmana, e però vi trattarò cose utili quanto mi sarà possibile. E voi e io, e io e voi, essendoci affadigati . . . ma che dich'io? Io n'ò avuto e ò diletto, e non m'è fadiga di fare che voi viviate come fedeli cristiani. E anco voi, credo; la fadiga v'è stata a sarà diletto a udire questi altri dì."

47. Siena 1427, I, 147.

sermons, when the crowd eventually numbered in the thousands. It is true that the Piazza del Campo provided an ideal arena for sharp observation: its hollowed-out shell slopes gently upwards from the Palazzo Pubblico where Bernardino stood, and he thus had an easy view of the listeners' faces and movements. But even if the recordings of other sermons are less complete than those given in 1427, there is little reason to suppose that he relaxed his vigilance outside Siena. The numerous interruptions are eloquent testimony to the preacher's ceaseless efforts to maintain a live current between himself and the crowd.

III. The Audience

Bernardino's sermons were not delivered into a vacuum and the group before the pulpit was not merely a pliant mass molded by the master preacher. What he actually said was shaped by the audience before him, and so his sermons reveal much about listener response and the continuous dialogue, spoken and unspoken, between the preacher and the crowd. The flow of the sermons was determined by Bernardino's perception of his listeners' needs, their capacities, and even their resistance to his message. Although they remain mostly anonymous to the historian, they were clearly a collection of individuals whose insistent humanity breaks through the sterile page via the echo of the preacher's voice. They are a reminder that sermons were not delivered as collections of words to be analyzed, but as events to be experienced.

Estimates of the size of the audience vary among the chroniclers and biographers. Many peasants and foreigners would have been necessary, though, to swell the Sienese crowd to the lavish "thirty thousand" which is reported. Yet for the most important sermons the number of spectators could easily have included most of the city. The Piazza del Campo, for example, is capable of holding over fifty thousand people—more than double the town's population during the early Renaissance—as it routinely does during the modern Palio. In a little town like Prato the number of those present was correspondingly smaller, but may have included most of the population; the merchant and eyewitness Marcovaldi reported that between three thousand and eight thousand people came, depending on the day.

Attendance at Bernardino's sermons, even among the devout, seems to have fluctuated greatly, determined by both the appeal of the subject matter and the day of the week. A Lenten or Advent course was an intensive experience, taking place every day for a month or more. And if the 1427 Sienese redaction is typical, sermons could last up to several hours at a time. Not everyone would have been willing to invest an entire month in steady sermon-going, despite the fact that they were conveniently held early in the morning (this early morning schedule also explains the preacher's bitter complaints against those who preferred to sleep instead of attending the sermon). Frequent complaints and entreaties on Bernardino's part, supplemented by advertisements for what was coming next, are signs that he often had to scramble to get a larger audience for subsequent sermons. Sometimes he would announce the coming agenda well in advance so that people could choose accordingly; Sundays, when the audience was largest, were the best times to lay out the subjects for the rest of the week.[48] The Florentine sermons of 1425 indicate that market days also brought in larger crowds. Bernardino probably hoped that individuals would at least choose those talks which had some applicability to their own sins. A more likely scenario is that, aside from market and feast days, the audience swelled when the most exciting sermons were given, especially the ones which led up to the public bonfire.

Given Bernardino's popularity, it is natural to assume that "everyone" came to hear him. Contemporary observers asserted that "*tutti*" visited his sermons, young and old, rich and poor, men and women. An anonymous friar who wrote a biography shortly after the preacher's death provides a partial breakdown of those who came to hear:

> The learned as well as the ignorant flocked to the holy man's sermons: the most famous theologians, skilled doctors and lawyers, every religious

48. Florence 1424, II, 72.

order. Also temporal lords, nobles, common people, merchants, rustics, mercenaries, prostitutes, and even Jews—people of every condition hurried to the sermons, most desirous to hear.[49]

And when the preacher himself describes his encounters in various cities, it seems that a broad spectrum of urban humanity was indeed present. He enjoyed bragging about his success, particularly in Lombardy, and liked to tell stories about meeting people from every walk of life. Yet just as it was important for those interested in his cult to claim that he attracted and was accepted by the entire society, Bernardino too tended to idealize what went on at a sermon, that "half-paradise." Although we will never know the exact composition of his audience, internal evidence from the sermons hints that it was not always as representative of society as either he or his hagiographers might have liked.

Recent studies of other preachers suggest that audience composition varied depending on who was giving the sermon. The challenging thirteenth-century Alleluia preachers, for example, were perceived by many as a threat to the established order and may not have attracted usurers, bankers, lawyers, or judges. And resident Franciscans preaching in fourteenth-century Florence probably had somewhat more proletarian listeners than their Dominican counterparts who aimed many sermons at the *popolo grasso*.[50] Bernardino's situation was not precisely analogous to either of these groups since he neither presented a threat to secular authority nor was a resident in the cities where he preached, except in Siena. The famous traveling Franciscans of the fifteenth cen-

49. Anonymous Friar, "Vie inédite de S. Bernardino de Sienne par un frère mineur, son contemporain," ed. Francois van Ortroy, *Analecta Bollandiana* 25 (1906): 313. "Propterea ad predicationem sancti concurrebant docti pariter et indocti, famosissimi quoque theologi, periti medici ac iuris utriusque doctores, necnon claustrales omnium religionum, domini temporales, nobiles, plebei, mercatores, cives, rustici, stipendiarii, et meretrices, quin etiam et iudei et cuiuscunque condicionis gradus avidius concurrebant."

50. Thompson, *Revival Preachers*, 101; Lesnick compares Franciscan and Dominican friars and their audiences in *Preaching in Medieval Florence*, 40–86.

tury, like their founder two centuries before, probably had a somewhat wider clientele, as well as larger audiences, if only because of the curiosity factor and the reputation which preceded them.

But while we can acknowledge that Bernardino had unusually broad appeal, his method of direct address and the persistence of certain themes within the sermons show that, although a rough cross section of lay society came to listen during the course of a visit, one category predominated. The most conspicuous group of people at the sermons clearly stands out in the paintings by Sano di Pietro which depict Bernardino before his audience. A cloth extending through the middle of the crowd divided it by sex, emphasizing the huddle of women gathered together, hair modestly covered by wimples and everyone kneeling in devout attention. Unlike Sano, contemporary moralists were less sanguine about the motives of female sermon-goers and often complained that women came to the sermons not because they were pious but in order to display finery and marriageable daughters, much in the same spirit as they (supposedly) went to Mass.

Bernardino, either because he was a sharp observer or because he had absorbed this contemporary stereotype, believed that many of his listeners came to socialize and tried to circumvent it by introducing the cloth which divided the sexes. Keeping the two groups apart kept everyone more focused on the preacher himself and maintained a minimal degree of order. However, it was sometimes difficult to control those who preferred to mingle. In one instance, when Bernardino was preaching in Verona, a soldier refused to stand among the men and defiantly placed himself on the women's side, despite the remonstrances of the preacher's assistants. In the end, the fellow noisily declared that he'd go off and gamble if he wasn't allowed at the sermon. (Bernardino triumphantly told his Florentine audience that the soldier was then punished for his impudence when he lost his arm in a gambling fight!)[51] In the preacher's eyes, the restrictive cloth not only controlled the women, but probably protected them from affronts such as the

51. Florence 1424, I, 423–24.

Sano di Pietro, "La Predica di San Bernardino nella Piazza del Campo" (Bernardino preaching in the Piazza del Campo). The painting is in the Museo dell'Opera di Duomo in Siena. *Courtesy of Foto Lensini.*

soldier's. It seems, too, that for reasons of propriety, the preacher tried to maintain the dividing line between the sexes during public reconciliations. In the Sienese peacemakings of 1425 and 1427, he sent the men to the Cathedral and the women to San Martino, in the opposite direction; the sexes may have had separate quarrels to reconcile, but the perceived danger here was that peacemaking generally involved kissing—and a possible chance of disorder.

The women in Bernardino's audience deserve special attention as a group, both because of their physical presence and the advice which he lavished upon them. As he surveyed his listeners from the pulpit, the preacher always looked out upon a mixed audience, but it was one in which women predominated on the average day. His female devotees were a constant and reliable presence during every discourse, from those on vanity and family matters to sermons on usury, sodomy, and faction. Bernardino's casual remarks in the course of the sermons are the best evidence for the large percentage of women. For example, when he compared God to a moneylender—our good deeds multiply like interest over the years—he exclaimed: "Oh, he is a great usurer, women!"[52] This was very early in his visit to Siena in 1425 and the number of listeners was not as large as it would become within the next few weeks; predictably, women were the core of his audience at this point. But they probably still outnumbered the men even when the preaching was its height. At one point late in his six-week visit to Siena in 1427, he exhorted wives to bring their husbands to the next day's sermon since his work would be for nothing if he reformed the women and not the men; he promised them all in return "a most elevated sermon" (*una altissima predicazione*).[53]

It is difficult to identify with precision the women who came to hear Bernardino. Unfortunately, he tended to categorize them only as "you women," while men were sometimes differentiated by occupation or sin: merchant, official, usurer, sodomite, partisan. In general, he

52. Siena 1425, I, 68.
53. Siena 1427, II, 877.

seems to be addressing the respectable dowager, virgin, or young married woman, but that does not mean that servants, slaves, and the wives of the poor were not present alongside their upper-class sisters, if they managed to find respite from the morning's work. Sometimes, in a particular discussion, it is not quite clear which social level the preacher is targeting. His ideal of spiritual friendship and cooperation between husband and wife, for example, was intended for everyone, but it might have had greater relevance to those *popolo minuto* listeners who had some possibility of forming companionate marriages.

There are few surprises in the nature of the messages Bernardino relayed to these women, whatever their marital or social status. When he holds up the Virgin Mary as the young girl's primary role model, or when he discusses the importance of obedience to one's husband and the superiority of widowhood to remarriage, we are hearing familiar variations on the traditional themes of preachers. Much of his advice would have reassured the men in the audience. "O woman," he counsels, "when you speak to your husband speak little, rarely, and softly."[54] At another point, he proclaims that the secular life should be obedient to the spiritual, just as the wife should be obedient to her husband.[55] Even his unspoken assumptions reflect traditional perceptions of woman's place. He likened the joy and lightness one feels after confession, for example, to that of a woman after giving birth—that is, birth to a male child.[56]

Vanitas was predictably one of his favorite targets, as it was for most medieval preachers. He believed that a vain woman was subject to all seven deadly sins: she walks out of the house in her finery, submitting to Pride; she sees one more beautiful than herself and thus

54. Ibid., I, 221, and Florence 1424, II, 14. Roberto Rusconi notes that Bernardino's description of the husband's duties "fit within that affirmation of masculine authority" which was being asserted in fifteenth-century culture; see "St. Bernardino, the Wife, and Possessions," in *Women and Religion in Medieval and Renaissance Italy*, ed. Daniel Bornstein and Roberto Rusconi (Chicago: University of Chicago Press, 1996), 182–96.

55. Florence 1424, II, 14.

56. Ibid., I, 8.

succumbs to Envy; etc.[57] It was a moral failure which had far-reaching consequences for both the individual and society. In all of his preaching he was obsessed with the domino effect of sin, and he portrayed female vanity as an escalating social blight that could engulf an entire city in damnation.[58] He especially condemned the vice because it set off homosexual behavior among men (i.e., women's vanity ruins families who cannot afford their dowries, which then turns men to each other so that they become sodomites). If the economic approach failed to persuade, Bernardino could switch tactics and tell women that too much makeup and adornment physically repelled their menfolk and turned them to sodomy for that reason.

Yet even his talks on vanity tried to get to the heart of women's insecurities instead of merely condemning the female body as a potent source of evil. He told Florentine women, for example, that vanity would *not* be a long-term surety for their husband's love. The virtuous woman, on the other hand, would not be abandoned in old age or misfortune; as she aged, she would grow "more wise, more honest, more prudent."[59] Alternating with his many negative judgments is Bernardino's admiration for his society's ideal female. Frequently, his praise of the virtuous woman was almost rhapsodic: he compared a good woman to the sun which gives life to all.[60] On the worldly plane, women exerted a civilizing influence upon men—those who lived without wives were like beasts. If we read his words as patronizing, we must not assume that they were received that way by the veteran sermon-goers who were accustomed to harsh treatment by misogynistic clerics.

57. Siena 1425, II, 91.

58. In fact, Bernardino was less tolerant than some of his contemporaries, such as Antoninus of Florence (who was willing to take social status and local custom into account when he assessed women's vanity). See Thomas M. Izbicki, "Pyres of Vanities: Mendicant Preaching on the Vanity of Women and Its Lay Audience," *De Ore Domini: Preacher and the Word in the Middle Ages*, 211–34.

59. Florence 1424, I, 409.

60. Ibid., I, 407.

Many scholars have pointed to Bernardino's use of domestic meta-phor as evidence of how well he understood women's lives. His home-ly images sought to draw in the urban housewife. For example, in one of his definitions of confession he compares it to a wife who washes her linens frequently to make them white and beautiful.[61] But more telling is the way in which he discussed complex family situations. In his advice not to neglect the soul for the body, he used the metaphor of the husband who abandoned his wife for a servant-mistress. How, he asks, would you women feel if your husbands, smitten by an "evil love," helped those servants if they were sick but would not do the same for their lawful wives?[62] It was an analogy designed to make his female listeners picture the conflict between the worldly and the spiri-tual in uncomfortably concrete terms. And because of his empathy with women, Bernardino tried to force men to examine their easy as-sumptions. In the following dialogue, he reproves a lack of realism on the part of prospective husbands when they seek wives:

> "How do you want your wife made?"—"I want her honest"—"and you are dishonest. That's not right. Beyond that, how do you want her made?"—"I want her to be temperate."—"And you don't ever leave the tavern!"[63]

Moments such as these attest to the preacher's awareness of at least some of the difficulties women faced in a male-dominated world.

We still know relatively little about the spirituality of ordinary women in this period. Because of the nature of the sources, the richly articulated scholarship on women and religion in the late Middle Ages has been concerned primarily with nuns, saints, and tertiaries;

61. Florence 1424, I, 8–9. In Siena 1427, I, 568–71, he notes the many labors women endure in the household—and the ease of the men: "Tutta questa fadiga vedi che ella è sola della donna, e l'uomo se ne va cantando."

62. Ibid., I, 51–52.

63. Siena 1427, I, 557. "Come vuoi tu fatta questa moglie?—Io la voglio onesta.—E tu se' disonesto. Anco none sta bene. Oltre: come la vuoi fatta questa tua moglie?—Io la voglio temparata.—E tu non non esci mai della taverna."

the average woman remains in the shadows, a silent witness to the exploits of the holy.[64] Yet these women formed the sturdy bedrock of the faith and were the primary conduits linking the religion of clerics to the Christian household. Bernardino directed his attention to women because he believed that they were more receptive to his message.[65] If we remember the extraordinary creativity of his earlier com-

64. A representative sampling of recent Italian scholarship is in Bornstein and Rusconi, *Women and Religion in Medieval and Renaissance Italy.* An excellent study of late-medieval Italian saints is in Anna Benvenuti Papi, *"In Castro Poenitentiae": santità e società femminile nell' Italia medievale* (Rome: Herder, 1990). In order to better understand the religiosity of laywomen, future scholarship must combine insights gained from devotional literature with detailed work in the archives. Samuel Cohn's *Women in the Streets: Essays on Sex and Power in Renaissance Italy* (Baltimore and London: Johns Hopkins University Press, 1996) traces broad changes in devotional practice as well as in social structures; see his chapters "Women and the Counter-Reformation: Authority and Property in the Family" and "Last Wills: Family, Women, and the Black Death in Central Italy."

65. Richard Trexler has claimed that Renaissance sermons in Florence were addressed to males, even though most of the audience was female, "The Florentine Religious Experience: The Sacred Image," *Studies in the Renaissance* 19 (1972): 37–38. This was not true in Bernardino's case, as I will continue to point out in this chapter and elsewhere. Origo's comments on Bernardino and women provide a general introduction to his sensitivity to female listeners, *The World of San Bernardino*, 43–75. And Bernardino may not have been atypical: Bernadette Paton has suggested that other Sienese preachers were also aware of women's role as "cultural catalysts" who aided the clergy through their informal transmission of the Word; *Preaching Friars*, 56–58. For a dissenting view which emphasizes Bernardino's misogyny, see Ida Magli, "L'Etica familiare e la donna in S. Bernardino," *Atti del convegno storico Bernardiniano in occasione del sesto centenario della nascita di S. Bernardino* (L'Aquila: Comitato aquilano del sesto centenario della nascita di S. Bernardino da Siena, 1980), 111–25. Magli claims that Bernardino had "un odio profondo per le donne" and emphasized their function in terms of male needs. I argue the contrary, because of Bernardino's own emphasis on the partnership between himself and his female listeners. Franco Mormando takes a middle position, noting both Bernardino's empathy with women and his misogynistic statements; see "Bernardino of Siena, 'Great Defender' or 'Merciless Betrayer' of Women?" *Italica* 75, no. 1 (Spring 1998): 22–40. A concise overview of clerical misogyny in the centuries preceding Bernardino is in Eleanor Commo McLaughlin, "Equality of Souls, Inequality of Sexes: Woman in Medieval Theology," in *Religion and Sexism: Images of Woman in the Jewish and Christian Traditions*, ed. Rosemary Radford Ruether (New York: Simon and Schuster, 1974), 213–66.

patriot, Catherine of Siena, an artisan woman who listened to sermons and then filtered them through her own religious consciousness, it becomes clear that even the disempowered could be active recipients of the Word. If women attended more frequently, they might have absorbed more of the "orthodox" message and were thus the section of the audience most quick to apprehend the fine points of the sermon.[66] Although Bernardino clearly did not expect to have a Catherine of Siena in his audience, he explicitly said that women possessed more faith than men.[67] He could also cite their receptiveness as a group in order to make a point about repentance and conversion. For example, he began a sermon on sodomy by reminding the men that the day before, when he had preached on vanity, the women stood with bowed heads; he was certain that they would throw away their various ornaments. He goaded the men to perform as well as their women: "Thus I have good hope of you."[68]

Bernardino regarded women as allies in, as well as objects of, reform, who could be trusted to convey the message of the Word at home. Indeed, he relied upon women to act on issues of great social importance. In his preaching against factionalism, for example, he praised women as peacemakers, alluding to the fact that in their role as marriage pawns, women could reconcile warring families as *mezzane*, or mediators. He also encouraged them to work behind the scenes in order to facilitate civic peacemaking.[69] What is striking is Bernardino's attitude that women were welcome and useful at these particular ser-

---

66. D'Avray, *The Preaching of the Friars*, points out that an audience can be sophisticated even if it is not literate: "Literacy is one criterion of the intellectual level, but not the only one," 42.

67. Florence 1424, I, 406. "Molto più fede ànno le donne che gli uomini . . ." When Bernardino describes the women of Jerusalem crying out in compassion as Christ went to Calvary, he remarks that "naturalmente le donne sono più piatose che non sono gli uomini e di più fede . . ."; Ibid., I, 135. Other preachers also acknowledged women's piety. See, for example, Michelle Menot's estimate that French women outnumbered men at sermons by four to one; Taylor, *Soldiers of Christ*, 172.

68. Siena 1425, II, 99.

69. Siena 1427, I, 384.

mons, telling us that, at least on one level, they were regarded as full citizens in the preacher's construction of the polis.[70] In other talks directed at specifically male sinners he often tried to enlist women as spiritual allies. Sometimes, Bernardino admitted, the usurer will refuse to hear a sermon on restitution, but the good wife can help the preacher in her own way:

> You know very well that spinach is fried in the pan with oil and salt, and that afterwards it is removed and placed in a serving dish with vinegar. So wives, do the same with him! Tell him he's going to the inferno, but that if he makes amends [i.e., restores usurious gains] God will pardon him. And if he says villainous things to you, bring out the vinegar that bites. Tell him that you don't want him to stay, that he's the son of the devil. In this way, remind him of his own good, give him some hot words—and you can make him amend.[71]

The spiritually adept wife could help teach her less pious husband "through good habits, honest words and ways and acts and deeds."[72] In other words, she served as the preacher's loyal proxy.

Judging from Bernardino's sermons, an effective preacher needed to appeal to his female listeners in order to accomplish his larger mission of individual and social reform. In fact, for the duration of the sermon, the public—hence gendered—space of the piazza underwent a

70. Decades later, Savonarola would not want women at his political sermons. See Luca Landucci, *A Florentine Diary*, trans. Alice De Rosen Jervis (London: J. M. Dent and Sons, 1927), 76–77.

71. Florence 1424, I, 371–72. "Tu sai bene che gli spinaci si friggono nella padella coll'olio e col sale, e poi si cavano della padella e mettonsi nel tegame coll'aceto e coll'agresto. Così fa ' tu, donna, a lui. Friggilo e ugnilo. Digli ch'egli anderà allo 'nferno, e poi, se rende, che Iddio gli perdonerà, e se si pente. E se ti dice villania, mettivi l'aceto e l'agresto che pugne. Digli che non vi vuogli istare, e ch'egli è figliuolo del diavolo, e a questo modo, ricordandogli el suo bene e dandogli de' caldegli, el potresti ridurre a farlo amendare."

72. Ibid., I, 407. Earlier preachers had made similar observations about their partnership with women: see Peter Biller, "The Common Woman in the Western Church in the Thirteenth and Early Fourteenth Centuries," in *Women in the Church*, ed. W. J. Shields and Diana Wood (Oxford: Basil Blackwell, 1990), 127–57.

remarkable transformation as the male preacher performed for a largely female audience, and they responded in turn. Individual reactions of
women to Bernardino are difficult to gauge, however. There are unfortunately no eyewitness accounts by female writers, but women do appear frequently in sermon descriptions as very active participants, taking part in dramatic exorcisms, as well as in peacemaking rituals and
the destruction of vanities. Despite the occasional sleeper or talker
who was rebuked during the course of the sermon, women also seem
to have been fairly attentive as a group. In a discussion on gossip,
Bernardino acidly pointed out that some people attended sermons just
to catch him in a mistake and that he would speak about these critics
one day. He asks for his female listeners' help: "Remind me about it,
O women, if I forget." When there was a really impressive response
from the female audience he commented upon it: a few days after
pleading with women to aid the unfortunate prisoners of the Sienese
commune, he reported back by thanking them all for their great charity. At other times he watched the women carefully and tried to provoke an emotional reaction: "O women, weep with me!" (*Doh, donne,
piagnete con meco!*)—the sense in this passage implies that they already
were. Collectively, they may have functioned as the preacher's chorus
with their tears, wailing, and shouts of "Misericordia!" Sometimes,
though, they were bewildered by Bernardino's vehemence; in one sermon he became so frenzied that the women must have registered
shock: "O women, am I outside of my sense? Do you think I've become crazy?"[73] The rhythm of the sermons was modulated by this
steady give-and-take between preacher and women.

Bernardino's faithful listeners, however, were not always as compli-
ant as he would have liked. They were particularly difficult to handle
whenever he spoke on the delicate topic of sexual relationships. Since
this lifelong virgin never hesitated to discuss the most intimate details
of married life, his preaching sometimes created scandal. Criticism

73. The examples are from Siena 1427: reminder, I, 141; thanks, II, 1111; weeping together, II, 1036; crazy? II, 1020–21.

seems to have been directed at him primarily from the female segment of the audience, and it resulted in an elaborate self-defense whenever he broached the topic.[74] Save for his talks on the YHS (which he realized made him vulnerable to heresy charges), this defensiveness is unparalleled elsewhere in the recorded sermons. When he spoke out against forbidden sexual practices, he imagined that people were saying his words "stank all the way to the brain." Preachers could be dangerously frank: Poggio Bracciolini tells the story of a preacher in Campania who, speaking against lust, warned his listeners not to place a pillow beneath the woman's hips for greater pleasure. Needless to say, his audience was eager to try this new sexual treat.[75] But Bernardino trusted preventative medicine, even when the prudish did not care for its taste: better to know an evil so that you avoid it rather than sin in ignorance.

The key point of disagreement between preacher and women was his insistence that it was better for young girls to know about sexual sins before they unwittingly engaged in them. Specifically, he warned them about husbands who wanted to practice sodomy ("Don't obey him. Rather, let him kill you.")[76] So he would order mothers to bring their daughters to these sermons without fail. This was unsuccessful enough to aggravate him. He begins one speech on marital love by accusing the women: "She who is wise has led her daughter here this morning to the sermon; she who is less than good has left her in bed. O, how much better you would have done to have led her to hear this

74. One defiant opener from a sermon on sodomy: ". . . l'un lato mi spegnie, l'altro mi tira indietro. Dall'uno lato mi pute; da l'altro ò odore di volervi trarre de' vizi vostri. Chi mi dice: 'Tace!' Chi mi dice 'Grida!' Ma considerando in me, è meglio el dire che 'l tacere . . ."; Siena 1425, II, 98. See also the retort in Florence 1424, I, 380–82.

75. Siena 1427, I, 587. Poggio's tale, real or invented, is in his *Facezie*, ed. Marcello Ciccuto (Milan: Biblioteca Universale Rizzoli, 1983), 166–67.

76. Florence 1424, I, 391. In the same sermon, Bernardino also warned against sex during menstruation because it would engender monsters "o con due coppie di mani, o con sei dita, o in mancamento della natura, o nascere uomini e femine perverse, pieni di lebbra o d'altri male."

true doctrine!"[77] He later scolds them for their neglect: although he asked them to bring the daughters, they have not obeyed, and he says irritably that he is excused on his part; he has done what he could. "You don't want to learn your own need? Your own damnation then." This reprimand was less than successful because a few minutes later, as he starts talking about the sexual obligations of spouses, he has to interrupt the sermon by pleading: "Don't go, don't leave; wait, so that you perhaps hear things that you haven't ever heard!"[78] That was precisely the problem—and the scandalized mothers were voting with their feet. As this tense exchange about sexual behavior shows, even great preachers like Bernardino could meet with various forms of resistance, some subtle and others not.

Most talks, though, were appropriate for cautious mothers and their offspring. As the core of his regular audience, women had the further responsibility to bring young children to the sermons. Bernardino hoped to see a variety of faces before him, young and old, so that his message could begin to penetrate at the earliest age and continue doing its good work until death. But this may have been unusual, even at those sermons which were more innocuous than those on sexual mores. On the first Sunday during his 1424 preaching in Florence, Bernardino had to ask parents to bring children to next week's sermon, from age "five years and above, both girls and boys."[79] A few sermons were meant specifically for younger listeners, though they seem more applicable to *giovani* than to *fanciulli* (the sermons on the value of study, for example, or on the Virgin Mary as a cultural ideal for girls).

77. Siena 1427, I, 539. Unlike another fifteenth-century Observant, Cherubino da Spoleto, who put the responsibility on male heads of household, who were supposed to set a good example: ". . . debbigli mandare alle predicazioni . . . o vero ci va' tu, e poi in casa racconta o fa raccontare la predicare, accioché quegli che non ci sono stati venghino a imparare alcuna cosa; se non tutto, parte." Quoted in Rusconi, *Predicazione e vita religiosa*, 191.

78. Ibid., II, 586.

79. Florence 1424, I, 66.

The most obvious of the messages designed for the young was the respect owed to parents and to elders in general. Like many of his contemporaries, he feared the potential hazards in a city where youth had the upper hand. His attitude can be summed up in one pithy statement: "He is young; therefore, he isn't wise."[80] Disobedience to parents resulted in disasters in this life and beyond. One story told about an evil young man who continually disobeyed his poor parents until he became a criminal and was finally hanged for his misdeeds. The corpse immediately began to age, proving that had he lived like a good son, the reprobate's natural life span would have been seventy years or more.[81] It is not clear from the tone of the sermons whether the young were present to absorb these baleful messages or if Bernardino wanted them preached again at home by stern parents. Parents, too, had obligations towards the child, and so the preacher spent even more time outlining the proper behavior of good fathers and mothers, promising them rewards in this life and the next. In particular, he focused on the responsibilities of fathers towards both their children and their households; for example, they needed to have everyone under their care go to confession and communion, or else they themselves would sin mortally.[82]

The sermons on fatherhood are one of the strongest indications that, although women made up the bulk of his regular audience, Bernardino also had men to whom he could speak. Most workers, particularly those in the laboring and artisan classes, were undoubtedly too busy to come during the week,[83] but the most devout men may been frequent sermon-goers, perhaps like those hooded confraternity

80. Ibid., I, 202.

81. Ibid., I, 194–95.

82. Ibid., I, 3, and II, 264.

83. Some lower guildsmen were part of the audience, however. At one point, for example, Bernardino calls out to butchers ("*O beccari . . .*"); Siena 1427, I, 517. And his encounters with individuals seeking advice include lower-class men: see the example of the barber who gave one-tenth of his earnings to the poor after hearing Bernardino preach; Siena 1427, II, 1220–21.

members depicted in a Vecchietta panel of Bernardino preaching.[84] Many sins which were favorite targets of his wrath—sodomy between males, usury, and factionalism—were gender-specific, although women could be guilty of complicity. And just as his domestic imagery was designed for female listeners, his metaphors of battles and sieges were probably aimed at their husbands. But men, too, could be enmeshed in domestic dilemmas. Just as a woman could be hurt by her husband's desire for a servant, so could a man be shamed by his wife's adultery. How would you feel, he asked the men, if your wife and her lover locked you out of the house and then made jokes at you?[85]

In Florence, at least, Bernardino assumed that he was addressing a basically literate audience, which argues for the presence of many males. If you have not confessed in twenty years, he advised, take a book with twenty pages and divide each sheet into four parts, one for each season of the year. Then search your memory year by year, season by season, until you are satisfied that you have written down all of your sins. This memory device was clearly intended for those men who possessed at least a rudimentary education and the willingness to order their consciences in the same manner as their account books. But Bernardino did not forget the unlettered, as he immediately assured them that the mind also writes everything in its memory and that you could achieve the same thing in your head.[86]

At least some of the literate men who came were *gente da bene*. Neroccio di Bartolommeo's painting shows a raised dais where a row of prominent citizens are seated, undoubtedly the governing officials of Siena. Since Bernardino preached at the invitation and with the blessing of these men, it is natural that they should have been present to hear his words. In at least one case, there was a restricted audience of the ruling class within the Great Hall of Siena's Palazzo Pubblico. For all of his fiery delivery and ruthless assessment of social sin, Bernardi-

84. Vecchietta's painting is in Siena's Pinacoteca.
85. Florence 1424, I, 56.
86. Florence 1424, I, 45–46.

no was not a challenging figure to ruling elites. His basic message was
spiritual regeneration, so there was little in his sermons that leading
citizens would have found threatening. Even his Apocalyptic sermons,
which promised the sure ruin of the city if the inhabitants refused to
repent, neither predicted nor advocated social change, despite the terrifying effect of his words. It is noteworthy that most of the written
criticism against Bernardino came from hostile clerics, and not from
laymen.[87]

His attitude towards the social hierarchy was comfortably conventional. In a discussion of how grave a sin it was to offend God, he
went so far as to say that it was worse to kill a citizen than a contadi-
no, a lord than a citizen, and so forth, trying to make his audience
progressively imagine how terrible it was to offend the greatest Lord
of all. Although he championed the poor, his own educated prejudices
occasionally slipped out, as when he began one exemplum with "a
worker, one of those, you understand, who don't know too much
. . ."[88] Bernardino, who saw himself as a plain speaker, probably had no
conscious intention of ingratiating himself with the ruling class; statements like these signify, rather, an unconscious acceptance of hierarchy, both worldly and divine. But ruling implied responsibility, too—
some of the preacher's harshest criticism was directed at unjust offi-

87. One of the exceptions is Poggio's diatribe against the Observants in "On
Avarice," trans. Benjamin G. Kohl and Elizabeth B. Welles, in *The Earthly Republic: Italian
Humanists on Government and Society*, ed. Benjamin G. Kohl and Ronald G. Witt with
Elizabeth B. Welles (Philadelphia: University of Pennsylvania Press, 1978), 243–47.
Bernardino is nominally excused from the general failings of his order, but the malice
underneath is apparent. Also see the complaints of a Milanese abacus teacher who
protested Bernardino's too-successful conversion of adolescents to the Observance;
Celestino Piana, "Un processo svolto a Milano nel 1441 a favore del mag. Amadeo de
Landis e contro frate Bernardino da Siena," in *Cateriniano-Bernardiniano*, 753–92, and
Mormando, *The Preacher's Demons*, 82–84.
88. Siena 1425, I, 93. Michael Mullett, however, speculates that social preaching
such as Bernardino's "helped to inspire popular complaint, protest and insurgency";
Popular Culture and Popular Protest in Late Medieval and Early Modern Europe (London: Croom
Helm, 1987), 123–25. In fact, Bernardino's fervent defense of the poor is embedded in
traditional assumptions about almsgiving, and the fact that his regular listeners were
middle- and upper-class females argues against his preaching as active social protest.

cials who oppressed the poor. The affluent and the powerful also may have felt uncomfortable when Bernardino denounced the deadly sin of pride. And, although his speeches on forgiveness were aimed at the entire audience, male and female, much of what he says about the vendetta seems to be targeted at those upper-class men who were most likely to practice it.

One specialized group of males, clerics, probably came to Bernardino's preaching, but it is difficult to prove their regular presence from the recorded sermons. At a few points the preacher addressed them directly: "O priests or friars, are you here? This morning I wish that there were many of you. But let us speak to those who have come."[89] It is impossible to know whether priests and friars (other than Franciscans) attended in large numbers or not, since Bernardino felt that it was indecorous to berate them publicly, despite the intense pleasure that such criticism would have afforded nonclerics; he told the Florentines—who were probably disappointed—that he would only deal with clerical sins in a private setting.[90] There were, however, points of criticism which came up as Bernardino preached to layfolk: priests' lewd behavior with women, for example, or their failure to condemn usurers and partisans. There were also sly comments aimed at unnamed preachers who failed to live up to his own high standards. Even though most of the criticism which Bernardino received was from clerics, we cannot know whether members of hostile orders came to study their enemy or whether they preferred to stay away. The sermons are silent on the matter.

One large group whose presence does reverberate in the sermons was composed of the skeptics, the jokers, the nonlisteners, and the

89. Siena 1427, II, 1110. The rare sermon is directed exclusively at clerics; see Siena 1425, II, 131–44 on the duties of those who have renounced the world. More frequently, Bernardino gave miscellaneous advice to priests in the course of sermons aimed at layfolk.

90. A ferocious defense of clerical privilege and secular incompetence to judge clerical sin is in Florence 1424, I, 223: ". . . non està a' secolari a impacciarsi de' fatti loro." Bernardino wanted no public discussion of priestly failings: ". . . non si vogliono riprenderli in publico ma in disparte."

hostile. Like the soldier who was determined to stand among the women, these were all potential disrupters of the holy message. Since Bernardino's ability to amuse and charm could draw the impious and the merely bored to the piazza, the attention span of some of the listeners fluctuated along with the preacher's bravura on a given day. On many occasions it was necessary to reprimand the audience for talking or even walking out before the sermon was finished, and at the beginning of at least one discourse, he could not continue without several sharp commands to attend to his words.[91] While he hoped that everyone would come—it was their duty as well as his chance to convert the ignorant—sometimes Bernardino wished that the ill-behaved would stay away altogether:

> Now listen to the things that I will say this morning since preachers usually say little about it and so little is heard by people. And, as I said before, the intelligent and the discreet will not leave but the crazies can either go away or be patient.[92]

The preacher was apparently taunted by men in the crowd who could not hear a sermon without making jokes (*beffe*). Occasionally someone would pretend to be shocked by the subject matter:

> A fellow who is sunken in lust will say: "Oh, what sermons! . . . Eh! eh! eh!" He makes jokes about it with words and deeds. Doh! Have you ever seen these lumps of flesh? Oh! They've stayed in bed this morning! Oh! They are comfortable! They'll become even bigger lumps![93]

Bernardino's quick wit made him no easy prey.

91. At the beginning of one sermon he asks: "Che cosa è giustizia? Giustizia è . . . (Guardare me, hai inteso? Guarda me!) Giustizia se può intendare in molti e varii modi; ma fra gli altri, guistizia è constanzia di perpetua volontà . . . (O dalla fonte, che state a fare il mercato, andatelo a fare altrove! Non odite, o voi dalla fonte?)"; Siena 1427, II, 710–11.

92. Florence 1424, I, 217. "Or odi cose ch'io ti dirò stamani, che poco s'usano di dire per li nostri pari predicatori, e poco sono udite da' popoli. E, come ti dissi di sopra, gl'intelligenti e discreti non si partono e pazzi ne vadino via o abbino pazienza."

93. Siena 1427, I, 615. "Dice colui che è invilupato in libidine: 'Oh, che prediche! . . . Eh! eh! eh!' Elli se ne fa beffe co' le parole e co' fatti. Doh! avete voi mai ve-

One difficult segment of the male audience was composed of the usurers who could be found in every town where Bernardino preached. His frequent advice on *mercanzia* was usually more applicable to petty shopkeepers than it was to the great merchant-usurers, but the latter more often appear as a major target. In both the Florentine and Sienese cycles he usually was not attacking Jews, but "crazy" Christian hypocrites who say to Christ, "I worship you, but I don't believe in you."[94] These men were the first to go to Mass (and the sermon?) because their avarice kept them awake at night. Bernardino tried to persuade his audience that usury disrupted the common good—when a usurer died, the whole town rejoiced, as if it was roasting a pig.[95]

The shame of usurers or their unwillingness to face their sins made them an especially touchy group. They did not care to be identified for what they were:

> There isn't a beast that doesn't answer to its own name. If they say "Cat! Cat!" immediately the cat flees. So does the usurer; he flees at once.[96]

Bernardino was extremely sensitive to how his words were being received, and he had no illusion that everyone listened with equal attention, understanding, or respect. In the case cited above, the problem was an all-too-human discomfort at being singled out. Yet sometimes this worked in the preacher's favor, resulting not in an angry response, but in a conversion. The anonymous biographer relates an incident in Vicenza when, during a tirade against usury, Bernardino inadvertently kept glaring at and gesturing towards a man who happened to be a notorious usurer. Stung by the humiliation and by the preacher's just reprimands, the usurer determined to change and began by seeking out the holy man in his cell. But when he spoke to Bernardino's confrères, they insisted that the preacher had only been discussing usury in gen-

---

duti di questi pezzi di carne? Oh! elli so' rimasti stamane nel letto. Oh! ellino stanno in agio! Elli si faranno e più be' pezzotti di carne!"

94. Florence 1424, I, 78.
95. Ibid., I, 84.
96. Siena 1425, II, 277.

eral terms. Nevertheless, the coincidence along with the public shame made the sinner take it all as a sign from heaven, and he decided to restore his usurious gains anyway.[97] This possibility for self-identification and subsequent conversion explains why Bernardino tried to get everyone to come to the sermons, even the recalcitrant.

But there could be no accommodation with a certain kind of sinner. A "stubborn" group of men was actively hostile to Bernardino:

> They flee from sermons or rather they never come, in order not to hear about their evil life, and to have no reason to raise themselves up from the dirt. Filthy no-good who doesn't want to hear![98]

According to Leonardo Benvoglienti, Bernardino's strong aversion to homosexuals began in his childhood. The pretty boy was supposedly chased by older Sienese men, but the future saint sturdily resisted with jeers and blows and on one occasion harassed the harasser with a band of friends. One admirer was present years later when Bernardino preached in the Campo and the memory of his evil intentions made the man dissolve into tears.[99] But it is unlikely that most homosexuals were as repentant as the shamed Sienese since the preacher complained that they laughed at his reproaches.

Bernardino sometimes labeled the "sodomite" as a man who practiced a specific sin, either with males or females, but generally he referred to him as a member of a separate category (that is, as a *type* of sinner).[100] Sodomites were thus marginalized as designated enemies, as

97. Anonymous Friar, "Vie inédite," 337–38.

98. Florence 1425, II, 277.

99. Benvoglienti, "Vie," 62.

100. Bernardino worried that young girls would be married off to "ribaldi soddomiti." In a brief but furious tirade, he warned parents that "forse uccidendola salvaresti quella anima, ove maritarla a simili uomini, perdono l'anima e 'l corpo, dandolo a' soddomiti arrabiati"; Florence 1424, I, 388. It is difficult to see how parents would be able to identify these "sodomites," unless they had some kind of public reputation as homosexuals; in this particular instance, Bernardino clearly did not distinguish between the "act" and the "persona," implying that innocent females would be victimized by men who enjoyed sodomy with other men. For a more extensive treatment of

were witches, heretics, and, to a lesser extent, partisans. As we have seen, one of the preacher's key techniques was the cultivation of an all-encompassing intimacy mingling empathy and humor with reproaches and mockery. The purpose was to create a dialogue which would draw the sinner in and cause him or her to repent. Bernardino did not bother wasting this relatively gentle technique on sodomites, whom he considered to be "hardened sinners" of the worst sort. Although he hoped that he could dissuade young boys from the practice, his normal tone was intensely threatening, with the adult sodomite distanced in his role as the unredeemable "Other." Instead, the usual dialogue which took place was with other members of the audience, especially parents and officials, who needed to be persuaded to root out the vice.

A particularly concentrated attack on sodomy which uses this distancing technique occurs in three sermons given on April 6, 7, and 8, 1424, in Florence. Bernardino addresses the Florentines at large rather than sodomites as a group whenever he offers his ultimate solution: "You need to punish by fire or fines in order to get rid of this vice which ruins your good name throughout the world!"[101] On April 6, he compares sodomites with animals: their lustfulness makes them "unbridled horses" and "obstinate pigs." This is then swiftly developed into an association of sodomites with demons: they are like the herd of swine into which Christ cast the legion of devils. The next step is an ominous warning about "those wild pigs who always go about at night, in the dark," destroying the state—and yet the Florentines refuse to take care of this public danger! The scarcely veiled association is with those other sinners of the night, witches and heretics. Both citizens and parents are blamed for failing to restrain the vice: the latter have permitted their sons to "become girls."[102]

Bernardino's preaching against sodomy, see Michael Rocke, *Forbidden Friendships: Homosexuality and Male Culture in Renaissance Florence* (New York and Oxford: Oxford University Press, 1996), 36–44, and Mormando, *The Preacher's Demons*, 109–63.

101. Florence 1424, II, 22.

102. Ibid., II, 35.

The next day, he depicts Florence as Lazarus, the dead man, "stinking to God and the world."[103] The tirade that morning includes everything from the coming of the Angel of the Apocalypse to accusations that the Florentines encourage laziness and sodomy by permitting the taverns to stay open twenty-four hours; the *ispeziali* make it worse by selling marzipan and sugared cakes! Throw out the idle, he demands, and "whatever male has become female" (*"chiunque è fatto di maschio femmina"*).[104]

In the culminating sermon, Bernardino's focus is on retribution and the just punishment of sodomites—and other Florentines—if they will not amend. He advocates burning again, this time explicitly in praise of the savage justice he once saw rendered in Venice. "I saw a sodomite burnt in Venice," he says, impressed; the Venetians, who do not spare the well-born, carry out "the justice that you do not." The burning of the sodomite is only a prelude, of course, to what he will suffer in the fires of hell. "All of the sodomites in the inferno will be coals burning so that the smoke goes all the way to the blessed in paradise" (i.e., so that they can savor the sufferings of the damned).[105] In this and other preaching against sodomites, Bernardino deliberately set them apart from other sinners—both now and in the hereafter—as unsalvageables.

The most intriguing subtext of the anti-sodomy sermons was the dilemma, as Bernardino saw it, of his predominantly female audience. While he chastised Sienese women for their vanity and coddled sons, he also tried to instill active hatred for their "natural enemies." Like the serpent, the sodomite was woman's nemesis, and she should flee whenever he approached. In one remarkable tirade, he showed he was on woman's side by explicitly putting himself in her place. He could

103. Ibid., II, 37.

104. Ibid., II, 45–46.

105. Ibid., II, 66–67. For the Venetians' treatment of homosexuals, see Guido Ruggiero, *The Boundaries of Eros: Sex Crime and Sexuality in Renaissance Venice* (New York: Oxford University Press, 1985), 109–45.

barely contain his wrath against the sin which harmed marriage: "Doh, if I could . . . oh, if I could, I would . . . ! If I was a woman, I'd certainly try to extinguish [that vice] in my husband!"[106] Bernardino was undoubtedly appealing to wives' jealousy of male rivals, as well as their attempts to protect their own bodies and souls.

The preacher's appeal to specific groups, whether beleaguered wives or usurious merchants, may have been matched by his words to partic- ular audiences as a whole. It is likely that crowds in different cities var- ied in their response, both in terms of attendance and pliability. Un- fortunately, because of the uneven nature of the sources, we can only speculate. Bernardino provides some useful information, however, from the point of view of an exceptionally well-traveled man. He was fond of characterizing the "personality" of a given town, much as his contemporaries did, and as many Italians still enjoy doing today.[107] His descriptions suggest that certain towns indeed responded to him differently and that this in turn affected his opinion of them. For ex- ample, the place that received his greatest ire was Rome, since its pop- ulace was so hostile to him when he was summoned to the city in 1426 on charges of heresy. As Bernardino put it to his beloved Sienese, "They wanted me roasted, they wanted me fried."[108]

Most of the personal encounters described in the sermons are from northern Italy, although the preacher did not distinguish between the personalities of its towns. The marked exception was Venice, which Bernardino saw in terms of the contemporary stereotype. La Serenissi- ma apparently made a profound impression on the friar from the Tus-

106. Siena 1427, I, 1157–58. For an individual woman's dilemma, see the story of the married "virgin" who for six years had only sodomy with her husband and decided to see Bernardino for advice; Siena 1427, I, 591.

107. Bernardino pointed out that the weak points of our natures as individuals or as inhabitants of certain cities always incline us to commit the same sins; Florence 1425, I, 189. Many Italians still indulge in regional stereotypes, labeling Siena and the Sienese as "chiusi," for example, or Emilians as especially "accoglienti."

108. Siena 1427, I, 183. "Di quello che s'è fatto a Roma non dico nulla; che quando v'andai, chi mi voleva fritto e chi arostito . . ."

can hills; his admiring description of its great harbor contains something of the open-mouthed wonder of a country boy visiting his first great metropolis.[109] He was even more impressed by that state's stable government and freedom from the plague of factions, and—as we have seen in the case of sodomy—he praised the Venetians for their efficient and ruthless execution of justice. Venice was always an ideal for Bernardino, a paradise of "Good Government" which he liked to use in his preaching against civil strife.

Perugia, on the other hand, emerges as the city for which he may have had the most genuine affection. This was understandable since the Perugians paid him the supreme compliment of revising their statutes after his visit there in 1425.[110] Bernardino returned on several other occasions and was always honored with immense enthusiasm, which continued after his canonization when the city constructed an oratory for the new saint, decorated with exquisite reliefs by Agostino di Duccio. Bernardino felt that the Perugians were as eager to turn towards good as they had been to embrace evil, an analysis in keeping with the city's political volatility. The Sienese preacher considered Perugia to be a model of conversion and liked to goad his own countrymen with its virtue. In a plea to those sinners who needed to repent instead of "returning to the vomit," Bernardino described Perugia as a place "according to my heart." People there frequented the churches, he said, and confessed often. He taunted the Sienese:

> I haven't heard anything about you, that you have done so well. Therefore: mend your ways, mend your ways! Do you want to be worse than those others?[111]

109. Siena 1427, I, 459.

110. The statutes are in Antonio Fantozzi, "Documenta Perusina de S. Bernardino Senesi," in *AFH* 15 (1922): 103–54 and 406–75. For the most notable change in the statutes, the abolition of Perugia's famous stone-throwing battle, a violent ritual game of the city's youth, see Claudia Cardinali, "Il santo e la norma: Bernardino da Siena e gli statuti perugini del 1425," in *Gioco e giustizia nell' Italia di Comune*, ed. Gherardo Ortalli (Treviso: Fondazione Benetton and Rome: Viella, 1993), 182–91.

111. Siena 1427, I, 183. "Ma non anco udito di voi nulla, che voi aviate fatto tanto bene. E però amendatevi, amendatevi. Volete voi essere peggiori che sieno gli altri?"

This ploy suggests that, within the limits of discretion, Bernardino may have made similar comparisons elsewhere, in hopes of using the spirit of *campanilismo* to his own advantage.

He displayed considerably less affection for the Tuscan rival of Siena. Admittedly, the two groups of Florentine sermons are less rich than their Sienese counterparts in those warm personal asides that would enable us to pinpoint his attitude. But when Bernardino made a judgment specifically on Florence, his tone was different from the pride he felt in the Perugians or the exasperated affection one hears in the sermons preached to the Sienese. Florence was an impressive sight in the 1420s, with its display of artistic and intellectual energy, and Bernardino did not fail to notice its achievements. But he berated the citizens for their tendency to "build chapels" instead of truly repent-ing.[112] In much of his criticism of Florence there is the ascetic's disgust with the comfortable and complacent rich. Even the city's intellectual prowess was double-edged, since Florence surpassed all other places in evil, as it did in good:

> As I've told you so many times, if a man has a noble intellect, so much more does he understand the good and thus also the evil [along with it]. Italy is the most intellectual country in the world, Tuscany is her most in-tellectual province, and Florence is the most intellectual city in Tuscany. Thus Florence has the most natural understanding in the world and therefore the greatest sins.[113]

His unrelenting attack on sodomites was another chance to criticize Florentine laxity. He painted an image of pampered Florentine youth whose lifestyle—sweetened by all that marzipan!—naturally encour-aged vice. It shocked Bernardino that a city with such nobility and *gen-tilezza* could be so sunken in filth: "Oh, how much you have to cry and

---

112. Florence 1425, I, 89.

113. Florence 1424, II, 64. "Come t'o detto più volte, quanto più l'uomo è di gen-tile intelletto, tanto più apprende el bene e così el male. La patria d'Italia è la più in-tellettiva parte del mondo, e Toscana è la più intellettiva provincia d'Italia, e Firenze è la più intellettiva città di Toscana. Adunque maggiore senno naturale che nel mondo sia debba essere in Firenze, e però maggiori peccati."

despair about!"[114] Like the appeal to *campanilismo*, this censure of particular vices in particular cities may have been a standard feature of his preaching, an effort to make his words personal in a civic as well as in an individual way.

Bernardino's special relationship to the Sienese will be discussed in the context of his preaching against factional strife. In addition to the Sienese propensity to engage in faction, he criticized the city's general backsliding in religious matters. But at least the preacher was able to comfort himself with the observation that the Sienese had the good habit of listening to a sermon until the end.[115] This is ironic in light of the frequent interruptions which are recorded in the 1427 sermons. If the Sienese were an especially "attentive" audience, then how much more disruptive were crowds in other towns?

This question introduces one of the most puzzling issues in any consideration of the real impact of Bernardino's words. The Sienese preacher initially laid the foundation of his celebrity in the northern towns of Lombardy and the Veneto. If modern Italians must strain to understand dialects far removed from those of their own region and from standard Italian, it must have been correspondingly difficult for fifteenth-century audiences to follow a Sienese preacher in an age before Tuscan was the linguistic norm. Could the Sienese have been so attentive because they could relish every play on words, the humor of each pithy anecdote, the complexity of the more serious discussions? It is true that Bernardino was a great success in the north. For example, he achieved a general pacification at Belluno, a town in the Venetian outback, and he was popular in Bergamo, a place noted even today for its distinctive dialect. Yet it is unlikely that the average Lombard woman would have comprehended the sermons in quite the same way as her Tuscan counterpart. Among urban audiences which included the uneducated and the untraveled, most of Bernardino's more subtle allusions must have been lost. He did try to include words from each

114. Ibid., II, 53–54.
115. Siena 1427, I, 164–65.

locality where he preached—in this he could have been helped by the resident Franciscan community—but the problem could not have been easily surmounted.[116]

Clearly more went on at a Bernardino sermon than the spell created by his honeyed tongue. Any discussion of the preacher and peacemaker which only takes into account his actual words is doomed to be incomplete. In the highly visual culture of Quattrocento Italy the sermon was a spectacle which combined both hearing and seeing, and the rapport between preacher and listeners was cemented not only by the mental bonds of words, but by audience participation. Bernardino's great success as a preacher was largely due to his ability to harness and direct his listeners' own energies until they were willing to surrender their vanities in a bonfire or their hatreds in a peacemaking.

IV. The Scene of the Sermon

Both the physical setting of the sermon and the appearance of the preacher himself contributed to a visual display which reinforced Bernardino's hold over his audience. A bell first summoned the faithful since the sermons were usually held in the mornings. Each sermon was preceded by a celebration of the Mass, a stimulus to the preacher who claimed afterward that he felt "light and bold" (*leggiero e gagliardo*) and thus in fighting form for the strenuous act of preaching which followed.[117] Although Bernardino often spoke in churches, as he did inside Florence's immense Santa Croce, he became associated with open-air preaching in the piazze of the towns he visited. For this he received permission from the pope to hold the Mass outside of the church.[118]

116. Ibid., II, 229.

117. Siena 1425, II, 313.

118. For the pope's permission, see Siena 1425, II, 116 and 229–30. Richard Trexler claims that "the emptying of the church in effect radically desacralized it"; *Public Life in Renaissance Florence* (New York: Academic Press, 1980), 53. However, Bernardino's custom of preaching in the piazza was essentially a practical measure—to have more room and, possibly, to attract passers-by. Besides, preachers had been using the convenient setting of the piazze even before Saint Francis's time.

Even when he began to preach inside, there was a practical reason why it was often necessary to move outdoors: eventually the sheer mass of listeners could not be accommodated by even the largest of buildings. In 1425 when he preached in Siena, he actually had to move from an outdoor space, the Piazza San Francesco, to the much larger Campo, which indicates that his audience grew as reports of the sermonizing made the rounds.[119] Two years later, he told his Sienese audience that he couldn't preach inside because "there isn't a church which could hold the half of you"—this in a city with a comparatively large Duomo. An occasional drawback of the outdoors, however, was that sermons could be interrupted by a sudden downpour, an event which Bernardino regarded as direct interference from the devil. Another disadvantage to preaching in the open was that it may have encouraged nonchalant behavior. The preacher was annoyed when people brought their casual attitudes even into a church: it was necessary to tell them not to spit, not to lean their elbows upon the altar, and to refrain from bringing their hawks and dogs inside.[120] The elementary nature of these warnings makes it easy to imagine the difficulties presented by a large crowd in a piazza.

A considerable amount of work was necessary in order to prepare the piazza for both Mass and sermon. Besides the erection of a pulpit, an altar had to be set up and seats for the worthies arranged. The expense for these preparations was borne by the commune, which also might have provided men to help assist Bernardino's companions.[121] Another expense was for candles: a description of the prelude to the sermons claimed that so much wax was burning that it was a wonder to behold.[122] If the Mass began early enough, the flickering effect of

119. Siena 1425, I, 145.

120. Ibid., I, 179–83.

121. Bernardino always seems to have traveled with companions, the best known of these his close friend Fra Vicenzo of Siena. See Gustavo Cantini, "I compagni missionari o socii de S.B. da Siena," *Studi Francescani* (1945), 262–77. Cantini speculates that Bernardino's fellow priests among his associates probably heard confessions after some sermons, 277.

122. Siena Biblioteca, MS. I. II.34 (henceforth referred to as "The Poetical Life" of

candles in the dawn must have been extremely pleasing. Paintings of the sermons do not depict the candles, but do show the pulpit and altar covered with rich cloth. In marked contrast to the adornment of this backdrop stood the preacher himself, a very icon of holiness in his simple Observant robe, his entire being testifying to his personal asceticism. Bernardino's appearance made one observer characterize him as a "Seraph."[123] The statue by Vecchietta now in the main hall of the Museo Nazionale (Bargello) in Florence gives some idea of the impressive demeanor of Bernardino as he preached: emaciated, toothless, yet commanding despite his frailty. The holy man's visage must have provided reassurance to the people massed below him, his blatant saintliness an integral part of the scene.

Bernardino's wizened body was belied by the physical energy he displayed throughout the course of the long sermons. Aside from the obvious exertion of talking for hours, he probably employed an active mode of gesticulation. Fifteenth-century Italian preachers made use of a wide range of gestures in order to get their point across to audiences. Giovanni da Capestrano, for one, shocked his northern European listeners by preaching "with hands and feet." Roberto da Lecce, a controversial preacher at mid-century, had a flamboyant repertoire that would have been familiar to late-antique ascetics. People were tremendously impressed by Roberto's Christ imitation when he stood silently for long periods with arms dramatically stretched out in the form of a cross.[124] Bernardino's mannerisms were probably not so extreme—the

---

San Bernardino) folio 19r. Andrea de Cascia, an Augustinian critic of Bernardino and the Observants, accused the Franciscans of wanting a showy setting for their preaching: ". . . nam ipsi, quando volunt celebrare, requirunt altare novum et in platea maiori cum magno apparatu, cum aureola et umbracula desuper, cum magna multitudine luminum, cum strepitu omnis generis musicorum, tubarum et campanarum . . ." in Longpré, "S. Bernardin et le nom de Jesus" *AFH* 29 (1936): 451.

123. "Poetical Life," fols. 18r and 26v.

124. Roberto was not the only preacher with heroic stamina: the fourteenth-century Giordano da Pisa could preach up to four sermons per day; D. Lesnick, *Preaching in Medieval Florence*, 113. For gesture in medieval culture see Jean-Claude Schmitt, *La Raison des gestes dans l'occident médiéval* (Paris: Gallimard, 1990), esp. on preachers, 278–84. Baxan-

"dolce" epitaph hints at this and contemporaries paid more attention to his powerful voice—but he knew how to use gestures effectively. Occasionally the sermons indicate that he singled out individuals with a pointed finger (for instance, when he discussed the plagues that would come "to you and to you and to you!") or made sure that a physical description of praying was accompanied by the appropriate gesture.[125]

Through both his voice and his gesticulation, Bernardino in his better moments was able to hold the audience's rapt attention. Descriptions of his uncommon ability to do so occur in both the eyewitness accounts and the lives of the earliest biographers. So pleasing were his sermons that for hours people forgot their cares: *"Poveri, richi, mezani, e ogni gente/ Di lor faccende non pensava niente."*[126] The perception that people were left awestruck was a common one. One Lucchese notary, looking back after the preacher's death, felt that it was a miracle in itself that he had been able to listen to Bernardino for so many hours. The sermon provided such pleasure (*gaudiam et letitiam*) that, despite an ailment which usually did not permit him to hold his urine for more than one hour, he suffered no pain or discomfort the whole time.[127]

dall discusses preachers' expressive repertoire in *Painting and Experience*, 64–66. Trexler also provides a useful discussion of the importance of gesture and formalized behavior in fifteenth-century culture in *Public Life*, 99–111. The Capestrano incident is in Moorman, *History of the Franciscan Order from Its Origins to the Year 1517* (Oxford: Clarendon Press, 1968), 471; Roberto's cross trick is described in Agostino Zanelli, "Predicatori a Brescia nel Quattrocento," *Archivio Storico Lombardo* 15 (1901): 106–107. See also Oriana Visani, "Pubblico e temi del quaresimale padovano del 1455 di Roberto Caracciolo da Lecce," *Giornale Storico della Letteratura Italiana* 157 (1980): 541–56, and "Roberto Caracciolo, un imitatore di Bernardino da Siena," in *Cateriniano-Bernardiniano*, 845–61. These preachers were far less constrained than their counterparts a century later; Frederick McGinness notes the stringent advice on preaching decorum during the Catholic Reformation, in *Right Thinking and Sacred Oratory in Counter-Reformation Rome* (Princeton: Princeton University Press, 1995), 29–49.

125. Siena 1427, I, 202, and Siena 1425, II, 292.

126. "Poetical Life," fol. 17r.

127. Dionisio Pacetti, "La predicazione di S. Bernardino in Toscana," *AFH* 33 (1940): part I, 304–306. The letter was written by Giovanni di Niccolò Nesis to Fra Bartolommeo da Siena on 3 June 1445.

One of the most effective ways of retaining people's interest was to encourage audience participation. Bernardino liked to emphasize the ideal relationship between speaker and listener and spent much time outlining their respective roles. He insisted that the audience was part-ly responsible for the sermon's effectiveness. Mental willingness and preparation were most important, but Bernardino also gave practical advice on how to arrange the day's chores efficiently so that one could come to the sermon with a free mind.[128] Aside from attentiveness and decent behavior (the preacher disapproved of those who laughed "like fools" when they heard him say something funny[129]), one should mull over the words of the sermon afterward, discuss them with friends, write them down, and try to incorporate them into one's actions. Lis-tening to sermons was meant to be an all-encompassing act which took place before, during, and after one actually entered the piazza; Bernardino even told the Sienese that he wanted to make them "all preachers."[130] This concept of "audience participation" was, of course, highly idealized. Participation during the average sermon was basically confined to some verbal response by listeners when Bernardino asked them rhetorical questions. Occasionally, they also followed his direc-tions to perform a certain action. In a sermon on sodomy, for exam-ple, Bernardino referred to the fire of Sodom; whenever you hear evil talk, he advised, spit upon the ground:

> Spit hard! The water of your spittle will perhaps extinguish their fire!
> And so everybody spit strongly!

This is exactly what the listeners proceeded to do, since the recorder added the note that the noise they made "seemed like thunder."[131]

There were certain sermons, however, in which audience participa-tion was of a very special kind. These did not rely on the decorum of

128. Siena 1425, II, esp. 295.

129. Ibid., I, 191.

130. Ibid., I, 130.

131. Florence 1424, II, 48. "Sputate forte! L'acqua del vostro sputo, forse, ispegnerà el loro fuoco. E così ognuno isputi fortemente!"

the ideal listener, but on a dramatic group response to a well-staged spectacle. The celebrity of popular preachers was built upon their orchestration of these special sermons and the rituals which followed. Bernardino's most famous preaching tactic was the display of the YHS at the conclusion of his sermons on the Holy Name. The emblem, its letters emblazoned like a golden sun against a blue background, served as an identifying motif for the Sienese saint in fifteenth-century altarpieces, just as Peter was associated with the keys or Catherine of Alexandria with the wheel. But it had quickly evolved into a kind of religious talisman even before Bernardino's death and canonization, seizing the popular imagination in a way which was very disturbing to some members of the ecclesiastical hierarchy. The accusations which followed Bernardino throughout the 1420s, reaching their pitch in 1426 and 1431 when he was in trouble for "heresy," were often prompted by jealousy because of his success. But there were also sober critics like the learned Augustinian Andrea Biglia who had more serious reservations about the emblem. Biglia felt that the crowd response to the YHS had the potential to sink into pure idolatry, and he was appalled by the fervor of Bernardino's audiences. The preacher may have effectively answered all criticism with his sound dogma—the tavoletta was meant to be no more than a reminder of the Holy Name itself and a visual substitute for factional emblems—but the possibility for "idolatry" existed nonetheless. In the minds of some listeners who still required very basic religious instruction and who had to be wooed away from the occult, the perception of the tavoletta and its meaning surely must have differed from the sophisticated ideas of the preacher.[132]

132. A concise overview of Bernardino's preaching on the YHS is Loman McAodha's "The Holy Name of Jesus in the Preaching of Bernardino of Siena," *Franciscan Studies* 29 (1969): 37–65. The important documents relevant to the controversy are in Longpré, "S. Bernardin et le nom de Jesus"; the tract by Biglia is edited by Baudouin de Gaiffier, "Le memoire d'Andre Biglia sur la predication de S. Bernardin de Sienne," in *Analecta Bollandiana* 53 (1935): 308–58. Also see Anna Morisi, "Andrea Biglia e Bernardino da Siena," in *Bernardino Predicatore*, 337–59; Daniel Arasse, "Andre Biglia contre Saint Bernardin de Sienne: L'Humanisme et la fonction de l'image religieuse," in *Acta Conventus Neo-Latini Turonensis, Troisième Congrès International D'Etudes Néo-Latines, Tours*, ed.

The actual use of the YHS during the sermons shows how well Bernardino grasped the uses of imagery in a culture so oriented towards the visual. Even though his own understanding of the emblem was entirely orthodox, the sight of the *tavoletta* encouraged an enthusiasm which bordered on the frenetic. Bernardino would dramatically hold up the YHS at the end of his preaching and what followed would not have reassured sober ecclesiastics like Biglia. The audience would suddenly begin to scream *"Gesù! Gesù!"* and *"Misericordia!"* amidst an outpouring of tears. Cries and sobbing were a common enough response to religious phenomena, ranging from the Bianchi shout of *"Misericordia e Pace!"* in their processions to the outburst caused by the appearance of Pope Eugenius in a Florentine piazza. Similar reactions are recorded for sermons given throughout the fifteenth century. The flamboyant Roberto da Lecce, with his trance-like arm extensions and his theatrical display of a crucifix and a crown of thorns, excited such a frenzy in the crowd that authorities became uneasy.[133]

Jean-Claude Margolin (Paris: J. Vrin, 1980), vol. 1, 417–37; and Bernardino's own defense of his doctrine in Florence 1425, I, 198: "Il primo rimedio è ricorrere a Dio, al nome de Gesù, Iddio e uomo. Non la lettera, non i colori, non gli addornamenti; Idio, Idio, Idio!" However, sometimes his zeal in propagating the YHS came across as extreme, as when he told the Sienese in 1425 that "niuna vale senza el Nome di Gesù," I, 203. Most of his listeners probably thought that he was referring to the *tavoletta* rather than to the Holy Name itself.

133. William Christian analyzes ritualized weeping in terms of individual contrition, purgation of sin, and collective penitence in "Provoked Religious Weeping in Early Modern Spain," in *Religious Organization and Religious Experience*, ed. J. Davis (London: Academic Press, 1982), 97–114. Bornstein, in a discussion of the *lauda*, "Peccatori, tutti piagnete," notes that people believed that "the emotional release of tears will actually cleanse the sinner's soul"; *The Bianchi of 1399*, 139. Collective emotional response was a standard part of popular devotion. In early modern France, for example, ritual fervor, including weeping, was inspired by visiting Capuchin preachers and served to delineate Catholics from a larger, mixed community; see Keith Luria, "Rituals of Conversion: Catholics and Protestants in Seventeenth-Century Poitou," in *Culture and Identity in Early Modern Europe, 1500–1800: Essays in Honor of Natalie Davis*, ed. Barbara B. Diefendorf and Carla Hesse (Ann Arbor, MI: University of Michigan Press, 1993), 65–81. The populace's devotion at the sight of Eugenius is reported by Vespasiano da Bisticci, *Vite*, 17–18. For Roberto, see Zanelli, "Predicatori a Brescia," 136.

Neroccio di Bartolommeo Landi, "Predica di San Bernardino" and "Miracolo dell'Ossessa" (Preaching of San Bernardino in the Piazza del Campo and Miracle of the Possessed Woman). The painting is in the Museo Civico in Siena. *Courtesy of Foto Lensini.*

The sight of Bernardino's YHS provided even more excitement. Not merely an outlet for pent-up emotion, its efficacy was such that it caused spontaneous exorcisms. On May 28, 1425, the recorder of the sermons in Siena reported that a woman who had been possessed for more than fourteen years was freed from her demons as soon as she saw the tavoletta; Francesco Mei, another eyewitness at this sermon, reported the same.[134] Bernardino was quite pleased by this manifestation of the power of the YHS to heal souls. He boasted that it had exorcised a demon at Padua and that, in the same city, a woman with a four-year flux of blood had been cured after seeing the emblem.[135] Distinguishing between true and false healings, he pointed out that unlike either Nature or the Devil, who were forced to work within *time*, God accomplished his miracles instantaneously—and thus the

134. Salvatore Tosti, "De Praedicatione S. Bernardini Senensis in patria civitate, anno 1425," *AFH* 8 (1915): 680; also see the recorder of the Siena 1425 sermons, II, 184.

135. Florence 1424, II, 163 and 199. Also Siena 1425, II, 182.

Paduan woman was cured within the moment. By propagating the cult of the YHS, Bernardino hoped to encourage miracles to continue even after his departure from a given town. One woman, for example, freed her child from a demon by placing the emblem on top of him. Another time, a man from the Mantuan contado came to the preacher with an unusual plea for help; a devil was following his daughter everywhere and even slept between them at night. Bernardino advised him to sprinkle holy water about the house as he recited the Holy Name. When the preacher returned years later, the man happily informed him that the formula had worked.[136]

After all the tears and healings came a more orderly form of audience participation. Francesco Mei and the recorder of the May 28 sermon in Siena said that a procession immediately followed the exorcism. Described in the "Aldobrandini Chronicle" (although this writer claimed it took place the following day), it was

> a beautiful procession, and it accompanied the Giesù with much burning wax; the Signoria was there and the nobles and all the people, and they carried the Nail, the Arm of San Sano, the Head of San Galgano, and other relics; there were many children and boys dressed in the outfits of the Compagnie, singing devout *laude*, going around the three parts of the city. And afterwards they displayed the Giesù again in the piazza and a possessed woman from S. Maria a Pilli was set free. Then the men from the Terzo of Camollia took the Giesù to the Church of San Francesco, those from San Martino took the head to the church of San Galgano, while those from Città escorted the Nail to the Ospedale . . .

Francesco Mei reported that all this was done *"flentes et gaudentes."*[137]

136. Florence 1424, II, 199–200.
137. "Aldobrandini Chronicle," Siena Biblioteca, MS C.IV. I., fols. 276v–277r. Siena 1425, II, 336. ". . . una bella Processione, e s'accompagnò el Giesù con molta cera ardente, et eravi la signoria, e l'honoranza, e tutto 'l popolo, e si portava el chiodo, el Braccio di S. Sano, la Testa di S. Galgano, e altre reliquie, e molti fanciulli, e garzoni di compagnie vestiti cantavano devote laude, cercando tutti i Terzi della città, e poi su la Piazza si mostrò un altra volta el Giesù, e fu liberata una spiritata da S. Maria a Pilli, di poi gli huomini del Terzo di Camollia accompagnoro el Giesù a Frati Minori, quel-

Aside from the honor which the procession paid to the YHS (i.e., the Giesù), this climax of Bernardino's preaching visit was meant to display a city united under Christ. Everyone was involved, from the governing elite to the entire *popolo*, and notably included were the two local saints, Ansano and Galgano. The procession began in the Campo, the political and geographical heart of Siena, and then visited each of the three major divisions of the town before returning to the piazza, which was, significantly, neutral territory—it belonged to no neighborhood.[138] It was this calculated atmosphere of civic unity beneath the protection of the YHS which provided the psychological readiness for any peacemaking. The author of a life of Saint Bernardino written shortly after his canonization remembered the scene which took place after the preacher showed the YHS:

> A pianger forte ognuno incominciava
> Perchè nel quore avieno compuntione
> Con carità l'un l'altro abbraciava
> Mai non si vede tanta divozione.[139]

> [Everyone began to cry/Because they felt compunction in their hearts/ They embraced each other with love/Never before was such devotion seen.]

Although this tearful outpouring of *carità* was not quite the same as the formal peacemakings which will be discussed later, it was the necessary prelude to a real pacification. Tears and embraces were immedi-

---

li di Città el Chiodo a lo Spedale, e quelli di S. Martino la Testa di S. Galgano . . ." It's not clear from the sources whether the demoniac who is exorcised after the procession is the same woman, or a different one, reported by the other chroniclers. Francesco Mei's account of the collective weeping is in Tosti, "De Praedicatione," 680.

138. For an analysis of social space in two Italian cities, see Edward Muir and Ronald F. E. Weissman, "Social and Symbolic Places in Renaissance Venice and Florence," in *The Power of Place: Bringing Together Geographical and Sociological Imaginations*, ed. John A. Agnew and James S. Duncan (Boston: Unwin Hyman, 1989), 81–103. Natalie Z. Davis contrasts Catholic and Calvinist ritual space and social relations in "The Sacred and the Body Social in Lyon," *Past and Present* 90 (February 1981): 40–70.

139. "Poetical Life," fol. 54r.

ately followed by the procession which united the entire city. Afterwards, the spontaneous emotional response of individuals sobbing in the piazza was quickly channeled by Bernardino into an orderly expression of union.

Civic harmony did not preclude social distinctions. Even though the sermon was a meeting place for all souls—*"poveri, richi, mezani, e ogni gente"*—so was it also a clear manifestation of social divisions: the rulers of the city seated apart on their dais, the benches for the *gente da bene* and perhaps also for the women, the separation of the sexes. In the YHS sermon it all culminated in the procession itself, a further statement of order and hierarchy.[140] Despite the frenzy which a great preacher could arouse, Bernardino's manipulation of the YHS was a kind of play between "Order" and a tightly controlled "Disorder." His sermons had little potential for erupting into civil disturbance because, unlike some later preachers such as Roberto da Lecce, Bernardino da Feltre, and Savonarola, the more conservative Bernardino was

140. Robert Darnton has characterized the procession in premodern Europe as "a statement unfurled in the streets, through which the city represented itself to itself—and sometimes to God," in "A Bourgeois Puts His World in Order: The City as a Text," in *The Great Cat Massacre and Other Episodes in Cultural History* (New York: Basic Books, 1984), 120. For Corpus Christi processions in northern Europe see Mervyn James, "Ritual Drama and Social Body in the Late Medieval English Town," *Past and Present* 98 (February 1983): 3–29, and Charles Zika, "Hosts, Processions, and Pilgrimages: Controlling the Sacred in Fifteenth-Century Germany," *Past and Present* 118 (February 1988): 25–64. Edward Muir closely examines processions in *Civic Ritual in Renaissance Venice* (Princeton: Princeton University Press, 1981), esp. 185–230. Also see Christopher F. Black, *Italian Confraternities in the Sixteenth-Century* (Cambridge: Cambridge University Press, 1989), 108–21. For a twentieth-century example which reflects longstanding Italian traditions surrounding the procession, see Robert Anthony Orsi in *The Madonna of 115th Street: Faith and Community in Italian Harlem, 1880–1950* (New Haven: Yale University Press, 1985), 33: "There is an iconography of the streets in dense urban communities like Italian Harlem: the street is a text composed by the people."

Trexler in *Public Life* interprets the post-sermon procession in the Renaissance as "an imperial and imperious demonstration that, through form, the freedom of nonform had been attained within form," 18. Although I essentially agree with this (abstrusely stated!) point, I believe that these neat expressions of civic unity were far less complete than Trexler makes them out to be.

unwilling to exploit the emotions of the crowd beyond a certain point. This helps to explain why he was such an acceptable figure in the eyes of secular governments. When the glittering procession returned to its starting point, the nobles and ecclesiastics in all their finery, along with the entire people, could look up for approval from the saintly friar who had inspired such a show of devotion, unity, and social cohesion.

A second highlight of Bernardino's visit also inspired individual and collective penitence. The day after the Sienese procession, he preached against witchcraft. Several weeks before, in preparation for what was to come, he had asked the audience to send all their gambling devices to him. At the end of the sermon on May 29, he united the material evidence of three major sins—witchcraft, gambling, and vanity—in a common blaze of destruction. A great pile of objects was massed to one side of the pulpit and set alight. The recorder says that the flames destroyed gaming boards, chessmen, and sackloads of dice, in addition to the vanities of both sexes (probably mirrors, false hair, high heels, and expensive clothing). Also thrown into the bonfire were books of enchantment and other *"malìe"* used in the practice of sorcery. These bonfires must have been immense: the one ignited in Perugia in October of the same year was "like a castle of wood" that endangered some nearby spectators. Agostino di Duccio's relief of a Perugian bonfire provides an interesting twist with weapons shown at the base of the fire, probably a sign of reconciled enemies, and a little devil with an erection leaping from the flames.[141]

These gestures of purification were not uncontroversial. When Bernardino staged a bonfire the previous year in Florence he complained that "murmurers" were speaking against him. Practical-mind-

---

141. *Cronaca della città di Perugia dal 1309–1491, nota col nome di Diario del Graziani*, ed. F. Bonaini, A. Fabretti, and F. L. Polidori, *Archivio Storico Italiano* 16 (1850): 31. Agostino's relief still adorns the facade of the Cappella di San Bernardino in Perugia. For the Sienese bonfire, see Siena 1425, II, 99; Bernardino's invitation to bring him the objects of sin is found in II, 199. The bonfire in Florence is found in 1424, II, 87.

ed people wanted to know why he didn't sell the evil goods and then donate the money to the poor. Bernardino's reply emphasized his faith in the power and utility of the visual. He explained that if your father was murdered with a sword, you would never think of profiting from that weapon by turning it into knives, since the very sight of them around the house would be unendurable.[142] Second, the bonfire as spectacle performed a useful service since the visual sense was stronger than the auditory. Those children who witnessed a bonfire would not forget it for the next fifty years, even though they failed to remember the actual sermon.[143] Bernardino thoroughly grasped the essence of what would remain in the minds of the young, the ignorant, and those who had difficulty with Tuscan dialect. They would at least retain a series of dramatic visual memories: the entry of the care-worn ascetic into their town, his attire and demeanor fulfilling all their expectations of what a holy man should be; the growing mass of listeners swelling the church day by day; the holy tavoletta, the exit of demons, and the candle-lit procession which followed; the wild bonfire; and, finally, the startling image of sworn enemies locked in an embrace.[144]

These images could supersede the listeners' memories of the actual content of the sermons. The author of the poetical life quoted above was scarcely interested in transmitting the words which precipitated the events; his memory of the sermons was reduced to a kind of shorthand where there remained only generalized talk of heaven, hell, and *carità*. Much more vivid to this author writing several decades later was

142. Criticism of Bernardino is in Florence 1424, II, 122; the knife story is on 10–11 of the same volume.

143. Siena 1425, I, 192 and 291.

144. For a negative appraisal of the populace's response to Bernardino when he entered Spoleto, see the virulent description by Andrea de Cascia in Longprè, "S. Bernardin e le nom de Jesus," 451–52. Andrea thought that Bernardino was blasphemously reenacting Christ's entry into Jerusalem: "illam bestiam" (i.e., Bernardino) was greeted with olive branches and accompanied by a huge crowd, thereby enraging the Bishop of Spoleto. See Edith Pasztor, "S. Bernardino da Siena e l'episcopato italiano del suo tempo," in *Cateriniano-Bernardiniano*, 715–39.

the memory of the crowd's enthusiastic response, embodied in procession, bonfire, and peacemaking.[145]

Even a description written only days after the author heard Bernardino speak emphasized many of the same things, although in this case the witness had a more sophisticated appreciation of what the preacher actually said. In a letter written to his brother on June 15, 1424, the Pratese Sandro di Marco de' Marcovaldi gave an account of the preacher who had just spent the last six weeks in their town. Written with all the fervor of the newly awakened—the letter begins "in the Name of Jesus" and ends with an entreaty for his brother to adopt the YHS—it documents Bernardino's ability to convert through words and ritual. Marcovaldi starts by enthusiastically describing the good friar as a "*chapitanno fortissimo*," a second Saint Paul, who had come to repair the sins of the world. He summarizes Bernardino's power to move souls:

> [He caused] every hardened sinner to come to confession and to penitence, and if all the sinners possessed hearts of stone and steel, he broke and opened them and made them turn to the path of salvation in the name of Jesus . . .

Marcovaldi himself felt such "*piacevolezza*" in Bernardino's preaching that he swears it will comfort him all of his life.[146]

Almost everyone in Prato attended the daily sermons. On feast days, the inhabitants of the surrounding countryside also came to hear, and the number of listeners swelled to six thousand. Even more people showed up at the bonfire which destroyed an enormous heap of vanities and gaming devices "to the confusion of Sattenasso and his followers." Finally, on the 12th of June and only three days before this letter was written, Marcovaldi sat down between two of his friends

145. "Poetical Life," fols. 21v–22v, 26v.

146. Ridolfo Livi, "San Bernardino e le sue prediche secondo un suo ascoltatore pratese del 1424," *Bullettino Senese di Storia Patria* 20 (1913): 458–69; text of Marcovaldi's letter on 460–66. ". . . ed ongni duro pecchatore fare venire a chonfesione ed a penittenzia; e se ttuti chuori di pechatori fossono di pessimo pietra e d'acciaio, tutti gli apre e speza, e falgli aprire e fagli tornare in via di salvazione nel nome di Gesù . . ." (I've left the irregular spelling as Marcovaldi wrote it), 460.

near the women's section and listened to the sermon on the Holy Name. Bernardino announced that everyone should have faith in the Name, carrying its letters in the heart and placing the visible symbol in the houses and on the piazze and gates of Prato.

Suddenly, only four *braccia* away from Marcovaldi, a woman whom he recognized as the wife of "*il Fiorentino*" began to scream; she had been possessed by a demon for twenty-four years. Bernardino descended from the pulpit with crucifix and YHS and repeatedly made the sign of the cross over her. Men, women, and children began to shout "Misericordia!" and finally the demon departed. Although Marcovaldi does not say so explicitly, it seems that this surge of audience participation speeded the exorcism. Two more evil spirits then fled other possessed individuals. The spectators were "stupefied," as if they had been "hit and beaten." To add credence to the story he was telling his brother, Marcovaldi pointed out that more than one hundred Florentine citizens were present who had never before witnessed a miracle like this one.

This and other accounts of Bernardino's preaching suggest that, during the sermon spectacles, the usual crowd reaction to the holy man was predictable in its almost ritual sameness. Indeed, the sermon itself could be characterized as a grand ritual where the expectations of both preacher and listeners met in a cathartic outpouring stimulated by the sight of the holy, and where the entire city—unified and hierarchically ordered—was dramatized on the public stage of the piazza. Bernardino was able to use his knowledge of crowd behavior in order to make people respond in predetermined ways. In the 1425 visit to Siena, for example, he cunningly manipulated the order of the sermons to achieve the maximum effect. After the talk on the YHS came the next day's bonfire, which was shortly followed by important sermons on justice, *carità*, and concord, suggesting an intentional buildup to at least individual reconciliations.[147] His adept handling of the lis-

147. The sermon on justice is in Siena 1425, II, 203–14; *carità* is 215–24; concord is 254–76.

teners' emotions and their reaction to him suggest that both sides knew what to expect; even if the audience was "stupefied," it had arrived in the piazza with the intention of becoming precisely that.[148]

Yet if the sermon was a ritual, it was also very much more. Behind the cleansing action of the bonfire and the fragile social concord engendered by the YHS pulsated an extraordinarily complex set of human reactions. Italian piazze, then as now, were secular arenas where people came to be amused, to display themselves, and to observe others.[149] This meant that the sermon's function as entertainment was

148. Trexler has described the rapport between preacher and crowd as closure of the "psychic distance between pulpit and audience, between one devotee and another, between all present and the spirit for which both reached . . ."; *Public Life*, 117. I suggest that this closure was always incomplete.

What passes for uninhibited emotional catharsis in a religious setting can in fact be something other than what it seems. See Meredith B. McGuire, *Pentecostal Catholics: Power, Charisma, and Order in a Religious Movement* (Philadelphia: Temple University Press, 1982), esp. 93–100. McGuire characterizes sudden outbreaks such as "speaking in tongues" as a kind of "controlled spontaneity" within the group experience, modulated by an authority figure and by the reception and interpretation of the speaker's message; she points out that the expectations listeners bring with them greatly contribute to the religious experience, 119.

149. In their search for coherent interpretations, many historians approach the devotional behavior of the past with more solemnity than did the actual participants; most studies of ritual tend to ignore the jostling crowd. A contemporary observer of Sicilian life puts the matter nicely after watching Palermo's festival of Santa Rosalia and the casual behavior of its participants: ". . . I wonder about the contrast between what I have seen today and the exquisite drawings of the seventeenth and eighteenth-century carts from which today's (festival) has drawn its inspiration. And in all justice I am forced to admit that perhaps the contrast is not so much between past and present as between intention and realization, that perhaps the ephemeral nature of the Festino has always been more tawdry and distracted than the official plans and the visitors' chronicles would lead us to think, its choreography plagued by mishap and disorder, its message distorted in the transmission and contested in the reception," Mary Taylor Simeti, *On Persephone's Island: A Sicilian Journal* (New York: Knopf, 1986), 271. Muir notes the tardiness, mistakes, and arguments over precedence which could occur prior to Venetian processions; *Civic Ritual*, 201–202. And Benjamin Klein has argued for an active, restless audience during English civic rituals; see "'Between the Bums and the Bellies of the Multitude': Civic Pageantry and the Problem of the Audience in Late Stuart London," *London Journal* 17, no. 1 (1992): 18–26.

openly acknowledged, exploited, and sometimes lamented by the preacher. And listening to the sermon was, above all, a voluntary act where the unspoken contract between speaker and listener could not always be sustained, thanks to resistance on the part of individuals and to the selective attention paid to the more exciting sermons by the audience as a whole. Bernardino was no shaman nor were his listeners merely acting out parts in a script which had already been written. The preacher was, instead, an active swordsman who fenced with his listeners and the piazza was their field of battle. His final goal was always inner transformation, even if within the context of public display. Tears, bonfires, exorcisms, and processions were satisfying because they were both the manifestations and the instruments of what he hoped was permanent conversion. But what the preacher intended was not always what his audience perceived.

The most moving event of all elicited many of the same reactions as the sermons described above. Peacemakings provided a good show, but were also meant to both symbolize and prompt internal forgiveness. The most difficult battle the preacher faced was the one he waged against the unforgiving heart: cleansing the soul of pride and the spirit of vendetta was not so easy as throwing vanities on a bonfire. The following chapters will show how Bernardino used his many skills, and his understanding of public ritual and inner conversion, in order to make peace.

CHAPTER TWO

Peacemaking: Community and Coercion

"Allora disse santo Francesco: 'Frate lupo, io ti comando nel nome di Gesù Christo, che tu venga ora con meco senza dubitare di nulla, e andiamo a fermare questa pace al nome di Dio.' E il lupo obbediente se ne va con lui come un agnello mansueto . . ."

The events which took place during Bernardino's sermons show that the interaction between himself and his audience was multilayered, created not only by his masterful rhetoric, but also by the listeners' expectations of what was supposed to happen. They actively responded to the preacher's words and to the visual elements of the sermon both as individuals and as participants in a group ritual where the boundaries between selves were dissolved. When people threw vanities on a bonfire, screamed in joy and fear at the sudden appearance of the YHS, and marched through the city in a solemn procession, the unity created by Bernardino and this willing audience exorcised, literally and figuratively, the demon of self-interest. Together, preacher and crowd forged their civic commitment to the conversion process. But there were inevitably those defiant wills who refused to be persuaded by either Bernardino or the group; their uneasy presence reminds us that people attended sermons for many reasons, not all of them devotional. The rapport between preacher and listeners was sometimes powerful, at other times wavering, and even the most successful of orators was not able to meld individual wills completely into his vision of social harmony. If the sermon was a type of liminal state which engendered "communitas," it could only be an incomplete one.

This is nowhere more evident than in the most spectacular events in Bernardino's repertoire, peacemakings. As the most emphatic statements of *carità* and Christian fraternity, they became one of the key elements in the Quattrocento view of his status as holy man and saint. Evidence given at his canonization trial sums up the way he was perceived by admiring contemporaries:

> Item, the aforesaid frater Bernardino was so famous and had the opinion of good men because of his astonishing life and doctrine, so that in each place he went, he reduced enemies to peace and concord, ended scandals, quarrels, and disagreements, and everywhere sowed *carità* and extinguished ancient hatreds.[1]

Preacher as peacemaker is a standard accolade in almost all contemporary descriptions of Bernardino, particularly in the first biography which was written by Barnabò da Siena shortly after his countryman's

---

1. Celestino Piana, "I processi di canonizzazione," 387. "Item quod praefatus fr. Bernardinus tanta fama et opinione bonorum virorum pollebat propter eius mirificam vitam et doctrinam, quod in omni loco quo ibat, inimicos ad pacem et concordiam reducebat, scandala rixas et discordias terminebat, pacem, concordiam, et caritatem ubique seminabat et inveterata odia exstinguebat."

death. Barnabò emphasizes Bernardino's peacemaking achievements in the troubled towns of northern and central Italy where he ended the discord between "Guelphs and Ghibellines." He did such a fine job of pacifying Siena, for example, that "it seemed as if all the citizens were of one mind and even soul." Barnabò does not explain how all this was accomplished, but another biographer, the anonymous friar, brings up the important role of the YHS in Bernardino's preaching against factions. Along with its use as a devotional symbol, its primary function was as a visual reminder of Christian unity. Everywhere, he writes, party signs on houses and walls, in churches, and over portals were replaced by this emblem of the Holy Name.[2] Remnants of the popularity of the YHS can be seen in Siena even today, not only on the facade of the Palazzo Pubblico, but also tucked in narrow *vicoli* where humbler versions are occasionally placed over doorways. Most fifteenth-century portraits of the saint are careful to picture him holding the emblem; each time they saw him depicted in this way, contemporary viewers would have been reminded of the role of both man and image in peacemaking.

It was Bernardino's Lombardy tour beginning in 1417 which set him on his path of a traveling peacemaker, aided by the YHS. Clusters of pacifications occurred in northern Italy during his early triumphs as a celebrity-preacher, notably in Cividale di Belluno, Crema, Verona, Como, Brescia, Bergamo, and Bologna. When Bernardino returned to central Italy in the early months of 1424, his sermons there also resulted in several notable peacemakings, in Assisi and Perugia during the summer of 1425 and in Siena in 1427. Sporadic peacemakings continued throughout his life, and one of his last accomplishments before his death march to L'Aquila was to pacify Massa Marittima, the town where he was born.[3]

2. Barnabò da Siena, *Vita*, 108; Anonymous Friar, "Vie inédite," 318.

3. Barnabò gives an itinerary in the *Vita*, 110–11. Pacetti has researched two specific peacemaking visits: for Belluno, see "S. Bernardino a Belluno nel 1423," *Bulletino di Studi Bernardiniani* 18 (1940): 142–53; for the Assisi-Perugia visit, see "La predicazione di S.

Unfortunately, despite this impressive list and his grand reputation, there remains only fragmentary evidence of what took place before, during, and after his peacemakings. This makes it far more difficult to understand the respective roles of Bernardino and his listeners during a pacification scene than in the dense layers of human interaction which can be traced in the general sermons. Nor is it always clear who was being pacified. Barnabò and other biographers praised Bernardino's role as a mediator between "Guelphs and Ghibellines," but this stock phrase, as well as other vague descriptions of the calming of "seditions" and "enmities," raises many unanswerable questions about the circumstances behind each peacemaking. The *Cronica ad memoriam*, written by an anonymous eyewitness to Bernardino's 1423 preaching in Vicenza, is typical: it tells us only that the Sienese "fece fare pace tra i cittadini."[4] The precise identification of who was involved and how they were converted was of little concern to the chroniclers. The focus in their brief descriptions is always on the result of Bernardino's sermons—that is, a big peacemaking, generally taking place in a piazza or a large church, where everyone took part. The descriptions are suspiciously generalized, making it seem as if every peacemaking was a spontaneous combustion of repentance ignited by the preacher's oratory and charisma.

It would be overly cynical not to admit that in some sense this *was* what took place, and the following chapters will attempt to delineate the genuine conversion which could underlie the ideal peacemaking. Just as the reaction to the sermon was an unruly blend of fervent re-

---

Bernardino a Perugia e ad Assisi nel 1425," *Collectanea Franciscana* 9–10 (1939–40): 5–28, 494–520, 161–88.

4. Cited by Gian P. Pacini, "Predicazione di minori osservanti a Vicenza: fondazioni, confraternite, devozioni," in *Predicazione Francescana e Società Veneto nel Quattrocento: Committenza, Ascolto, Ricezione* (Atti del II Convegno Internazionale di studi francescani) Padova, 26–28 Marzo, 1987 (2nd edition, Padua: Centro studi antoniani, 1995), 254. Bernardino preached for more than two months in Vicenza; the anonymous reporter claims that there were more than "thirty thousand citizens and *contadini*" present at the sermon and procession on June 3.

pentance and casual behavior, so too did the peacemakings encompass
a variety of motivations and responses on the part of those involved.
The narratives, on the other hand, are essentially sanitized versions of
a messier process. Clearly, the narrators wanted people to remember
not the process itself but the end point, or at least what was hoped for
as the "final result" in those first enthusiastic days after a peacemaking. And so the content of the sermons, the actual peace ritual, and
the mechanics of local politics which surely must have been working
behind the scenes are all underplayed or ignored. This makes it difficult to see the peacemakings in context, as the evidence has left us only
the blurred images of united cities, images that were no doubt very
satisfying to Bernardino and to his contemporaries, but which shroud-
ed hard realities beneath a soft veil.

The meager information about Bernardino's peacemakings can be
supplemented, however, by looking at the tradition within which he
worked. The Sienese friar was certainly not the first, nor would he be
the last, in a long line of Italian peacemakers. Ritualized forgiveness
was a familiar punctuation in the lives of his listeners. We need to look
at some of the traditional options available to the fifteenth-century
preacher and his audience in order to recreate what went on during
these elusive events, whether in the public arena where the ritual took
place, in the descriptions left by contemporaries, or in the minds of
those who participated.

I. The Preacher and the Wolf

The inescapable model for Bernardino and every other Franciscan
peacemaker was of course Saint Francis, who had become part of the
collective memory of his order and of society at large. A good starting
point for understanding what happened at a peacemaking is the famous passage from *I Fioretti*:

> And Saint Francis said to the wolf before everyone: "And you, Brother
> Wolf, do you promise to observe the peace pact, so that you will offend
> neither men nor animals nor any other creature?" And the wolf, kneeling

and bowing his head, with gentle movements of head, tail, and ears, showed that he wanted to observe each article of the pact. Saint Francis said, "Brother Wolf, I want you to swear here before all the people, just as you promised me outside the gate, that you will not deceive me about the surety I've made for you." Then the wolf raised his right paw and placed it in the hand of Saint Francis.[5]

And so proceeded an ideal peacemaking. The beautifully pristine story of the Wolf of Gubbio contains, despite its guise as fable, most of the steps which would have been familiar to late-medieval Italians: the savage tamed by the sweet words of a peacemaker, the aggressor's oath— here pronounced in proxy by the saint—not to violate the legal contract of peace, the public ritual. Nothing is missing except, for understandable reasons, the *bacio di pace*, or kiss of peace. The passage is in effect a metaphor of a flawless reconciliation; embodied within it are the various elements of a real peacemaking, at once secular and religious, legalistic yet highly emotional.

By the time Francis was making his rounds in the early thirteenth century, there already existed a legal apparatus which tried to ensure that negotiated peaces would remain unbroken. To be effective, a peacemaking needed to be embodied in a legal contract. These documents, or "instruments of peace" (*instrumenta pacis*), were signed by feuding parties in the presence of witnesses, and then notarized. Although the exact components of each treaty varied according to circumstances, they generally had the following characteristics in common: a promise to keep the treaty forever (*in perpetuam pacem*), a corre-

---

5. *I fioretti di San Francesco*, introduction by Cesare Segre, notes by Luigina Marini (Milan: Rizzoli Editore, 1979), 126. "E santo Francesco, dinanzi a tutti, disse al lupo: 'E tu frate lupo, prometti d'osservare a costoro il patto della pace, che tu non offenderai né gli uomini né gli animale né niuna criatura?' El il lupo inginocchiasi e inchina il capo e con atti mansueti di corpo e di coda e d'orecchi dimostra, quanto è possibile, di volere servare loro ogni patto. Dice santo Francesco: 'Frate lupo, io voglio che come tu mi desti fede di questa promessa fuori della porta, così qui dinanzi a tutto il popolo mi dia fede della tua promessa, e che tu non mi ingannerai della mia malleveria ch'io ho fatto per te.' Allora il lupo levando il piè ritto, sí lo pose in mano di santo Francesco."

sponding promise that heirs would also observe the peace, a bond of surety and a financial penalty if the treaty was infringed, and the names of witnesses. A peace treaty could be either a promise by an injured party to give peace (*pacem dare*) to an offender and a reciprocal promise by the offender to also keep the peace, or an agreement between parties who have engaged in mutual hostilities. Only occasionally is the reason for the dispute given in these laconic thirteenth-century records.[6] The signing of the pact was sometimes part of a public ceremony similar to that enacted by Francis and the repentant wolf. The documents usually stipulate that the two enemies exchange a kiss of peace, along with the signing of the *instrumentum* and an oath sworn on the Gospels. Otherwise, the nuances of the ceremony have been lost, which makes it difficult to analyze variations based on social status or degree of injury. But in some feuding cultures, ritual humiliation of the offender is also an integral part of public peacemaking. In Albania, for example, the loser begged for a truce by crawling towards the victor with a gun hung around the neck, while in sixteenth-century Scotland killers would hand a naked sword to their foes.[7] The Wolf of

6. For a representative selection of private peace documents from the thirteenth century, see Gino Masi, *Chartum Pacis Privatae Medii Aevi ad Regionem Tusciae Pertinentium* (Milan: Società Editrice Vita e Pensiero, 1943). One colorful exception to the reticence of these sources is from 1290: a certain Giovannini Benvenuti, "irato animo et malo modo," had entered the house of his enemy Tura Ranieri "cum uno cul[tello in] latus, minando eidem quod segaret ei venas . . . ," 229.

7. See Christopher Boehm, *Blood Revenge: The Anthropology of Feuding in Montenegro and Other Tribal Societies* (Lawrence, KS: University Press of Kansas, 1984), 133–36, and Keith M. Brown, *Bloodfeud in Scotland* (Edinburgh: J. Donald, 1986), 54; Brown says that the homage ceremony was thus a way of restoring honor. Comparative ethnography is helpful in pointing out possible variations within peacemaking ceremonies. In late-medieval London, for example, the reconciliation ritual could depend on the status of the parties: equals would share food and drink, while status differences were expressed through gestures of humility, such as the offering of casks of wine; see Barbara Hanawalt, *Of Good and Ill Repute: Gender and Social Control in Medieval England* (New York and Oxford: Oxford University Press, 1998), 29–30. Among Fijians, the peacemaking ceremony (*i soro* = "surrender") is conducted as an elaborate show of public humility on the part of the offender; Klaus-Friedrich Koch, Soraya Altorki, Andrew Arno, and Letitia Hickson, "Ritual Reconciliation and the Obviation of Grievances: A Compar-

Gubbio kneels humbly before the townsmen and bows his shaggy head, and Bernardino tells a miracle story about a Spanish lord who begged for mercy at his enemy's feet, bare-headed and wearing only a shirt, but otherwise there is little evidence of ritual submission in Italian peacemakings.[8] Perhaps most reconciliations would "take" only if some equivalence in honor was acknowledged between the two parties.

The need for a legal document, public oath, witnesses, and financial sanctions attests to the potential violence simmering just beneath the tranquil surface of the ritual. Feuds had to be terminated legally and with multiple safeguards because of the deep suspicion which usually existed towards one's new "friend." As late as the fourteenth century, for instance, vendetta was still legal in Siena; the injured party was supposed to present an instrument of peace to the offender in token that he would not pursue his rightful desire for vengeance.[9] According to Sarah Blanshei, in thirteenth-century Bologna the authority accorded to the *instrumentum* (or *pax*) could even fluctuate, pulled by alternating pressures between a lenient, personalized concept of justice embodied by the "self-help" of the vendetta, and an abstract and im-

---

ative Study in the Ethnography of Law," *Ethnology* 16, no. 3 (July 1977): 279. The peace ritual of the Moroccan Rif is perhaps the most extreme example: the killer has to approach his enemies, hands tied behind his back and knife between his teeth. Along with money, the killer's family provides a sheep, which will be slaughtered by the said knife; see Raymond Jamous, "From the Death of Men to the Peace of God: Violence and Peacemaking in the Rif," in *Honor and Grace in Anthropology*, ed. J. G. Peristiany and Julian Pitt-Rivers (Cambridge and New York: Cambridge University Press, 1992), 167–91. On the other hand, Stephen Wilson notes "an absence of shaming rituals" during Corsican peacemaking; see *Feuding, Conflict, and Banditry in Nineteenth-Century Corsica* (Cambridge and New York: Cambridge University Press, 1988), 259.

8. Florence 1424, II, 242–43. But Jennifer Selwyn reports that, during one peacemaking by the Jesuits in Naples, feuding noblemen asked for pardon with ropes around their necks; "Planting Many Virtues There," 272. Perhaps this dramatic penitential scene was in keeping with the Jesuits' tactic of arranging theatrical "mortification rituals" which spurred public conversions, 317–19.

9. William Bowsky, "The Medieval Commune and Internal Violence: Police Power and Public Safety in Siena, 1287–1355," *American Historical Review* 73, no. 1 (October 1973): 13. Bowsky notes that the need for the private *instrumentum* was in fact a sign that the government was not able to protect the offender.

personal severity which demanded punishment rather than reconciliation. In lenient periods, diminished fines accompanied the *pax*, while in harsher years—those dominated, Blanshei shows, by the *popolo*—private peaces often gave way to perpetual exile.[10] Some communes were more consistent in their attempts to control the vendetta and the impetus behind the signing of peace pacts may have come more often from government itself than from private initiative. In 1295, the Florentine commune forced the Manelli to make peace with the Velluti one month after Lippo di Simone Manelli had been killed ("wounded twenty times or more") in retaliation for a murder his family committed twenty-eight years previously. The public peacemaking which took place July 17 in San Piero Scheraggio was an impressive affair, with the Priors and the Capitano del Popolo in attendance. (Donato Velluti, however, notes in his diary that the Manelli were still filled with rancor.)[11] Although the stronger governments of the fifteenth century had even more success in curbing feud, the desire for vengeance did not disappear nor did the need for the assurance offered by a legalized peace. Gene Brucker has found evidence in the Florentine *Notarile* of a traveling notary who was still legalizing private peace agreements in the *contado* at the end of the Quattrocento.[12]

It is important to keep in mind the emotions which lay behind the dry formalities. The hard process of negotiation was sometimes

10. Sarah Rubin Blanshei, "Criminal Law and Politics in Medieval Bologna," *Criminal Justice History* 2 (1981): 1–30.

11. *La cronica domestica di messer Donato Velluti*, ed. Isidoro del Lungo and Guglielmo Volpi (Florence: G. C. Sansoni, 1914), 14–18.

12. Marvin Becker, "Changing Patterns of Violence and Justice in 14th and 15th-Century Florence," *Comparative Studies in Society and History* 18, no. 3 (July 1976): 281–96. But Trevor Dean critiques "the decline of the vendetta," arguing that historians must differentiate between the relative tolerance shown by Tuscan, especially Florentine, governments and the firmness of signorial states; see "Marriage and Mutilation: Vendetta in Late Medieval Italy," *Past and Present* 157 (November 1997): 4–11. The peacemaking notary found by Gene Brucker is Ser Piero di Pellegrino Marsilii, who traveled on a circuit from the 1480s to 1505; his record book (two volumes) is in the Archivio di Stato di Firenze, Notarile antecosimiano, M 216.

prompted by religious conversion, which meant that secular peace-making and its spiritual counterpart were often intertwined, as in the case of Francis and the wolf. The decision to clasp one's enemy in a fraternal embrace was especially prominent during Italy's periodic bouts of religious revivalism. For example, the Great Devotion, or "Al-leluia," of 1233 was a revival inspired by charismatic mendicant preach-ers who helped legislate social change, preached against heretics, and arranged individual and large-scale peacemakings. This early move-ment had much in common with that of the Bianchi penitents of 1399: processions, preaching, tears, and what would seem to be—at least, on first glance—spontaneous and violent conversions. Flagellant move-ments also left peacemakings in their wake.[13] In all of these cases, many of the reconciled were careful to sign notarized contracts.

The need to transform "peace" into a negotiable commodity should not disguise what were sometimes spur-of-the-moment deci-sions. For example, a Sienese law of 1309 suggests that the decision to make peace could occur quite suddenly: it stipulated that all shops should be closed on August 15 except for those selling "festive candles and things needed for the dead, and instruments of peace, and final testaments."[14] A century later, Bernardino was well aware that sermons given on feast days could sometimes prod enemies into repentance and forgiveness. He advised the *podestà* not to work on holy days—unless, that is, the official became involved in some holy work, such as peace-making.[15]

In the case of large-scale reconciliations, spontaneous conversion was especially likely in times of crisis. In one thirteenth-century case

13. For an extended discussion of the preacher-peacemakers of 1233, see Thomp-son, *Revival Preachers and Politics,* and for the Bianchi, see Bornstein, *The Bianchi of 1399.* For the flagellants and peacemaking, see John Henderson, "The Flagellant Movement and Flagellant Confraternities in Central Italy, 1260–1400," in *Religious Motivation: Bio-graphical and Sociological Problems for the Church Historian,* ed. Derek Baker (Oxford: Basil Blackwell, 1978), 150, 155–56.

14. Cited in Bowsky, *Siena Under the Nine,* 276.

15. Siena 1425, II, 267.

reported by Salimbene, an eclipse of the sun frightened people into making peace, with the *podestà* himself preaching on this terrible occasion.[16] Political crisis more often inspired mass peacemakings among citizens. One of the more dramatic instances occurred in 1260, on the eve of the Battle of Montaperti, as the Sienese showed their collective determination to defeat the Florentines by staging a big peacemaking in the cathedral which lasted all day and part of the night.[17] On December 7, 1375, a general peacemaking in Perugia was the necessary prelude to overthrowing the despised tyranny of the papal governor:

> Everyone together, the *santo popolo* of Perugia on Friday morning, everyone together, young and old, *gentiluomini* and *popolari*, having forgotten every injury and discord, and all reduced to one will, peace and concord, went into the piazza, everyone shouting in unison: "Long live the *popolo* and death to the abbot and pastors of the Church!"[18]

This seems to have been the general pattern for large-scale peacemakings, battle cry excluded. Most often reconciliations were proceeded by a sermon (or harangue) delivered by either a cleric or public official. The peacemaking in Siena, for example, followed a sermon given by the Bishop. In Florence in 1301, a desperate Dino Compagni gave a rousing speech to his fellow citizens, imploring them to heal their factional differences.

The physical setting of the mass peacemakings was ostensibly neutral ground, whether the cathedral, the town's main piazza, or, in Compagni's case, the Baptistery where he tried to make belligerents re-

16. Salimbene de Adam, *Chronicle*, trans. Joseph L. Baird with Giuseppe Baglini and John Robert Kane (Binghamton, NY: Medieval and Renaissance Texts and Studies, 1986), 156.

17. At least this is what a later Sienese chronicler reports. See "La Sconfitta di Montaperti," in Siena Biblioteca, MS. A. IV. 5, 4v–5v.

18. *Cronaca di Perugia (Diario del Graziani)*, 220. ". . . il santo popolo di Perugia, un venerdì mattina, tutto in comune, piccoli e grandi, gentiluomini e popolari, avendo dimenticato ogni ingiuria e discordia, e ridotti tutti ad un volere, pace e concordia, baciando l'uno inimico l'altro, andarono in piazza, tutti concordemente gridando: 'Viva il popolo, e muora l'abbate e li pastori della chiesa . . .'"

call their common baptism at the font where they had become Christians and Florentines.[19] The usual scenario, then, was a persuasive oration of some kind followed by tears, embraces, and the kiss of peace with "everyone" supposedly involved. Reconciliation under these circumstances was on a grand scale, involving large numbers of people or even, the chroniclers boast, the entire city. This brand of peacemaking resembled several of the reconciliations in thirteenth-century *instrumenta* which involved many members of warring *consorterie* or the followers of a powerful noble arrayed against the citizens of a neighboring town. The solemn ceremony of the oath-swearing and the kiss of peace must have been a magnificent sight, with its numerous participants and spectators and display of deep emotion.

What is surprising is the cursory treatment of what must have been visually and psychologically impressive events. Analysis of the collective peacemaking ritual is difficult, given that few sources provide more than a brief synopsis of what actually took place. One Genoese record from 1169, cited by Jacques Heers, gives a rare glimpse of a theatrical public display: the bishop and clergy preached on a platform surrounded by torches, alongside a cross with relics of Saint John the Baptist at its foot. Salimbene reports a peace procession in Parma where exiles returned "amidst the ringing of bells and the sounding of trumpets."[20] Most narrators, however, abbreviated their accounts by merely explaining that "so-and-so made peace," "everyone reconciled," or "enemies exchanged the kiss of peace." For a culture whose written records display both great attention to legal details and an obsessive interest in the workings of human personality—both of which formal peacemakings must have provided in abundance—the scanty notice is worth examining in itself. These crystallized descriptions, intriguing though they may be, tell us little about the real human interactions

19. *The Chronicle of Dino Compagni*, trans. Daniel E. Bornstein (Philadelphia: University of Pennsylvania Press, 1974), 66–67.

20. The Genoese peacemaking is in Heers, *Parties and Political Life*, 198–99; Salimbene's description is in his *Chronicle*, 461.

which took place. A report about Francis of Assisi in Bologna, for example, implies that peacemaking took place immediately, once the belligerent nobles gathered in the piazza were moved to tears by his powerful words.[21] The lack of attention paid to ritual in this and similar reports may mean that the ceremony of peacemaking enjoyed a kind of "longue dureé" in Italy (notice that the spectacle of 1169 took place a half-century before Francis's preaching) and that, like the Mass or baptism, its basic lineaments were well-enough established to be taken for granted.[22]

But a far more suggestive explanation for the lack of detail in these sources is that, by ignoring most of the ritual and all of the social context, contemporaries unconsciously telescoped these peacemakings into pious, indeed monotonous, accounts of civic unity, just as Bernardino's chroniclers said little about his pacifications, save the end result. Whether one took place in thirteenth-century Bologna, fourteenth-century Perugia, or fifteenth-century Siena mattered not at all to the narrators who smoothed out the difficulties which must have been involved in so fragile an enterprise. Time, place, and circumstance rarely affect the general pattern because the major concern was to show that peacemakings *worked*, and that all was well that ended well. The narrators wanted to leave the impression that these were sponta-

21. Despite his contemptible appearance, Francis was able to speak so effectively that "multae tribus nobilium, inter quas antiquarum inimicitiarum furor immanis multa sanguinis effusione fuerat debacchatus ad pacis consilium reducerentur," cited by Delcorno, *La predicazione nell'età comunale*, 66–67.

22. Peacemaking in Corsica centuries later followed the medieval Italian pattern very closely, with a treaty drawn up by a notary, the presence of family representatives and local witnesses and guarantors, a public embrace, and sometimes concluding with attendance at a religious service (or, in one documented case, a banquet); see Stephen Wilson, *Feuding, Conflict, and Banditry in Nineteenth-Century Corsica*, 257. Jacques Le Goff believes that "Italy very early showed a tendency towards rigidity of ritual in the realm of symbolic gesture, since it was quick to employ writing in connection with these ceremonies, and what is written down is more difficult to change than what is not." See "The Symbolic Ritual of Vassalage," in *Time, Work, and Culture in the Middle Ages* (Chicago: University of Chicago Press, 1980), 264. The point may also be valid for the ritual of peacemaking, since it, too, was customarily accompanied by a written document.

neous, unanimous, and successful events, so what they have left us is an abstract tableau of *Pax et Concordia* which seems to be frozen outside of real time and real life.

One way to move behind the scenes of these tranquil narratives is to examine the intermediaries who were involved in peacemaking. An integral part of feuding societies is recognition of some individual or group of persons who can mediate quarrels, whether through informal means or by assuming a formal and publicly recognized position as peacemaker.[23] In the case of individual feuds within small communities, the tightly woven social bonds between kin and neighbor often exert pressure to settle disputes, the paradox being that it is those same bonds which encourage tension in the first place. Peacemakers within the community are intimately familiar with the details of the quarrel, and understand the personalities on both sides; in most cases, if they have a personal relationship with the disputants, it is also to their own advantage to make a lasting peace. For instance, in the small, local communities of sixteenth-century Scotland, kinsmen, lords, and dependents acted as the usual mediators, while in nineteenth-century Corsica informal peacemakers were often important personages with a large kindred to buttress their authority.[24]

In the Italian setting, concerned friends, relatives, and neighbors similarly served as informal *mezzani*, or go-betweens. Catherine of Siena, for example, seems to have functioned as a local peacemaker through her services as a "good neighbor," admonishing individuals to reconcile through both her speech and her numerous dictated letters.[25]

---

23. In legal terminology, mediation does not give the third party the right to impose a settlement, while arbitration does. Negotiation, on the other hand, takes place without the assistance of a third party at all. For a concise discussion of these terms, see Ian William Miller, *Bloodtaking and Peacemaking: Feud, Society, and Law in Saga Iceland* (Chicago: University of Chicago Press, 1990), 261.

24. Max Gluckman, "The Peace in the Feud," *Past and Present* 8 (November 1955): 1–14; Keith Brown, *Bloodfeud in Scotland*, 54; Stephen Wilson, *Feuding, Conflict, and Banditry in Nineteenth-Century Corsica*, 255–64.

25. For example, her friend and biographer Raymond of Capua reports how Catherine calmed down Nanni di ser Vanni, a troublemaker who was "always starting

Informal community pressure was sometimes elevated to an official status when moral persuasion was reinforced by government mandate. In their desire to preserve order, communes occasionally appointed their own *pacieri*, or peacemakers, from among the citizenry. Their duties might be relatively simple, as in fourteenth-century Siena where the governing body of the Nine chose two peace officials for each company of the urban militia; these were then supposed to report all infringements of private peace agreements to the *podestà*. Contemporary Florentines went further when, in May 1349, they gave eight men powers to force antagonists to sign *instrumenta* and to post bond for good behavior. Later in the century, other *paciales* appointed by a *balìa* were supposed to do the same thing, except that they could neither interfere with homicide vendettas nor arrange truces for a period longer than three years.[26] Tuscan governments, then, were able to exert a certain amount of power over private feuds, but often placed limits on the coercive authority they gave to their own officials.

There were obvious strengths and weaknesses to any system, whether ad hoc or official, which relied on middlemen who were part of the community. Their understanding of how individuals related to one another in a particular setting was counterbalanced by deep suspicions that local peacemakers, even churchmen, were not always impartial.[27] If large-scale mediation was needed it was often expedient to use foreign arbitrators, in keeping with the long-standing tradition of hiring foreigners for key political posts such as *podestà* and *capitano*. Papal legates, for example, were sometimes sent in to mediate between fac-

---

private feuds"; *The Life of St. Catherine of Siena*, trans. George Lamb (London: Harvill Press, 1960), 212–15.

26. For Siena, see Bowsky, "Police Power and Public Safety," 12; the Florentine examples are from Brucker, *Florentine Politics and Society, 1373–1378* (Princeton: Princeton University Press, 1962), 128–29, and *Civic Life in Renaissance Florence* (Princeton: Princeton University Press, 1977), 63.

27. But urban bishops were still acting as peacemakers as late as the sixteenth century. The reform bishop of Modena, Egidio Foscarari, was a trusted mediator; see Michelle Marie Fontaine, "Urban Culture and the Good Bishop in Sixteenth-Century Italy" (Ph.D. diss., University of California, Berkeley, 1992), 140–51.

tions. Even the quixotic emperor Henry VII attempted to become a peacemaking outsider. When he entered the peninsula in 1310, he tried to use his authority to force peacemakings between factions in the towns of Lombardy. But, predictably enough, the results were both unimpressive and temporary, since he was soon manipulated by the partisan families he sought to reconcile. Neither pope nor emperor could really fulfill the requirements of a true "outsider" since their supposed impartiality usually disguised their own intense political agenda; "peacemaking" on their terms often became a springboard to political domination. Witness the machinations of Pope Boniface and his supposed peacemaker, Charles of Valois, and the consequences of their brutal interference in the struggles between Blacks and Whites in Florence.[28]

All true peacemakers, whether foreign or part of the community, had to navigate between Scylla and Charybdis, their idealistic stance threatened by personal ambition and partisanship. One solution was to call upon acknowledged religious figures. There are still mediators (*shorfa*) in the Moroccan Rif, some of whom are designated as "saints"; these holy men are in essence absolute outsiders who come from peaceful patrilineages and who must be invited to intervene (which implies that the parties concerned already want to reconcile).[29] Christianity, too, has a long-standing tradition of using its own holy men as peacemakers. From the early Desert Fathers through Francis of

28. For cardinal-legates as peacemakers, see the futile visits to Florence by Cardinals Latino, Matteo de Aquasparta, and Niccolò of Prato in Dino Compagni, *Chronicle*, 8, 24, and 66. Bowsky depicts the emperor as a very active, if mostly ineffectual and unrealistic peacemaker, in *Henry VII of Italy: The Conflict of Empire and City-State, 1310–1313* (Lincoln, NE: University of Nebraska Press, 1960), esp. 66–87. Randolph Starn discusses the dangers of "partisan peacemaking" in *Contrary Commonwealth: The Theme of Exile in Medieval and Renaissance Italy* (Berkeley and Los Angeles: University of California Press, 1982), 48–59.

29. Jamous says that the peaceful conduct of these special patrilineages is considered to be a virtue, even though most kin-groups normally consider such behavior to be "a proof of cowardice"; "From the Death of Men to the Peace of God: Violence and Peacemaking in the Rif," 79.

Assisi, asceticism could bestow an aura of being withdrawn from human affairs, making saints ideally suited to mediate within them. The column-saints of late antiquity, such as Simon Stylites, found that the desert itself was no barrier as word of their powers of judgment spread alongside reports of their miracle working; problems and quarrels were brought to them for resolution, with the suppliants ranging from peasants to the emperor himself.[30] In late-medieval Italy, Catherine of Siena's status as holy woman permitted this daughter of artisans to interfere in the quarrels of the great. More than a century earlier, the Alleluia preachers of 1233 ably blended their outsider status and miracle working with intervention in communal affairs, functioning as both holy men and arbitrators with the power to impose settlements.[31] Even the modest Francis of Assisi knowingly disengaged himself from his native town in order to be acknowledged as a holy man and outsider. Once, when he was preaching in Perugia, his sermon was interrupted by a group of riotous knights riding through the piazza. So he "turned to them and said with great fervor of spirit: 'Listen and take heed to what the Lord has to say to you through me his servant; and do not say that this is a man from Assisi.'"[32] Although he was a native son of Perugia's traditional foe, his status as God's messenger served as proof that he had erased all partiality.

30. I owe my discussion of holy men as "insiders-outsiders" to Peter Brown's classic article, "The Rise and Function of the Holy Man in Late Antiquity," *Journal of Roman Studies* 61 (1971): 80–101. For one later example of an ascetic-peacemaker see H. Mayr-Harting, "Functions of a Twelfth-Century Recluse," *History* 60, no. 200 (October 1975): 337–52.

31. For the brilliant career of John of Vicenza, see Thompson, *Revival Preachers and Politics*, 39–79. However, even holy men as spectacular as the Alleluia preachers were not completely above suspicion. Salimbene reports that the friar Gerard of Modena was made *podestà* of Parma in hopes that he could reconcile its factions. Some, however, expressed dissatisfaction with him because it was suspected that "he had leanings towards the imperial party"; *Chronicle*, 52.

32. *Scripta Leonis, Rufini et Angeli, Sociorum S. Francisci*, ed. and trans. Rosalind B. Brooke (Oxford: Clarendon Press, 1970), 151: "Et conversus et illos beatus Franciscus, cum fervore spiritus dixit: 'Audite et intelligite, que Dominus per me servum suum vobis annuntiat; et non dicatis quoniam iste est Asisinatus.'"

Francis and his immediate followers and, later, Observants like Bernardino, fulfilled the qualification of true impartiality on two counts. Not only did they come from outside most of the communities where they served as *pacieri* but, in their almost complete renunciation of the world, they were perceived as being above family and party interests. Bernardino and his colleagues in the Observance occupied a unique place within this tradition of friar peacemakers. Their renewal of Francis's ascetic spirit helped them to be "outside" secular society, but their astute adaptation of that spirit gave them special advantages within the consolidated political world of the fifteenth century. It is significant that the Observants began to make their impact as popular preachers following the end of the Great Schism, and that Bernardino became a celebrity in 1418, soon after the Council of Constance elected the unification pope Martin V. In a church and society weary of the long travesty of the Schism, the Observants were the right men for the right time, finding a fertile field in which to sow the Word of God.

Unlike the late-antique hermit Simon Stylites, an outsider even in the psychological sense thanks to his aberrant behavior, the Observants did not need to spend their lives atop columns in order to display their self-imposed distance from the world. They made ideal peacemakers for their time because they possessed the zeal and emaciated physical appearance of traditional holy men, yet were not quite strange enough to alienate sophisticated urban audiences. Nor were they as deliberately eccentric as Francis, even if there were a few notable exceptions like the bizarre and enormously successful Roberto da Lecce. Although he could stand twenty minutes at a time, motionless, with his arms stretched out in imitation of Christ on the cross, Roberto was a far cry from the column-saints of fifth-century Anatolia; they had the same trick in their repertoire, but could perform it for hours at a time! Had Roberto tried this sort of thing on his restless spectators, my guess is that many would have laughed and then drifted away. Quattrocento Italians still appreciated ascetic heroics, but really responded to a holiness which was measured rather than extreme. The

Observants possessed what was in essence a kind of institutionalized charisma; harnessed by the discipline of their order, their holiness fulfilled audience expectations, but was never really surprising. And even though they rejected the temptations of the world, they wisely never expected their listeners to do the same. Bernardino, for one, presented the path to salvation as concrete and attainable, usually counseling not rigor, but moderation.[33]

Finally, the greatest Observants were traveling preachers, always on the move, and hence political outsiders wherever they preached. Bernardino seems to have deliberately cultivated his role as outsider when he preached peace in Lombardy. He explicitly says that factions were willing to listen to him because he belonged to neither side (*"La cagione si è, che il conviene che tenga o da l'una parte o da l'altra, e io sul saldo"*).[34] His position as an outsider was more problematic when he preached peace in his hometown in 1427; in this case, Bernardino relied on his status as a preacher-ascetic with the privileged tongue. Explaining why he had refused their bishopric, he told the Sienese that such a position would disqualify him from speaking frankly.[35]

Paradoxically, outsiderness for the Observants did not mean that they held themselves aloof from official connections. Great supporters of the restored papacy and of strong governments, they were unlikely to cause political problems for established hierarchies. Their return to Franciscan idealism was thus coupled with a concern not to stir up trouble for either secular or ecclesiastical authorities, although there was the occasional exception, such as the unruly late fifteenth-century

---

33. Arthur Fisher sums up the paradox of the Observants: "By this neat combination of the urban mission and the desert, heroic distance from society could be translated into power within society . . . "; in "The Franciscan Observants in Quattrocento Tuscany" (Ph. D. diss., University of California, Berkeley, 1978), 27. A good introduction to the nature of charismatic authority and the tension between renunciation and the world is by Charles F. Keyes, "Charisma: From Social Life to Sacred Biography," *Journal of the American Academy of Religious Studies* 48, nos. 3–4 (1982): 1–22.

34. Siena 1427, I, 325.

35. Ibid., I, 525. ". . . ella mi sarebbe stata serrata la metà della boca."

friar Bernardino da Feltre, expelled from Florence in 1488 because he was unwilling to refrain from ferocious verbal attacks on the Jewish population.[36] The greatest Observants, however, were accomplished and well-educated men with a fine understanding of how the political world operated. Francis had not been naive, by any means, but his studied innocence was a contrast to later peacemakers whose practicality and accommodation were barely cloaked by their ascetic demeanor. The political tact of the Observants made them ideal *pacieri* in Quattrocento towns where a freelance mediator like Francis would not have been appreciated by lord or oligarchy, or where aggressive personalities like the Alleluia preachers might have seemed too threatening. Success in the fifteenth century usually depended upon the cooperation of rulers, as was the very invitation to preach in the first place. In the case of Francis, a few truly spontaneous peacemakings may well have occurred, but the reconciliations of Bernardino and his fellows were far more carefully planned. Among the individual preachers involved, however, some variations were still possible since Observant peacemakers could draw upon several traditional options.

One possibility open to the peacemaking preacher was to take an extremely active role in the implementation of a peace agreement, building upon some common understanding of how reconciliations should be organized. The mediation of Giacomo delle Marche, contemporary and colleague of Bernardino, provides an instructive example of how preacher and government could work hand in hand in order to pacify a town, with the holy man's personal charisma here supplemented by vigorous legislation. In November 1444, Giacomo, already a seasoned peacemaker, was invited to preach in Terni. Less than two decades before, the government had tried to ensure an ongoing peace by appointing secular *pacieri*, referred to as the Ten Good

36. This Bernardino insisted on "complete freedom to preach from the pulpit, and he said that it was necessary for the salvation of souls"; from *The Society of Renaissance Florence: A Documentary Study*, ed. Gene Brucker (New York: Harper and Row, 1971), 248–49.

Citizens. Giacomo's plan when he came to Terni was to develop a more extensive organization of *pacieri* along the same lines. After his sermons had presumably created a widespread desire for reform, debates were held in the city council on the exact steps to take. One enthusiastic friend of the preacher proposed what seems to be an unrealistic number of *pacieri* for a town as small as Terni: he wanted no less than 150 peacemakers and, furthermore, planned to give them far-reaching power, including the right to imprison those who destroyed the peace and to impose heavy fines of 100 gold ducats. A more cautious voice suggested less intrusive peacemakers who could not force hostile parties to reconcile (sign an *instrumentum*?) but could make them swear to a truce which would ensure that neither side could take the offensive. This proposal suggests that even as late as the mid-fifteenth century, there was a perception that some governments still had limited powers to impose a negotiated peace.

Optimism won the day. What is surprising is the radical solution which was eventually adopted, thanks to the advice of Giacomo himself. He and the council—which cast 100 white beans in favor and only one vote against—set up a body of what became more than 350 *conservatori e difensori della pace*. These were to meet twice each year, at Christmas and Pentecost, and whenever else the Priors of Terni so desired. Their lifelong duty was to quell "discord," but the statute unfortunately did not provide specifics as to how they were to go about this delicate task. Informal social pressure may have been the real means, since the underlying idea of the reform seems to have been a citywide network which caught everyone in its web. *Conservatori* who violated the terms of the *societas* would be dismissed and their relatives to the third degree prohibited from serving.[37]

Several points can be made about Giacomo as peacemaker. First, the friar clearly had zealous supporters within the government itself,

37. The legislation and other documents surrounding Giacomo's visit to Terni can be found in Alberto Ghinato, "Apostolato religioso e sociale di Giacomo delle Marche in Terni," *AFH* 49 (1956): 106–42 and 352–90; the specific peacemaking material is in Part II.

powerful enough to exert sufficient pressure to obtain an overwhelming consensus in favor of the reform. There must have some kind of agreement among important citizens even before the famous outsider was invited in, and thus the very invitation to preach implied a group of people who were willing to listen—and who were already inclined towards a general peacemaking. This was probably the usual case. Fra Giacomo received at least one other official invitation when, before his trip to Terni, he had been asked to serve as *paciere* in Rieti in early October of 1444.[38] Other Observants received similar requests. In 1438, for example, Alberto da Sarteano, one of the other so-called Pillars of the Observance, was invited to make peace in Brescia by Francesco Barbaro, the Venetian official then governing the town. At that time, Brescia was under attack by the *condottiere* Piccinino, and Barbaro hoped that a formal peacemaking would be one way of defending the city against him.[39] Bernardino, too, was asked to preach by anxious governments. One well-documented case involved the town of Belluno, a Venetian dependency in the far north of the peninsula. In 1423 the town sent two ambassadors to formally request his aid. The aftermath of a relatively brief visit by Bernardino was a public peacemaking, the adoption of the YHS, and the destruction of the infamous *rotuli*, or lists of family names which indicated who could and who could not hold public office.[40]

In most cases, conflict mediation took place in the context of a

---

38. Angelo Sacchetti Sassetti, "Giacomo delle Marche paciere a Rieti," *AFH* 50 (1957): 75–82.

39. Zanelli, "Predicatori a Brescia," 92–93. Alberto did not come on this occasion, but did respond when issued a subsequent invitation in 1444; see Guido Lovati, "La predicazione del B. Alberto da Sarteano a Brescia (1444–1449)," *Miscellanea Francescana* 37 (1937): 65. Other examples of Observant peacemaking: In 1441, Frate Silvestro di Paolo di Siena persuaded eight thousand people in Piacenza to swear an oath to keep peace; cited in Fisher, "Franciscan Observants," 237. See also Bertagna, "Frater Silvester Senensis, O.F.M.—Concionatur Saeculi XV," *AFH* 45 (1952): 152–70. The Sicilian Matteo of Agrigento arranged notarized peaces in Spain in the late 1420s; see Agostino Amore, "Matteo d'Agrigento a Barcelona e Valenza," *AFH* 49 (1956): 255–335.

40. Pacetti, "S. Bernardino a Belluno nel 1423."

more comprehensive moral reform. In addition to setting up the society of *conservatori*, Terni passed new statutes which imposed heavy fines on usury and blasphemy, prohibited certain games, and regulated sumptuary laws. All of these sins were standard targets of fifteenth-century preachers and a whirlwind of miscellaneous social legislation could be pushed through the town council during the visit of an especially charismatic friar. Bernardino himself tried similar government reforms in both Perugia and Siena. But even though he subsequently bragged about his success as a peacemaker in Perugia, the collective memory concentrated on other aspects of his visit there in 1423. For example, the *Chronicle of the Graziani* does not say much about his peacemaking but lavishes attention instead on the bonfire and on the overall emotional impact of the sermons. In Brescia in 1422, Bernardino not only made peace but also succeeded in temporarily stopping the scandalous races of bulls and prostitutes.[41] Peacemaking was often only one part of a more sweeping desire to "clean up" a city, with reconciliations taking place in a temporary but fervent atmosphere of good will and determination to reform urban morals from top to bottom.

Finally, in the Terni episode, Giacomo was not only a catalyst for an already desired reform but a participant in the actual proceedings. His close partnership with the government led him to set up a detailed program; his vigorous personality made him not only willing to preach peace but also to stay long enough to oversee the official deliberations. Since we do not have any evidence of what he actually said on this oc-

41. Fantozzi discusses Bernardino's reforms in "Documenta Perusina" and provides the relevant documents. For Bernardino's visit to Brescia, see Zanelli, "Predicatori a Brescia," 86–87. For the full range of reforms inspired by mendicant preaching, see Mario Sensi, "Predicazione itinerante a Foligno nel secolo XV," *Picenum Seraphicum* 10 (1973): 139–95. The general background to social legislation in Italy and the role of Quattrocento preachers is in Diane Owen Hughes, "Sumptuary Law and Social Relations in Renaissance Italy," *Disputes and Settlements*, ed. John Bossy (Cambridge: Cambridge University Press, 1983), esp. 80–83. Hughes discusses Franciscan preaching and anti-Semitic legislation in "Distinguishing Signs: Ear-Rings, Jews, and Franciscan Rhetoric in the Italian Renaissance," *Past and Present* 112 (August 1986): 3–59.

casion, Fra Giacomo's style as a mediator ends up seeming more bureaucratic and unemotional than it probably was in fact. But his peacemaking in Rieti was structured in much the same fashion: secular *pacieri*, financial penalties for non-attendance at meetings, and the signatures of 427 citizens who promised to observe the peace. The reconciliation which took place was essentially a large-scale version of the *instrumentum pacis* ceremony as scores of citizens swore on missals held by the friar and important officials.

This kind of tightly controlled pacification, however, was not the only style available to the fifteenth-century preacher and his audience. In those cases where peacemaking was a culmination of a long visit aimed at total moral reform, charisma and oratorical fireworks played an even more prominent role in the conversion. In 1448, the youthful and flamboyant preacher Roberto da Lecce came to Perugia for an extended stay (from January to April) and produced quite a different show than the sober scene arranged by Giacomo. When Roberto preached peace, he dramatically displayed a crucifix, which caused everyone to scream "Iesu Misericordia!" and cry for a half-hour without stopping. Afterwards, the city immediately proceeded to elect four citizens for each part of the town to serve as *pacieri*. A practical yet highly emotional step was also taken to diffuse factional allegiances: all family *bandieri* (standards) were removed from the churches, and the statue of Perugia's erstwhile ruler, Biordo dei Michelotti, was taken down. Significantly, the one *bandiera* which was *not* taken down was that of Braccio da Montone, whose sister was currently wife of a Baglioni, the dominant family in Perugia. Fra Roberto also arranged various processions meant to whet the populace's appetite for both moral transformation and entertainment. All kinds of theatrics were involved, including the participation of a barber in the guise of a "*Cristo nudo con la croce in spalla.*" His own imitation of Christ converted the barber as it did several others, but after a few months as a pious friar the barber abandoned the convent, took a wife, and was "a greater *ribaldo* than ever before." Did a similar relapse await those who exchanged the kiss of peace during these exciting sermons? The chronicler is prudently silent on this point.[42]

Bernardino's style as a peacemaker seems to have been substantially different from both the tough negotiator Giacomo and the frenzied Roberto da Lecce, indicating that preachers could be flexible both in their performance and in the way they were used by local governments. When he visited Siena in 1425, in a format which was probably typical of his longer preaching missions, he embedded a speech on Concord, and its accompanying peacemaking, within a total of fifty sermons which dealt with a wide range of topics. He saved the peacemaking until the forty-third day and made sure to give it on a Sunday, when he must have had a large crowd; the sermon itself was also sufficiently generalized to induce "everybody" to reconcile, from feuding families to quarrelsome spouses. Two years later, when he was invited to Siena specifically as a *paciere*, his sermons were once again a careful, controlled presentation of the subject matter, this time with peacemaking the dominant, but by no means exclusive, topic.[43]

Bernardino himself provides the most detailed account of his peacemaking. It is revealing of the low-key and occasionally ambiguous way in which he confronted urban discord. In this case, he needed to work very quickly since he was in the town for only a brief period. Factional conflict in Crema in 1421 had resulted in the exile of around ninety men along with their families. Bernardino went there at the time of the grape harvest, which meant that he had to speak at night in order to muster an audience. He says little about the content of his preaching, except to say that he never directly referred to the touchy exile problem but neither did he "keep silent about anything there was

---

42. *Cronaca di Perugia (Diario del Graziani)*, 597–603.

43. Jesuit peacemakers cultivated a similar style, grounding pacifications within a context of total moral reform. But even though they built on the tactics of earlier peacemakers such as Bernardino, their preaching campaigns reinforced the "emerging institutional identity" of their order, as Jennifer Selwyn persuasively argues in "Angels of Peace," 250. Hence their peacemaking was far more systematic than Bernardino's.

to say" (*"parlavo in genere e non in particolarità, e non tacevo nulla che fusse di dire"*). This cryptic treatment of faction was characteristic of Bernardino's approach, at least if we judge it by the careful way he avoided direct political references when he pacified his hometown six years later. Whatever was actually said, it was both lengthy—when he stopped at dawn he had already been preaching for four hours—and effective. Individuals approached Bernardino (*"a uno a uno"*) and requested his advice. He asked them how the problem had come about, and they in reply advised him to speak to the *signore* of Crema, Giorgio de' Benzoni.[44] Bernardino proudly notes, as he tells the Sienese this story, that the *signore* was close to him (*"era molto mio domestico"*). He therefore talked freely to Benzoni, advising him to do good (*"nel bene operare"*). But the preacher excused himself from becoming involved in the actual peace negotiations; instead, he preferred to "let God and them work it out together and I'll do my own art of preaching." It seems that Bernardino preached again after his talk with Benzoni—the narration does not make the sequence clear—and received either his encouragement or his permission to speak frankly. In his sermon, Bernardino warned the Cremaschi that the suffering innocents cried out to God for a vendetta against those who had wronged them. His threat made such a powerful impression that the Cremaschi summoned a council "in which there was such union that it was a marvelous thing." The result was that the exiles were allowed to return.

Bernardino's good work was not quite finished. Still functioning as a good *mezzano*, he left Crema to visit one of the exiles who held a *castello* nearby. Did Bernardino leave the city as Benzoni's messenger? Perhaps the Cremaschi felt it necessary for someone impartial to convince the exiles that it was indeed safe to return (and they may have

---

44. The Benzoni were Crema's most prominent Guelph family. In 1414 Giorgio Benzoni became a formal vassal of the Duke of Milan, but long-term enmity with the Cremaschi Ghibellines was not put to rest, since the latter were angry about confiscated property. See *Historia di Crema*, raccolta da gli annali di M. Pietro Terni per A. Fino (Venice: Domenico Farri 1571; reprint, Crema, 1988), 34v–38v.

hesitated sending one of their own into an enemy's stronghold). When the lord of the *castello* heard about the impending reconciliation he laughed at the friar in disbelief, but his skepticism abruptly dissolved when yet another messenger came to confirm the good news. Joyously returning to Crema, the exile met a former enemy in the piazza, and they happily embraced and went off together for dinner. Bernardino's story does not indicate whether this was a formal peacemaking or a chance encounter. Meanwhile, another enemy who had been occupying the exile's house willingly departed, and that very night the former exile "slept in his own bed, among his own things." Subsequently, everyone else who had appropriated the man's belongings likewise restored them, and so it happened with the other exiles and their former adversaries. Bernardino complacently ends this success story by asking his listeners: "And how pleasing do you think all this was to God?"[45]

Several points of comparison with Fra Giacomo's mission at Terni show how individual preachers could make subtle variations upon the peacemaking theme. First, it seems that Bernardino, like Giacomo, had an audience who was eager to hear him; the fact that they came to the sermons in the middle of the night implies that the Cremaschi felt the famous stranger had a message worth listening to. On the other hand, the presence of so many weary bodies in the midst of the harvest season suggests that pressure from above was already operating, even before Bernardino delivered his first word. When individuals sought his help with the exile problem, he noted that people seemed united in their desire to solve it, *"senza nulla contrarietà."* The preacher also had connections with the city's lord, or at least developed them quickly, since he boasted of their friendship. Finally, the sermon(s) on peace

---

45. Bernardino's account of the Crema peacemaking is in Siena 1427, I, 367–69. The *Historia di Crema* only makes a brief reference to his visit: "Venne à questi tempi à predicar' in Crema il Beato Bernardino de l'ordine de' frati Minori; da cui fù fondato il Monastero di Santa Maria di Pianengo. Egli fece ancora pinger quel nome di GIESV, che vedesi à raggi d'oro sopra la porta del Duomo verso mezzo di," 36v. Apparently, the peacemaking was a minor incident in the troubled history of fifteenth-century Crema.

encouraged positive action about a sentiment which was already current. Bernardino probably did not persuade hardened hearts in this instance, but his sermons must have resonated in those listeners who were already half-convinced to reconcile even before the preacher delivered his first word. The council meeting was a further demonstration of the unified purpose of the town, or at least of its leading citizens, and the path to reconciliation was now secure. Giacomo's similarly quick work in Terni and the voices which supported him in the council also suggest that peacemaking preachers did not work in a vacuum. Charismatic prestige and moving oratory, essential as they might be, were in fact not primary catalysts, but often did their work a few steps later in the process. The presence of the preacher was meant to solidify a groundswell of preexisting support.

But the differences between Fra Giacomo's tactics and Bernardino's are more striking than the similarities. The latter would have nothing to do with the implementation of the exiles' return since his duty, as he plainly stated, was only to preach. He let the Cremaschi themselves work out the details—and very complicated they must have been—which a peacemaking on such a grand scale involved, concentrating instead on his power to move souls, in this instance apparently with the threat of hellfire. Despite the fact that he was a leading official in the Observance, Bernardino seems to have had a strong personal aversion to handling detail. At one point during his Sienese sermons, he implores his listeners not to bother him with private confessions or complaints; what he did best, he said, was preach. He refused to get involved in private disputes because he lacked the necessary authority. Whenever someone begged him to mediate a quarrel, Bernardino pointed out that he had neither the retainers nor the policemen to force the other party into compliance. "Oh, this isn't up to me!" he exclaimed irritably.[46] It seems as if he was very careful to guard his ener-

---

46. Siena 1427, II, 803. "Io trovo che se niuno ha quistione niuna, ellino capitano a me, dicendomi:—Doh, frate Bernardino, io vi prego per l'amor di Dio, che voi mi facciate una grazia: egli e quistione fra tale persona e tale, e potreste operare molto bene

gy for his primary role as preacher, and preferred to work with groups rather than individuals. The same attitude was clear in his mass peace-makings. He was a different breed from some of his more forceful colleagues and from earlier, more activist preachers such as those of the Great Alleluia. Like Francis, he was always suspicious of the direct participation of clerics in secular affairs: at one point, he vehemently condemned the Sienese tradition of having monks serve in the post of *camarlengo*, or communal treasurer.[47] Bernardino's strong sense of his identity as Preacher led him to view the reformation of morals and peacemaking in a somewhat different context than that created by Fra Giacomo. Certainly, he advocated strong laws to frighten evildoers into good deeds, but he was averse to involving himself in anything but the dissemination of the Word.

For Bernardino it was the sermon which created the moral and emotional context for the peacemaking between souls. What happened afterwards he would leave to others and hope for the best. When he preached peace in Siena, the reconciliation sermon finally took place on the forty-second day; after just three more days he was finished and off to another town. Moreover, the peacemaking itself occurred immediately after the sermon, when he instructed his listeners to proceed to the churches. What they did there neither Bernardino nor his chroniclers say, though it is likely that there was a formal exchange of the *bacio di pace*. Perhaps some citizens eventually drew up *instrumenta*, in addition to their verbal agreements, but this did not concern Bernardino.[48]

---

mettendoli in concordia.—Bene—dico io—che vuoi tu che io facci?—Vorrei che tu mandaste per lui.—Ma io no ho famigli e non ho birri da farcelo venire, e forse non vorrà altro che a suo modo. Doh, questa non è cosa da me!"

47. Bernardino said mockingly that if he were made *camarlengo*, he would steal even more than the others did; Siena 1427, II, 1104. Much earlier, the thirteenth-century Dominican Humbert of Romans stated that "the preacher must be careful not to involve himself in business which reeks of the world . . ." and he included peace negotiations in this category; "Treatise on the Formation of Preachers," in *Early Dominicans: Selected Writings*, ed. Simon Tugwell (Ramsey, NJ: Paulist Press, 1982), 184–370.

48. Jean-Claude Maire-Vigueur has searched the Sienese archives and found no

What really happened at the peacemaking in Crema? By the time he visited the exile, Bernardino would have us believe that the fine points had been worked out by others and that this had all been accomplished within the space of a few days. He makes no mention of the steps which might have been involved, nor tells us if there was a formal ceremony to seal the bargain. Were secular *pacieri* established to help maintain the new peace? How were people convinced to hand back property? It would be especially naive to think that the process of restitution was as smooth as Bernardino describes; like the disbelieving exile, the historian can only be amazed that forgiveness could take place so easily under these circumstances.[49] We can only speculate about those unhappy individuals who are prudently silent in Bernardino's happy version of the event. All that remains in the preacher's story is a benevolent lord, the smooth translation of property back to its original owners, the relief of one joyful soul, and a united city.

II. The Fox and the Bird

Bernardino, in telling the story of Crema to the factious Sienese, was only interested in the moral message it would convey. It functions, like other descriptions of peacemaking, as an encapsulated narrative of civic order seemingly detached from social reality. In a discussion of the connection between narrativity and moralism, Hayden White has commented upon the narrator's desire "to have real events display the coherence, integrity, fullness, and closure of an image of life that is and can only be imaginary . . ."[50] Whenever Bernardino or others describe a peacemaking, their accounts often display this urge towards

---

trace of notaries at work during Bernardino's peacemakings: "Bernardino et la vie citadine," in *Bernardino predicatore*, 272. But given the long-established peacemaking tradition, it is difficult to believe that the seriously reconciled would not have followed up their peacemakings with *instrumenta*.

49. On the confiscation of exiles' property, see Heers, *Parties and Political Life*, 183–84.

50. Hayden White, "The Value of Narrativity in the Representation of Reality," in *On Narrative*, ed. W. J. T. Mitchell (Chicago: University of Chicago Press, 1981), 23. For an analysis of the vendetta as "formulaic narrative," see Trevor Dean, "Marriage and Mutilation," esp. 24–36.

closure. This does not mean that they were misrepresenting reality, only that reality has been edited in the service of an ideal. Perhaps this was also part of the peacemakings as they actually took place. These big public demonstrations of unity were opportunities for Italian society to present itself as it wanted to be, hence they were conditioned by what people felt *should* happen.

Accordingly, large-scale peacemakings sometimes were not so much a "solution," but a last, desperate attempt on the part of a world divided by irreparable faction. We can see this, for example, in the chronicles of Dino Compagni and Giovanni Sercambi, astute politicians directly involved in the events of late thirteenth-century Florence and of Lucca a century later. Compagni's disillusionment and despair and Sercambi's pervasive cynicism focus, again and again, on the hopelessness of people's chance of living in harmony with their neighbors; the peacemakings they describe are last-ditch efforts which fail completely. Dino Compagni's chronicle can be read as a tragic series of failed or perverted attempts to make peace. The emotional peacemaking held in the Baptistery was apparently a front for malign spirits: "Those wicked citizens, who there displayed tears of tenderness and kissed the book and showed the most ardent good will, proved to be the leaders in the destruction of their city." At least the stubborn Gianfigliazzi were not such hypocrites. After a general reconciliation arranged by Cardinal Niccolò di Prato on August 26, 1304, this family refused to join in the big celebration, and Compagni notes that "the good people talked about this a lot, saying that the Gianfigliazzi did not deserve peace."[51]

Sercambi's Lucca is just as bleak. He recounts the story of a peacemaking held in 1392 when the *gonfaloniere di giustizia* and certain *anziani* mandated a general reconciliation among the factions. An Augustinian master of theology from Arezzo preached a generic peace sermon, "saying much about peace and concord and how good it was to live well." Everyone present—and also those who were not—were ordered

---

51. Compagni, *Chronicle*, 39 and 66.

to make peace by swearing on a cross. Sercambi then adds, darkly, that "after such a sacrament and promise there entered into the hearts of the citizens worse thoughts than before."[52] But, in the few days or even moments which surround these grand scenes of reconciliation, both men describe, as Bernardino describes, a world perfectly at peace, with "everyone" tearfully participating. We can look at peacemakings like these from a bird's-eye view and conclude that they were meant as public assertions of unity, as morality plays acted out on the streets. People expected a preacher to make peace when he visited and they provided a wide range of traditional options to help him in his task, such as the *instrumentum pacis* or the appointment of secular peacemakers. Hopefully, the audience would be persuaded to act on its own ideal, responding in familiar ways to the call for repentance.

At least this is what Bernardino and other reporters would have us believe . . . and therein lies the problem. Both the sanitized versions and real peacemaking as civic theater function as what the anthropologist John McCreery calls "potential ritual." Simply put, this is what both narrators and scholars hope the ritual meant, as they construct an overall picture of its possibilities and tie up most of the loose ends. "Effective ritual" is quite another matter; individuals of course have their own reaction to any given ceremony.[53] When we try to understand what went on during peacemaking ceremonies, it is important to remember that real human beings were involved and that they sometimes did not care to play their designated roles. Peacemakings were intense human dramas, vessels into which the participants could pour a variety of conflicting impulses and motives.

Clearly, a certain amount of coercion, whether subtle or blatant,

---

52. The oath which the Lucchese swore on the crucifix was to "non tenere a secta nè far divisione di Lucha e di perdonarsi insieme." From *Le cronache di Giovanni Sercambi, Lucchese*, ed. Salvatore Bongi (Lucca: Tipografia Giusti, 1892), vol. I, 270–72.

53. John McCreery, "Potential and Meaning in Therapeutic Ritual," *Culture, Medicine, and Psychiatry* 3, no. 1 (March 1979): 53–72. Edward Muir notes that rituals can be ambiguous, opening up "a labyrinth of dissonance rather than a neatly unified vision of society"; *Ritual in Early Modern Europe* (Cambridge and New York: Cambridge University Press, 1997), 4.

must have been involved in order to get "everybody" to join in. The defiant attitude of the Florentine Gianfigliazzi must have been far more common than the narratives care to tell us. For instance, the Genoese peacemaking of 1169 cited earlier obviously combined moral persuasion and outright pressure on the part of civic and ecclesiastical authorities. As the archbishop preached to the crowd, he harangued a party leader who was shamed by his words, but who swore he would forfeit his honor if he made peace with his enemies. Only when the consuls of the commune, along with the clerics, approached the man did he finally swear peace on the Gospels. The exhilaration caused by this "conversion" resulted in crowd and clergy swarming on the enemy house and forcing them, in turn, to make peace. In fourteenth-century Rome, Cola di Rienzo's peacemaking apparatus institutionalized coercion:

> This was the procedure followed there [i.e., in 'The House of Justice and Peace']: two enemies came in and gave guarantees of making peace; then, when the nature of the injury had been established, the man who had done it suffered just what had been done to the victim. Then they kissed each other on the mouth and the offended man gave complete peace. A man had blinded another in one eye; he came and was led up the steps on the Campidoglio and knelt there. The man who had been deprived of an eye came; the malefactor wept and prayed in God's name that he pardon him. Then he stretched out his face for him to draw out his eye, if he wanted to. The second man did not blind him, but was moved by pity; he forgave him his injury. Civil suits were likewise settled promptly.[54]

Rough justice, indeed.

Explicit force, in this case supernatural, also lay behind the supposedly effortless peacemakings inspired by the Bianchi processions of 1399. The Bianchi deserve a closer look because of their proximity in time to Bernardino, who was nineteen when these white-robed penitents swept through Tuscany. Predominantly a lay devotional move-

54. *The Life of Cola di Rienzo*, trans. John Wright (Toronto: Pontifical Institute of Medieval Studies, 1975), 46.

ment, the Bianchi nevertheless acted with the general approval of the religious establishment. Unlike the earlier flagellant movements, this lay devotion was a relatively well-ordered type of religious revivalism. Participants took vows to process for nine days, to fast during the day, and to sleep outside the walls of the towns they visited. In other words, the Bianchi practiced a strict but time-limited piety, which set them apart from the world but still made their devotion accessible to a large group of people. A wide variety of persons took part (just as they did at Bernardino's sermons), including the most surprising types: the immensely rich and self-centered merchant of Prato, Francesco Datini, was one of these unlikely, though temporarily earnest, participants. And, as at Bernardino's sermons, a certain holiday atmosphere prevailed, despite the movement's origin as an attempt to placate an angry God. Furthermore, the Bianchi penitents aimed to effect change within the sinful world around them. Wherever they went, their processions were typically accompanied by the opening of prisons, private peace agreements, and miracles.[55]

Whether manifested in weeping Madonnas, bleeding crucifixes, or apparitions, miracles were prominent allies in the Bianchi crusade. Not least among these miracles were the *"infinite paci"* which were made between enemies. Whenever the penitents filed into town with their cry of "Pax et Misericordia!" some of the inhabitants were moved to reconcile. In Pistoia, three *pacieri* handled these peacemakings. One important sermon there culminated in tears and kisses, with a notary, ser Niccolò di Grimo, on hand to make the ceremony legally binding. The

55. Along with Sercambi of Lucca, the major Tuscan chronicler of the Bianchi is Ser Luca Dominici, *Cronache* (Pistoia: A. Pacinotti, 1933), vol. 1. In addition to Bornstein's comprehensive study, see the articles by Arsenio Frugoni, "La devozione dei Bianchi del 1399," in *L'Attesa dell'età nuova nella spiritualità della fine del medioevo* (Todi: Presso l'Accademia Tudertina, 1962), 232–48; and Diana Webb, "Penitence and Peacemaking in City and Contado: The Bianchi of 1399," in *Studies in Church History: The Church in Town and Countryside*, ed. Derek Baker (Oxford: Basil Blackwell, 1979), 243–56. Datini's participation in the movement is discussed by Iris Origo, *The Merchant of Prato* (London: J. Cape, 1957), 316–20, and Joseph P. Byrne, "The Merchant as Penitent: Francesco di Marco Datini and the Bianchi Movement of 1399," *Viator* 20 (1989): 219–30.

genuine religious enthusiasm aroused by the Bianchi and the sudden peacemakings which resulted from it followed well-established patterns of "spontaneity," thanks to instant conversion in a public setting and the cooperation of grateful civil authorities.[56]

Far more revealing, however, are the few detailed stories about individuals. The two main Tuscan chroniclers of the Bianchi, Giovanni Sercambi and the Pistoian Luca Dominici, emphasize the movement's universal appeal, but also the considerable resistance it sometimes aroused. Several stories concern people who were somehow forced into forgiving their enemies through the intervention of the divine. Sometimes this supernatural push was spectacular, as in the case of the stubborn Florentines who only made peace after being frightened by a crucifix whose nails visibly grew before their eyes. More often, intervention involved physical punishment: the young son of an unwilling person dies, or the obstinate one is himself stricken with illness until he relents.[57] Naturally, miraculous force and subsequent conversion were most effective if many people were present. Sercambi relates how one man, seeing his enemy walking in the Bianchi processions, decided that this vulnerable moment would be an ideal time to attack. But at the very church door where the sinner lay in ambush, God showed that He had other plans. Just as the man raised his sword to smite his defenseless enemy, his arm suddenly froze in midair and he was unable to move it until he made peace. Sometimes the Bianchi themselves were the instruments of God's retribution. Dominici claims that in the Bolognese *contado* one mountaineer who resisted peacemaking was chased through the woods by a group of determined Bianchi. Suddenly struck by fever, he collapsed and was carried back to his house, where he remained gravely ill until he finally relented.[58]

Uncomfortable pressure, whether human or divine, was probably a

56. Dominici, *Cronache*, 67–88.

57. Ibid., 135, 88, 197.

58. Sercambi, *Cronache*, 308; Dominici, *Cronache*, 134. Bornstein discusses additional miracles of coercion in *The Bianchi of 1399*, 146–58.

standard part of religiously inspired peacemakings, like those of the Bianchi. As early as the eleventh century, monks involved in the Peace of God movement used many of the same tactics as the fifteenth-century penitents. They primed their audiences with well-planned spectacles deftly timed to coincide with holy days when many people would be present, and then used psychological pressure to force conversions to peacemaking. In one remarkable incident, the monks stop an impending vengeance with their solemn procession: as the murderer takes cover in a church, the lord who wants to punish him is shamed into making peace when the monks dramatically set their relics on the ground inside. Manipulated by the watchful eyes of a large audience and the baleful presence of the relics, the lord gives in, with more than a hundred knights following suit.[59] Given the sensitivity of fifteenth-century Italians to public image, one can imagine the heady effect of miracle-working combined with social pressure. Both the Bianchi and preachers like Bernardino arranged their peacemakings so that they were intensely public events, and the apparent consensus and attendant miracles were reported by dazzled witnesses, who thus prepared the ground for later participants.

Bernardino himself is the primary witness for his own peacemaking victories. The most revealing account comes from his visit to Cremona, in Lombardy. Everyone in his audience agreed to make peace

---

59. Reported by Geoffrey Koziol in "Monks, Feuds, and the Making of Peace in Eleventh-Century Flanders," in *The Peace of God: Social Violence and Religious Response in France Around the Year 1000*, ed. Thomas Head and Richard Landes (Ithaca, NY: Cornell University Press, 1992), 245–50. Koziol's analysis is similar to my own: the monks were not from Flanders, but outsiders from Hainault; they had the open support of the major political authority, the Count of Flanders; people sought them out even before they arrived to make peace; and they worked by singling out one sinner, who thus served as the example for other conversions. Medieval Irish monks also enlisted saints and relics to enforce the peace and take vengeance on the violent; see Lisa M. Bitel, *Isle of the Saints: Monastic Settlement and Christian Community in Early Ireland* (Ithaca: Cornell University Press, 1990), 152–56. In early modern Naples, resistance to peacemaking took place during Jesuit conversion rituals; see Jennifer Selwyn, "Planting Many Virtues There," 271–75.

except for a teenaged girl whose father had been murdered. Despite the remonstrances of relatives and others, she adamantly refused to enter the church where the reconciliations were taking place. Suddenly, a terrible nosebleed persuaded her to surrender. The girl was then helped into the church where she was immediately healed.[60] Only once do we see a brief shadow of failure pass over Bernardino's efforts. Apparently, it was sometimes possible for an entire crowd to resist the preacher's message. During the culmination of the great peacemaking sermon of September 28, 1427, he warns his Sienese audience that he did not want another *scandalo* like "that other time," when a woman had fainted (which he interpreted as a bad sign). Apparently, he must have expected good results at some earlier sermon, but his plans went awry:

> Never do I remember so few peaces made at any sermon than at that one. Therefore, because I'm a little more experienced than you are, I pray you to pay attention and for no one to get up from his seat for any reason.[61]

Bernardino goes on to preach a successful peacemaking and so he says no more about this embarrassing fiasco. What went wrong? Perhaps too much excitement caused the woman to faint in the crush of people, or perhaps there was either confusion or simple reluctance to join in. Whatever the reason, the mysterious incident shows us that even when the preacher had the audience in the palm of his hand, as he generally did during the Siena sermons of 1427, a serious misstep was still possible. The ritual could be as fragile as the conversions which

---

60. Florence 1424, II, 241; Bernardino claims that there were twenty thousand people present at this episode. Thompson reports an earlier peacemaking miracle where public pressure was one of the primary mechanisms of conversion: the preacher Ambrogio Sansedoni led his Sienese audience in a public prayer in the Piazza del Campo, which promptly changed the mind of the man who had been resisting peace; *Revival Preachers and Politics in Thirteenth-Century Italy*, 151–52.

61. Siena 1427, II, 1253. ". . . mai non mi ricorda che a tal predica si facesse meno paci, che a quella. Adunque, perché a queste cose io ci so' un poco più sperto di voi, vi prego che voi stiate attenti, e che niuno si parta da sedere per niuna cagione."

inspired it. Bernardino liked his peacemakings to be enthusiastic but orderly, and the unexpected could disintegrate that perfect mood.

Far more often, peacemakings are described in terms of two un-equal groups of participants: those who are willing and those who are not. The obstinate are relegated to a mere handful, and their resistance is eventually overcome. And yet their ominous presence serves as more than a warning to the lukewarm. Like sodomites, heretics, and witches, they are singled out because they refuse to take part in the general con-sensus established by their neighbors. The Cremonese girl who had to be forced into forgiving her enemies was, significantly, quite young; she may not have understood that what was being asked of her was some-thing less than a complete change of heart. She was punished because she was unable to go along with the decision of the group to "kiss and make up," a decision which may well have been completed from the moment her city invited Bernardino to preach there. In most of the mass peacemakings described in this chapter, the social pressure for forgiving one's enemies must have been relentless.

The few who resisted becoming part of this pretty picture of social harmony provided instructive examples of selfish and hardened hearts, the supposed catalysts of civil discord in the first place. By showing that only a stubborn minority refused to reconcile, Bernardino and his contemporaries could comfortably avoid any deeper discussion of the political, economic, and social reasons which lay behind faction and vendetta. That handful of stubborn souls who cannot forget their past relationships in order to forge them anew are targeted as outsiders re-sponsible for the problem. We might characterize the peacemaking rit-ual as a kind of exorcism, a dramatic expulsion of what is wrong—the vengeful hearts of the wicked—from the healthy social body.

But there was another form of resistance to peacemaking which was far more dangerous than the refusal to join in. A medieval exemplum says it best: a fox tries to convince a little bird that peace has been de-clared between the birds and their predators. The bird is at first hesi-tant to give his enemy the kiss of peace, but he consents when the fox

agrees to close his eyes . . . whereupon the little bird is promptly devoured.[62] Italian society had a corrosive fear of the false friend and the
false peace. The peacemaking ritual could in fact veil one's true intentions and give the cunning an opportunity to strike at unsuspecting
foes. We see this potential deception in one of the Bianchi stories reported by Dominici. The chronicler attributes a psychic miracle to a
young preacher-girl who had established her religious credentials
thanks to a visitation by the Virgin. The prescient girl interrupted one
of her sermons in order to evict a woman who had made a false peace
in order to bide her time for a vendetta.[63] For some, feigned forgiveness was merely another way to deceive an enemy. During the struggles
between the Whites and Blacks in Florence, the Donati faction mas-
tered the art of dissemblance in order to manipulate peacemaking for
its own ends. In October of 1301, the Blacks' strategy was to visit the
Priors in small groups and ask them to pacify the city ("we offer you
our goods and persons, in good and loyal spirit"). The Whites grew
foolishly relaxed. Looking back over the catastrophic results, Dino
Compagni ruefully notes, "We sought to make peace with them when
we should have been sharpening our swords."[64]

The stories of the Wolf of Gubbio and the bird who was eaten by
the fox show us the very different ways in which society could use the
peacemaking process. On the one hand, late-medieval Italians responded with intense enthusiasm to the call for peace, while on the
other, they remembered to look over their shoulders, just in case the
call proved to be false. When a town "unanimously" participated in
one of these moving scenes of public forgiveness, it was trying to convince itself that, potentially at least, all could be well in this world of
sinners. Like the bonfire, public peacemakings provided stirring images to remember and hence moral examples for future action.[65] The

62. Tubach, *Index Exemplorum*, 281.

63. Dominici, *Cronache*, 202.

64. Compagni, *Chronicle*, 35–36.

65. Richard Trexler says that mandatory participation in Florence's San Giovanni
celebration "forced unity upon participants by committing them to the public show

dramatic peacemakings which took place were enshrined in the social memory, proof that an ideal state of harmony was in fact possible. This is why certain troubled cities such as Brescia and Perugia called in one preacher-peacemaker after another during the course of the fifteenth century.[66] In the long run, these general pacifications often did not "work," but in the short term they must have provided one acceptable arena in which a handful of enemies were able to engage in a permanent peace, without losing face. It would be overly cynical to suggest that no one took them seriously. Just as Buonaccorso Pitti, seasoned gambler and man of the world, was inspired by the Bianchi to sign an *instrumentum* with the relatives of someone he had killed, some of those pacified by Bernardino must have considered it a permanent commitment.[67]

More importantly, we need to see peacemakings in Renaissance terms, rather than judge them merely on their ultimate success or failure. They were expressive acts,[68] complex events which sought to embrace contradictory impulses. Far from following a static formula, a single peacemaking was extremely flexible: it could be a civic consensus

---

of solidarity ... they then spent the next years living up to the public actions they had been forced to take," *Public Life*, 270. For a general introduction to memory and culture see Paul Connerton, *How Societies Remember* (Cambridge: Cambridge University Press, 1989).

66. The Florentines, too, in desperate straits during the last years of the Albizzi regime, tried to stem the rise of factionalism with similar proposals. See Luca di Filicaia's suggestion in 1429 that the pope send a cardinal-peacemaker; Brucker, *Civic Life*, 488. Although Brucker sees this as "another anachronistic proposal," it was clearly still one accepted possibility in a wide range of options available to fifteenth-century governments.

67. *Two Memoirs of Renaissance Florence: The Diaries of Buonaccorso Pitti and Gregorio Dati*, ed. Gene Brucker, trans. Julia Martines (New York: Waveland Press, 1967), 62.

68. Barbara Myerhoff defines ritual as "a form by which culture presents itself to itself" and says that "all rituals are efficacious in some degree merely by their taking place. They are not purposive and instrumental, but expressive, communicative, and rhetorical acts"; see "A Death in Due Time: Construction of Self and Culture in Ritual Drama," in *Rite, Drama, Festival, Spectacle: Rehearsals Towards a Theory of Cultural Performance*, ed. John J. MacAloon (Philadelphia: Institute for the Study of Human Issues, 1984), 155 and 170.

proclaiming newfound unity, a temporary embrace of enthusiastic brothers and sisters in Christ, an opportunity to present a magnanimous face and make a legal peace with honor (perhaps by negotiating and then signing an *instrumentum*) and, finally, a convenient mask for those who would retaliate in the future.

If Bernardino was effective at all, it was because he could ably mediate within two distinct forms of moral pressure. He clearly saw his big peacemaking sessions as the embodiment of two parallel processes: "There are two peaces," he said, "the one within and the other without" (the *pace di dentro* and the *pace di fuore*).[69] During public reconciliations one could be shamed by the participation of one's neighbors and by the knowledge that the audience would see one's own reluctance to take part; everyone remembered who wept, who shed a demon, who repented and made peace. Coercion by the enthusiastic (or calculating) majority could be implicit, as in the concern over a potential loss of face, or explicit, through physical force or the attempt to harness people's fear of divine punishment. This external peacemaking, the *pace di fuore*, was shaped by a relatively fixed ritual tradition, by the collusion between peacemaker and civil authorities, and by intense public pressure to make everyone conform.

Yet by placing these outward shows of unity within the context of a total moral reform Bernardino was really searching for the *pace di dentro*, the true peacemaking that took place in the heart. His special gift as a preacher was an ability to enter the minds of individuals and understand their hopes and fears in relation to others, his real goal a conversion which would then be reflected in an external sign, the ritual of peacemaking. But the *pace di dentro* was never easy to arrange in a culture where the fox still held sway.

69. Siena 1427, I, 383.

CHAPTER THREE

The Poisoned Word

"La lingua non ha osso, e fassi rompere il dosso."

In a peacemaking sermon to the Florentines, Bernardino tells the story of a priest who wanted one of his parishioners to forgive an enemy. Taking him to a church to recite the Our Father in Latin, the priest stops the fellow just as he reaches *"dimitte nobis debita nostra et nos dimittimus debitoribus nostris,"* asking him if he really understands the meaning, which is that God will forgive him as he forgives others. "Oimme!" declares the man in great surprise. "I did not think of that!" According to Bernardino, the man then "immediately left to pardon" his enemy.[1]

In his role as peacemaker, the hypothetical priest

1. Florence 1424, II, 236.

uses reason to convince the sinner and the story happily ends with enlightenment and a quick decision to make amends. In the neat little world of the exemplum, the peacemaker as catalyst needs only to point out the error of the man's ways for there to be a sudden and complete change of heart, just as the miracles in the Bianchi tales force a "conversion" during public peacemakings. But real hearts were not so easily moved. Many people might take part in a peacemaking ritual—whether because of government initiative, public pressure, or the sheer excitement of the moment—but the attractiveness and the constraints of this *pace di fuore* needed to be accompanied by an inner transformation if the peace was to be genuine.

Unfortunately, comprehending the *pace di dentro*, the inner peacemaking, is a frustrating task when we first examine Bernardino's actual words on civil discord and its remedies in the soul. What did he actually say that would soften at least some hearts into forgiveness? Surprisingly, it seems that when people were emotionally moved to make peace, it may have had little to do with the preacher's innovative ideas. Indeed, we would search in vain for any kind of "originality" either in his formulation of the problem or in his proposed solutions. For the most part, he never strayed from a few basic ideas which he repeated with stubborn conviction.

Paradoxically, it is this very lack of originality or analysis which explains how Bernardino convinced his listeners to "change," whether permanently or for a few happy days. His sermons on faction, on gossip, the match that ignites conflict, and on the psychology of forgiveness were satisfying because they drew upon deeply felt beliefs and anxieties. By bringing these to the surface, by threatening, entreating, but seldom surprising his audience, he was able to convince some listeners to identify with his message. It may be that we are best led to a conversion, religious or otherwise, not by new ideas but by the affirmation of old ones; perhaps it is easiest to be most deeply moved by what we already feel to be true.[2] Bernardino's great gift was in sensing

2. Daniel Lesnick, in "Dominican Preaching and the Creation of Capitalist Ideol-

what his audience wanted to hear, and then doing his best within this limitation. His sermons thus provided a comfortable setting in which listeners were able to accept a certain amount of criticism, but none which actually threatened their way of life. Just as the peacemaking ceremony was the culmination of a series of traditional responses to the preacher, so was the message itself a composite of traditional advice that rarely challenged basic assumptions.

Of course, both Bernardino and his audience believed that the precise opposite was taking place, that the message precipitated a radical change of heart. It is true that the preacher ostensibly challenged vendetta's code of honor when he pleaded for an alternative, and that he spoke directly and movingly to those troubled individuals who felt oppressed by a suffocating world. But Bernardino never entirely rejected the beliefs that caused conflict in the first place. This means that his sermons reveal some of the inner contradictions of a society in which true peace was far more elusive than the success of the *pace di fuore* would have us believe. When he spoke on faction, vendetta, and forgiveness, he confronted unsolvable dilemmas: how to criticize faction without attacking the social hierarchy; how to convince the individual that it was possible to survive in a hostile community; and, most difficult of all, how to resolve honorably the conflict between Christian pardoning and blood vengeance.

I. "Guelphs and Ghibellines"

When Bernardino preached directly against faction, he was prudent enough to skirt most political specifics. Although he did not hesitate to give frank and often complex advice on usury or sexual behavior, revealing a subtle understanding of the real world, he was reluctant to

---

ogy in Late Medieval Florence," *Memorie Domenicane* 8–9 (1977–78): 221–37, also portrays Giordano da Pisa as a "cultural agent" in relationship to what his listeners in Florence wanted to hear; Giordano's role, however, seems to have been more dynamic than Bernardino's since he was preaching at a time of rapidly changing ideology about capitalism and the good Christian.

discuss faction in a similarly realistic fashion. In some circumstances, he deliberately chose to avoid the subject altogether, even if a particular audience might have benefited from such preaching. It is remarkable, for example, that he refrained from pointing out party conflict when he spoke in Florence in 1424 and 1425. Maire-Vigeur claims that he did not preach against it there because the city on the Arno represented the kind of strong government he so much admired.[3] Given Florentine politics during this period, with the split between the Medici faction and the other oligarchs widening as the decade progressed, we should suspect a rather different motive. Gene Brucker points out that Florence maintained an image of stability during the early 1420s, but that internal criticism of the regime was growing during this time.[4] Since peacemaking was usually a mutual enterprise on the part of both preacher and government, Bernardino probably understood all too well that those currently in power in Florence would not have welcomed open talk of dissension. His sermons on concord are accordingly structured in the most general way, emphasizing peacemaking between feuding individuals.

Bernardino's language was strangely evasive even when he did speak out against party strife. He avoided almost all mention of the *monti*, or Sienese factions, when he preached in his hometown in 1427, although he was specifically asked to calm civic discord. Whenever he discusses *parzialità* in this sermon course, the nature of the unrest cannot be discerned from the virulent sermons which speak not of Dodici or Noveschi or Gentiluomini, but of unnamed and somewhat stylized "partisans." Occasionally he even drags in those old warhorses, the Guelphs and Ghibellines. This outdated terminology may have held some minimal power in Florence, where "Guelphism" was a kind of

3. Maire-Vigueur, "Bernardino et la vie citadine," 260. One of Bernardino's few, brief references to partisans is in Florence 1425, III, 100–101.

4. See Gene Brucker, *Civic World*, esp. 443–71 for a discussion of the city's political life during these years. For the eventual results of this calm before the storm, see Dale Kent, *The Rise of the Medici: Faction in Florence, 1426–1434* (Oxford and New York: Oxford University Press, 1978).

rallying cry for certain conservatives, but its application to fifteenth-century Sienese politics was completely anachronistic; the city's factional configuration was highly peculiar, with the years following the downfall of the Nine in 1355 giving birth to institutionalized factions, the hereditary *monti,* and where disaffected nobles frequently caused turmoil. Of course Bernardino was aware of the political realities of his native Siena. As in the case of the Florentine sermons, the careful avoidance of specific examples reflects not a lack of political acumen but a prudent evaluation of his own role, one that he did not care to jeopardize by abusing either those who held power or the malcontents who were hoping to seize it. The fact that he spoke relatively freely on certain subjects yet curbed his tongue when discussing politics indicates that preachers, at least those who hoped for repeat invitations, had to develop some sense of the boundary between plain speaking and confrontation. As Bernardino neatly put it, a preacher must approach a delicate subject as a rooster walks on dung: by stepping carefully.[5]

By framing his words within the safe abstraction of Guelph-Ghibellinism or a vague *parzialità,* the preacher could say what needed to be said while his listeners tolerated yet another discourse on "the evils of faction." Of course, if the historian is frustrated by the lack of concrete information and the dusty terminology, the contemporary audience certainly was not. Everyone present could automatically assign real names to the shadowy figures denounced from the pulpit, especially when the preacher spoke during emotionally charged situations. If Bernardino's sermons on faction cannot be used as sources which inform us about contemporary politics, this does not mean that audiences perceived them to be timid or abstract. The sermons must have functioned as up-to-date social criticism, with listeners avidly filling in the appropriate blanks—that is, when they chose to do so.

Apart from discretion, there is a larger cultural issue lying behind

---

5. Siena 1427, I, 574. He was referring to marital sodomy, but the metaphor is even more applicable to his treatment of faction.

Bernardino's misty picture of discord. As J. K. Hyde has pointed out, medieval Italians did not really spend much time reflecting on strife, despite the fact that they lived amidst it. The sketchy theory which they did formulate was "so satisfying that very few men were prompted to look beyond it." According to Hyde, strife was associated with the following ideas: disaster followed peace and prosperity in this transient world; the Devil played a major role in fomenting party struggle; certain sins like avarice and envy were key in the genesis of faction.[6] For the most part, Bernardino's ideas remain within this traditional schema. By depicting the struggle between competing groups as a kind of moral drama, he and his contemporaries could shift the blame from institutional structures to individual folly. The locus of the problem was thus identified as the heart rather than the system. And so Bernardino was content to paint faction in broad and colorful strokes, treating it as a sin rather than as a complex situation. For example, there is no acknowledgment of the patron-client relationship so integral to Italian politics, nor is there an understanding, as there would be in Machiavelli, that not an ideal "unity," but rather a balance of power (which implies conflict) contributed to healthy political life.[7] Bernardino is not even much concerned with the *gara d'ufici*, or struggle for offices, an important issue raised by astute commentators like Dino Compagni. What emerges from his preaching is a streamlined scenario of vice at work: the proud and the greedy join together to form parties which, if left unchecked, will dismantle the structure of civilization. The solution is for individuals to repent by forgiving their enemies and severing all factional ties. If they refuse to do so, they will be punished in this world and the next. Because Bernardino saw him-

6. J. K. Hyde, "Contemporary Views on Faction," in *Violence and Civil Disorder in Italian Cities, 1200–1500*, ed. Lauro Martines (Berkeley and Los Angeles: University of California Press, 1972), 273–76. See also the discussion in Heers, *Parties and Political Life*, 27–39.

7. Edward Peters, "Pars, Parte: Dante and an Urban Contribution to Political Thought," *The Medieval City*, ed. Harry A. Miskimin, David Herlihy, and A. L. Udovitch (New Haven and London: Yale University Press, 1977), 129.

self not as a catalyst for political change but as a herald of God come to warn erring souls, this scenario, with its stark opposition of Good and Evil, suited his purpose of appealing to individual Christians.

The best way to outline the preacher's method is to begin with his Latin sermons, the formal writings he composed from the late 1420s onwards, a decade after he had already established himself as a peace-maker.[8] The basic similarity between these sermons and those preached in *volgare* in 1427 suggests that Bernardino did not change his message for particular audiences, aside from adding his customary bits of local color. He presented the same body of material wherever he visited, since politics might vary from place to place but the human personality did not.

The most striking feature of the Latin sermons is the emphasis on the moral and material evils of faction, especially the horrors which it unleashed upon the community. The focus is on lurid description rather than analysis, with disgusting and exciting details used to capture the crowd's attention. Bernardino unabashedly uses the most primeval preaching technique, with enough hellfire to entertain his listeners and possibly terrify them into reform. This is in contrast to his usual style with its shifts between humor, calm instruction, and intermittent bursts of anger. Here a higher level of fury is sustained; like sodomites and witches, partisans were the recipients of a special kind of wrath.

Although the preacher naturally points out that partisans will be damned in the afterlife, his most terrifying warnings describe the fire and destruction which will take place in this world, once faction ruins the *patria* and everyone in it. *Partialitas*, the division of one citizen from

---

8. The relevant sermons are in Bernardino's *Opera Omnia*, ed. PP. Collegii S. Bonaventurae (Quaracchi: Collegio San Bonaventura, 1950–65): "Contra Guelphos et Ghibellinos et quascumque alias divisiones et partes," I, 308–20; "Contra insignia distinguentia inter partes," I, 321–32; "Contra partialitates cordis, oris et operis; et maxime contra Guelphos et Ghibellinos," III, 437–49; and "Prophetia beato Ioanni evangelistae revelata de eisdem partialitatibus cordis, oris, et operis," III, 450–59.

another, divides and annihilates towns and cities, Church and Empire. The images Bernardino conjures are reminiscent of the Lorenzetti frescoes showing the results of *Cattivo Governo*: faction destroys buildings and flocks, fields and vineyards, while trade and the arts are abandoned. Worse, the fate of those who are partisans or their victims is exceedingly gruesome, and the preacher lingers on the gory details, including raped and disemboweled women, infants flung against walls, and men who are burnt, suffocated in dung, or forced to eat their own body parts before being put to death.[9] Bernardino says he witnessed the horrors of factionalism himself when he preached in Lombardy.

Faction thus incited, in Machiavelli's phrase, "the beast in the man," a kind of cannibalism devouring human society. In fact, Bernardino claims that cannibalism literally takes place, since partisans have been known to feed on one another's flesh.[10] The charge is not a familiar one in the annals of late-medieval Tuscany,[11] but an aside in the *Decameron* hints that there existed at least a fear of bodily desecration by one's enemies. In the Ninth Day, First Tale, a hopeful lover plans to pose as a corpse in order to gain entry to his lady's house. But as he approaches the graveyard, he begins to have second thoughts, worrying, among other things, that her kinsmen might want to "wreak vengeance upon it in return for some wrong he [i.e., the dead man] has

9. Ibid., I, 312 and 323. Even more lurid descriptions of the ruin faction brings on a city can be found in Sercambi, *Cronache*, I, 373.

10. *Opera Omnia*, III, 453.

11. But see Giovanni Villani's account of the killings of Walter of Brienne's official, Guglielmo d'Asciesi, and his son during the 1343 rebellion in Florence, when the victims were supposedly dismembered and eaten by the angry crowd; cited by Edward Muir, "The Cannibals of Renaissance Italy," *Syracuse Scholar* 5, no. 2 (Fall 1984): 5–14. Muir shows how cannibalism, real or perceived, was a ritual act intended to shame an enemy, who was thereby reduced to the status of a "butchered hog," 12. Trevor Dean, on the other hand, is more skeptical than Muir (and Bernardino) about the reality of cannibalism and ritual mutilation; see "Marriage and Mutilation," 24–31. However, the admittedly scattered evidence is still too strong to be dismissed as projection on the part of storytellers, even if vendetta narratives, like peacemaking vignettes, are highly structured.

done them. She tells me not to make a sound, no matter what may happen; but what if they were to gouge my eyes out, or wrench out my teeth, or cut off my hands, or do me some other piece of mischief, where would I be then?"[12] That such fears were not wholly unfounded is indicated in a Sienese case cited by Daniel Waley: in 1273, nine men who were present at a homicide were condemned *in absentia* and the heaviest fine was placed on the person who had mutilated the corpse.[13] Recently, Edward Muir has found more detailed evidence of mutilation and "cannibalism" in his superb analysis of faction and vendetta in the Friuli. Tracing the links between the hunt and the feud, Muir shows how the vendetta was both depicted and acted out as predation. Contemporaries repeatedly noted the wolfish (or rabidly doglike) quality of those who pursued vengeance. The body of the defeated enemy was at the center of cultural perceptions and practices involving tracking, slaughter, and butchery, while the ultimate degradation was to have one's unburied corpse consumed by animals. At the very least, a cannibalism by proxy took place, with pigs and hunting dogs standing in for the human predator: in the grisliest scene described by Muir, witnesses in 1512 claimed that the factional leader Antonio Savorgnan lay dying as an enemy's dog devoured his brains.[14] Bernardino may well have heard comparable stories when he preached in northern Italy a century earlier.[15]

12. Giovanni Boccaccio, *Decameron*, trans. G. H. McWilliam (London: Penguin, 1972), 685.

13. Daniel Waley, *Siena and the Sienese in the Thirteenth Century* (Cambridge: Cambridge University Press, 1991), 97–98.

14. Edward Muir, *Mad Blood Stirring: Faction and Vendetta in the Friuli* (Baltimore: Johns Hopkins University Press, 1993), esp. 220–38. Edward Peters notes a similar connection between bestiality and discord in Dante's *Commedia*, "Pars, Parte," 116.

15. And this may have been a common scare tactic in preaching. Giacomo delle Marche gives a horrific list of the evils of faction, including attack by animals and forced self-cannibalism, in his sermon on "Partialitate," *Sermones Dominicales*, ed. Renato Lioi (Ancona: Biblioteca Francescana, 1978), vol. 2, 23: ". . . virgines deflorantur, uxores et vidue violantur, horrenda homicidia, puerorum crudeles neces, dire carcerationes, tormenta crudelissima. Quidam suffocantur, quidam conburuntur, alii fame

In the preacher's mind, the animal frenzy of partisans and their willingness to rend not just an individual corpse but society itself proves that they have abandoned human reason. All rationality is blinded in the city where factions hold sway, with the inevitable results of injustice, war, and destruction of the *patria*. Bernardino understands the simple, brutal formula at work when a partisan has legal power over enemies: "If a friend offends, a great wrong is considered insignificant; if an adversary does wrong, his offense is felt to be great . . ."[16] He wants people to regard these partial judges with the contempt they deserve, and bluntly labels factionalism as *"stultitia summa et consummata."*[17] At other times, he calls it "insane." Their folly is evident in the way various factions distinguish themselves through minor differences in eating and drinking, or in vehement preference of one fruit or tree to another.[18]

The most important visual mark of a partisan was his fanatical allegiance to factional banners and insignia, a devotion which was impressed upon children as soon as they left their cradles.[19] As propagator of the YHS and master of visually powerful sermons and peacemakings, Bernardino was acutely sensitive to the way in which the visual could marshal loyalties, for good or for evil. Outward signs reflected inner states. A wedding ring, for example, reminds both the world and the woman who wears it that a wife is supposed to be faith-

---

pereunt, alii in stercore proiciuntur. Aliis preciduntur membra, manus, lingua et aliquando ipsimet eadem coguntur conmedere, alii precipitantur a turribus, alii in fluminibus et puteis, alii dantur canis, alii relinquuntur lupis, alii assantur vivi."

16. *Opera Omnia*, I, 309.

17. Ibid., I, 314.

18. Ibid., I, 325. The Venetians tried to prohibit these signs (including flowers and ribbons) among the Friulian Strumieri and Zambarlani; see Muir, *Mad Blood Stirring*, 89–90. Like Bernardino, Giacomo delle Marche made the connection between party designations and human folly. He sarcastically notes: "Dicunt enim quod Deus est guelfus; Ioannes evangelista ghibellinus, Baptista vero guelfus; leo vero guelfus, sed aquila ghibellinus. Sed unum vellem scire: asinus quid est? De qua parte?" See *Sermones Dominicales*, vol. 2, 24.

19. *Opera Omnia*, I, 330.

ful in thought, word, and deed.[20] The preacher felt that party emblems
worked in much the same way, since they reinforced an allegiance at
the same time as they proclaimed it. Like the legitimate images of
Christ and the saints, these evil signs excited the spirit (*ad animae excita-
tionem*), albeit negatively.[21] One is reminded here of the excited spirits
aroused by that most spectacular visual display of all, the bonfire of
vanities. By throwing the instruments of one's sins upon the public
flames, one symbolically renounced those sins in the presence of others. In his understanding of the importance of the visual in his culture, Bernardino made his own original contribution to the discussion
of faction when he singled out insignia as a cause, as well as a manifestation, of the problem. Even if he deliberately simplified the political
and social roots of faction, he drew upon his expertise in psychology,
knowing that it was essential to arrest the spirit of party strife before
it gained an emotional hold and infected others. His solution was to
replace party emblems with the holy sign of the YHS, thus reminding
the hesitant where their true loyalties should be.

The emotional allegiance symbolized by emblems was so powerful
that it catapulted faction into another category of sin. The fools who
blindly followed these emblems and parties, and willingly died for
them, were martyrs for Satan.[22] Partisanship was not only a crime
against nature and human reason, but idolatry, "denial of the faith and
treachery against Christ"; it was, in fact, outright heresy, since the only
true "party" should be that of Christ and His Church.[23] Factions were
thus destructive of religious order (and perhaps threatened the fragile
unity which Bernardino and other fifteenth-century preachers advocated on behalf of the restored papacy). Also, by focusing on party allegiance as a type of heresy, the preacher could better confine his sanctions to the individual soul. Each listener who followed the banner of
Satan abdicated his place in the Christian community. Partisans

---

20. Ibid., I, 326.   21. Ibid., I, 330.
22. Ibid., I, 326.   23. Ibid., I, 309.

should be branded as heretics who must be denied prayers after death and burial in hallowed ground. The parish priest shares in this burden of conscience and will be damned if he cares for a partisan's soul. Bernardino likewise threatened the artisans who were guilty of fashioning party banners.[24] Each person, whether party loyalist, negligent priest, or greedy artisan, had a clear-cut decision to make: was it to be Christ or Satan, peace or destruction, salvation or damnation? Even if he evaded the larger social problems involved, the preacher was confident that individuals, the essential components of the factions, might be persuaded and saved.

Both unable and unwilling to attack particular institutions or governments, Bernardino chose to target the sinful person; his goal was to reach one heart which might then extend forgiveness towards an enemy. In fact, in his actual peacemaking sermons, the substance of his argument for forgiveness seems more appropriate for ending the vendetta, or private enmity. This explains why most of his reconciliations were probably not between parties. For example, although he specifically preached against "faction" in Siena, witnesses at his canonization trials do not mention any reconciliations among groups, but only peaces concluded between individuals and families.[25] Even the peacemaking in factious Perugia almost certainly did not involve parties. On the very day the Priors, inspired by Bernardino, approved various changes in the town statutes (November 4, 1425), they also asked Rome for a copy of a bull against members of Perugia's popular party.[26]

24. Ibid., I, 319–20, 328.

25. Piana, "I processi di canonizzazione," no. 1, 158: "Interrogatis de nominibus eorum, dixit de d. Thoma de Ragazaia qui nominibus eorum qui inimicitias capitales habebat cum familia illius de Thomasinis, ac Iacopo d. Barci qui graves inimicitiae habebat cum pluribus civibus civitatis praedictae; qui omnes fr. Bernardini opera ad bonam concordiam sunt reducti." Also see no. 2, 388, where another witness lists additional names, including the Piccolomini.

26. Maire-Vigueur, "Bernardino et la vie citadine," 269. The author distrusts biographers who praise Bernardino for reconciling factions, and says that this was in fact

Bernardino may well have been content to cast a wide net with his vague preaching against "partisans," and then draw in whomever he could, satisfied to pacify hostilities of any kind. Of course, the distinction we make between faction and vendetta was not so sharply drawn in the minds of the preacher and his contemporaries, where the personal and the political were always deeply intertwined. As a category of sin, faction lay at one end of a long continuum which began with human choice, and included private and family hatreds. Myriad personal quarrels, most of them inaccessible to the historian, inevitably fed into larger political rivalries. Particularly in smaller towns, a single vendetta might well escalate into a major crisis. Even the cessation of one feud—preferably before it came to blows—would have contributed to community peace.

This sense of vengeance as catastrophically linked to faction and a menace to the entire society is fundamentally different from many anthropologists' understanding of feud in both non-Western cultures and in medieval Europe. Classic feuding societies are described as pastoral or rural, and either "stateless" or resistant to the intrusions of a "modernizing" central authority. The feud is seen both as a way of competing for scarce resources and as a useful form of "self-help," a means of handling conflict as well as generating it, in the absence of a fully developed legal system. In the most extreme functionalist argument, Max Gluckman has articulated "the peace in the feud," and the importance of cross-cutting kinship ties in the eventual restoration of equilibrium. Other structural characteristics include honor as the general playing field, scorekeeping, and an understanding of the rules of the game.[27] Some form of the blood feud was prevalent throughout

---

not a standard part of the preacher's repertoire. The peacemaking in Assisi indicates that feud, rather than political faction, was at the heart of Bernardino's mission. See the *Cronaca di Perugia (Diario del Graziani)*, 313: ". . . e dicevase che in Asese aveva gran fruto, maxime di far pace con quelli che erano stati gran tempo in nimicizia chi per la morte del padre, chi de' fratelli, e chi de figli . . ."

27. See Max Gluckman for "The Peace in the Feud." Jacob Black-Michaud, *Cohesive Force: Feud in the Mediterranean and Middle East* (Oxford: Basil Blackwell, 1975), argues that

Europe during the early and central Middle Ages, but afterwards maintained a vigorous survival mostly in places such as Scotland and the Friuli.[28] Although these early-modern areas were certainly not "stateless" and had functioning lawcourts (another arena for quarreling and vengeance), they were in some ways still "frontier regions," with feudal social structures and agrarian economies.[29]

---

material scarcity is an integral part of feuding cultures. However, others have challenged or modified parts of these theories. For example, Paul Stirling in *Turkish Village* (New York: Wiley, 1965), 247–54, says that feud in this region was "disorganized and unsystematic," and also disagrees with Gluckman's claim that unresolved feud cannot exist in the village setting. In a look at a famous family quarrel in America, Altina L. Waller notes that Appalachian feuding was not narrowly a "self-help" phenomenon, but also actively pursued in the courts; see *Feud: Hatfields, McCoys, and Social Change in Appalachia, 1860–1900* (Chapel Hill: University of North Carolina Press, 1988). Good overviews of the structural characteristics of feud are included in Christopher Boehm, *Blood-Revenge*, and Stephen Wilson, *Feuding, Conflict and Banditry in Nineteenth-Century Corsica*.

28. For the Merovingian period, see J. M. Wallace-Hadrill, "The Blood-Feud of the Franks," in *The Long-Haired Kings, and Other Studies in Frankish History* (New York: Barnes and Noble, 1962), 121–47. In "Feuding and Peacemaking in the Touraine Around the Year 1100," *Traditio* 42 (1986): 195–263, Stephen White argues that "the prevalence of feuding among upper-class males may have provided a sort of rationale for their efforts to establish, consolidate, and perpetuate their own political and ideological hegemony," 202. William Ian Miller has provided one of the most complete analyses of feud in a medieval society; see *Bloodtaking and Peacemaking* and "Choosing the Avenger: Some Aspects of the Bloodfeud in Medieval Iceland," *Law and History Review* 1, no. 2 (Fall 1983): 159–204. Miller notes a "balanced exchange-model" in Icelandic sagas; repayment was essential in both gift giving and vengeance.

29. See Muir's description of social and economic conditions in the Friuli; *Mad Blood Stirring*, 16–48 and 77–107. Feud survived even later in several rural areas of northeastern Italy. See Osvaldo Raggio, *Faide e parentele: Lo stato genovese visto dalla Fontanabuona* (Turin: Einaudi, 1990), and Angelo Torre, "Feuding, Faction, and Parties: The Redefinition of Politics in the Imperial Fiefs of Langhe in the Seventeenth and Eighteenth Centuries," in *History from Crime: Selections from Quaderni Storici*, ed. Edward Muir and Guido Ruggiero (Baltimore: Johns Hopkins University Press, 1994), 135–69. Both works examine the relationship of periphery to center. Keith Brown in *Bloodfeud in Scotland* notes that feuds can be avidly pursued within lawcourts, 44, and, as in late-medieval Italy, private feud in sixteenth-century Scotland was often channeled into larger political enmities. Brown also points out that the Scottish crown did not "suppress" feud, but mediated change with the input of the nobility, 234. Jenny Wormald,

With the exception of Flanders, urban Italy in the late Middle Ages had perhaps the most distinct variant of feud which fits less easily into the classic anthropological mold.[30] Dynamic and economically sophisticated, with highly differentiated social strata that nevertheless permitted some mobility for aggressive individuals and families, the cities of the Italian peninsula possessed a complex legal system and rapidly evolving notions of both kin obligations and communal government.[31] In the worst scenarios, the control of the state became the

---

"Bloodfeud, Kindred, and Government in Early Modern Scotland," *Past and Present* 87 (May 1980): 54–97, agrees that private and public justice were complementary, and also notes that the local community was more important in the feud than obligations to an extended kindred. For another late example of a feuding society, see R. R. Davies, "The Survival of the Bloodfeud in Medieval Wales," *History* 14, no. 182 (October 1969): 338–57.

30. David Nicholas says that Flemish cities were disrupted by vendettas (made even more complicated by a system of bipartite, rather than patrilineal, kinship), but he also believes that in many ways "Flanders remained a frontier society"; *Medieval Flanders* (New York: Longman, 1992), 135 and 199–201. For the settlement of blood feud in Ghent, see Nicholas, "Crime and Punishment in Fourteenth-Century Ghent," *Revue belge de philologie et d'histoire* 48, no. 2 (1970): 298–334, and no. 4 (1970): 1141–76.

31. The best introduction to violent conflict in late-medieval Italy is Martines, *Violence and Civil Disorder*. However, there is still no commanding overview of the feud in Italian cities. We need more case studies like Muir's work on the Friuli, especially in places besides Florence, so that regional comparisons can be made. According to John Larner, at the end of the Quattrocento the vendetta was still going strong among leading families in the admittedly tumultuous Romagna; see "Order and Disorder in the Romagna, 1450–1500," in *Violence and Disorder*, 38–71. Thomas Kuehn notes that, even in Florence, "the courts could absorb feud, not abolish it," with legal action itself becoming a form of vendetta; "Dispute Processing in the Renaissance," *Law, Family, and Women: Towards a Legal Anthropology of Renaissance Italy* (Chicago: University of Chicago Press, 1991), 75–100. Following Kuehn's lead, historians need to move beyond the basic questions of when and how urban feud was "suppressed" in order to understand the nuances of how it actually worked (although this will be difficult, given the wider range of variables in Italy than in, say, the streamlined and insular society of Iceland). What were the internal dynamics of the feud; how far did kin obligations extend; what was the feud's relationship to rural power bases; how did it change over time; how did it function as a form of ritual display among males? An early attempt to answer some of these questions was made by Anna Maria Enriquez, "La vendetta nella vita e nella legislazione fiorentina," *Archivio Storico Italiano* 19 (1933): 85–146, 181–223. Daniel Waley has pointed out that feud in late-thirteenth-century Siena took place

focus of the expanded feud, or faction. Furthermore, personality itself was organized around a fundamentally different sense of social space than that possessed by feuding Saharan nomads, Icelandic homesteaders, or Appalachian farmers. Both the size and design of Italian cities meant closer living quarters than in most feuding cultures, and this had far-reaching implications for both social relationships and the concept of the self. Within the dense urban setting, levels of tension could quickly escalate because there was little distance to speak of, no place to retreat to with honor. Dino Compagni's bitter portrait of the Florence of the Blacks and Whites, with its population of approximately one hundred thousand, is probably the best description of how a feud can escalate into a citywide conflagration: the Donati and Cerchi literally lived next door to each other and found countless opportunities to challenge and attack. When Compagni and other writers described feud, they in no way saw it as the potentially stabilizing factor it is claimed to be for those societies which rely on "self-help." Instead, Italians believed that both private vengeance and large-scale faction precipitated the collapse of civic life.

Bernardino also realized how cities and the intense interactions they produced could result in a defensive human personality. He did not see himself as effecting structural change, but instead concentrated on trying to guide and reassure the individual soul by tapping into its deepest fears about menacing social relationships. The preacher thus devoted his energy to the area where he had some hope of practical success. The most vigorous part of his message was on faction's initial trigger, the violent impulse of the person who submits to the spirit of malice and vendetta. The Latin sermons on faction stress the relationship between the heart, the mouth, and the actions which result from envy and hatred. Naturally, the best place to arrest hatred was in the

---

among middle-class merchants as well as nobles; see "A Blood-Feud with a Happy Ending: Siena, 1285–1304," in *City and Countryside in Late Medieval and Renaissance Italy: Essays Presented to Philip Jones*, ed. Trevor Dean and Chris Wickham (London: Hambledon Press, 1990), 45–53.

heart, its birthplace, but it was the second step in the chain which really interested Bernardino. Once a person has conceived hateful
thoughts about another, evil words will pour from the mouth, spark-
ing some kind of physical response (either in the offender or the
offended). The sequence implies an almost inevitable progression
from the carelessly flung word to the drawn sword. In an attempt to
suppress humanity's worst impulses, the preacher hoped to intervene
before vicious words were spoken at all. It is precisely this insistence
upon the power of speech which is at the center of his understanding
of civic strife and peacemaking. Bernardino's partial solutions make
more sense when we examine what he and his listeners believed to be
the true origin of faction and vendetta: uncontrolled human emotion
and the unholy word.

II. Words and Swords

It is natural that a sculptor of language would understand its power
to create both good and evil. Words can shape our inner nature, just as
Bernardino shaped other men with his speech, and as his own strong
sense of self was carved as he spoke from the pulpit. He knew that,
like wedding rings or party banners, words become signs and rein-
forcers of a particular allegiance. In a sermon against blasphemy,
Bernardino noted that angels praise God while devils curse Him; one's
spiritual country was revealed by what issued from the mouth:

> You see that the soul is of eternal life. It conforms itself in such a way
> that it returns to its homeland. How does one recognize a Frenchman? By
> his talk. And the German from amongst others? By his talk. And thus
> one also recognizes who is for God and who is for the devil—by talk.[32]

Just as words identify one's natural and spiritual *patria*, so could they
also determine one's attitude towards the factions. Careless words

---

32. Siena 1425, I, 155. "Vedi che l'anima è di vita eterna. Conformala per modo che
essa ritorni alla patria sua. A che si conosci el francioso? Alla favella. E similmente el
tedesco e gli altri? A la favella. Anche si conosce chi è di Dio o del diavolo alla favella."

could turn into an informal oath when an excited person shouted his support for a particular party. One rather dangerous suggestion Bernardino made for resisting faction was to answer a partisan battle cry with a bravely shouted *"Viva la parte di Dio!"* This "Hurrah for God's Party!" was meant as a way of psychologically resisting both social pressure and the excitement of identifying oneself as a partisan; the assumption here is that verbalization is a catalyst for emotional response.

The word which most concerned Bernardino, however, was not the one shouted openly on the street, but the sly whisper behind the back. As a professional observer of human nature, the preacher understood all too well the impulses that dragged people into violent conflict. Prominent among these was the urge to gossip. To us, this may seem a relatively minor sin compared to other hostile acts, but not so to Bernardino. The theme of *detrazione*, or backbiting—*chiacchiera*, or idle chatter, is a less malevolent form of gossip—was one to which he turned again and again, especially in the 1427 sermons where he carefully traced its role in the genesis of faction. It is no coincidence that the four sermons on gossip which he gave on the sixth through ninth days of his visit were immediately followed by a series of hard-hitting talks against party strife. Their proximity forced listeners to link the sins of *detrazione* and *parzialità*. In the opening minutes of the first sermon, delivered on August 20, Bernardino makes the linkage explicit with a snappy proverb: *"La lingua non ha osso, e fassi rompere il dosso"* ("The tongue has no bone, but breaks the back").[33] The tongue of the detractor, he later claims, was the first cause of Guelphs and Ghibellines cutting each other to pieces.

His metaphors are strikingly similar to those he uses to describe partisans, forming an ominous procession of bestial images whose central figure is the predator. In fact, his *thema* for this group of sermons is the dragon of the Apocalypse, who is also associated with the

33. Ibid., I, 232.

serpent in Eden: *"Draco iste quem formasti ad illudendum ei; omnia ad te expectant"* (Psalm 103 [104]: 26). But he quickly departs from this particular monster in order to describe a large menagerie. Detractors, too, are beasts of prey who consume their victims. Like rabid dogs, their bloody mouths hang open, crazy to bite.[34] Their mouths stink like those of lions who devour other creatures. They are bloodsuckers, flies in the ears of dogs. Like birds who feed on snakes, they enjoy eating evil things. And like pigs, they happily put filth in their mouths.[35]

Worst of all is the human beast who devours his own. Throughout the sermons, Bernardino displays his finely tuned sense of the expressive tactics used by this predator: with feigned reluctance, the gossip pretends something is weighing him down until his companion asks what is wrong. "I have a great melancholy," he says with sadness, then piously adds, "What I'm about to say, I say for a good end! God knows it!" Then follows the vicious attack. Bernardino compares this type with a scorpion who licks with the tongue, embraces with the claws, then finally stings with the tail.[36] This is an active, planned slander far beyond ordinary gossip and akin to ambush: a master of deception ("with a thousand devices"), the malefactor assumes a false voice and waits by the door of a good woman, whispering, "So-and-so, are you there? are you there?" (*"Tale, secci, secci?"*). At other times, he will write an evil letter and let it be found, or compose nasty *canzonette*.[37] The detractor, then, is presented throughout these sermons as a vicious beast who feeds on reputation.

Even more pronounced is the association between slander and con-

---

34. Ibid., I, 237–38.

35. Ibid., I, 243, 267, 316. Giacomo delle Marche also describes detractors as filthy and poisonous beasts in his sermon, "De Detractione et Eius Iniquitate," *Sermones Dominicales*, vol. 3, 209–19. Like a pig, the detractor ignores good things in order to wallow in filth: "In orto invenit lapides pretiosos, herbas odoriferas, aurum et argentum et non vult; sed statim cum invenerit stercus, cito ponit os sicut pedes illud; sic detractor," 218.

36. Siena 1425, I, 229–30.

37. Ibid., I, 272.

tagion. Malicious gossips are filthy, like cockroaches who delight in dung: "O little children, when you hear someone saying ill of another, call him a cockroach!"[38] Like cats, however, they are careful to cover their waste.[39] But the real danger is what happens once gossip is unleashed in a city. Bernardino paints a venomous picture of that backbiter who first sighs heavily in order to feign innocence, and then goes on to destroy someone's reputation. Like a poisonous snake who merely touches a fountain, the speaker contaminates everything: "And in the same way does the evil tongue immediately poison a city, a country, a province." Once slander starts, it quickly goes out of control, and Bernardino compares its inflammatory nature to that of dry wood and flame. Words, like banners, ignite both partisans and those who respond too easily to every *infamia*. A sensible person, on the other hand, is like mature wood which does not easily ignite, while others are like tiny pieces of kindling which immediately become inflamed.[40]

Poisonous snakes, flies, cockroaches, excrement, dry wood—Bernardino is especially worried about the way in which gossip contaminates the larger society. For urban audiences who lived with fire and plague, the disease/flame/poison analogies were probably even more terrifying than images of bestiality or the hunt. When he preached against sodomy, for instance, Bernardino stressed the way in which that sin tainted others.[41] Like sodomy, gossip is characterized as infectious disease. It kills more than just its intended victim since the slanderer damns himself as well as the ten others who listen to him; each repeats the tale to another ten people, who then repeat it in turn. That first hundred turns into a thousand and, the preacher claims, "in a

38. Ibid., I, 269.
39. Ibid., I, 251–52.
40. Ibid., I, 156–57, 183, 210–11.
41. Ibid., II, 101: if there was one bad man among twenty good ones, "quello gattivo gli guasta, e per ragione si guastano, che l'uno apuzza l'altro." And Bernardino fears that youths will be corrupted by dishonest and contaminating words in Florence 1424, II, 44.

short time the whole world is killed."[42] The conclusion of his introductory sermon on *detrazione* is an eloquent plea against gossip as an infectious agent which spreads hatred:

> O Rome, how much evil has happened to you! What has been the reason
> for it? The evil tongue. It is the begetter of insults. O Patrimony, how you
> are undone! It has always generated contention between city and city. O
> Lombardy, how many are dead because of the evil tongue? It has undone
> many lands and many cities. It has started many fires, caused many homi
> cides and many patricides . . . it has been the desperation of hope, it has
> been the enemy of every virtue.[43]

Bernardino's obsessive warnings against "murmurers" (*mormoratori*) were not an isolated phenomenon, nor was his pairing of the twin evils of gossip and faction.[44] They were, instead, part of a deep-seated fear within Italian culture, the darker side of the humanists' optimistic belief in the power of words to bind people together. Words also had the capacity to maim and kill; they could break human society as well as create it. The terms *romore* and *scandalo* echo throughout the chronicles like recurrent nightmares, often preceding accounts of civil strife. Corso Donati's humorous insults against the Cerchi, for example, sped through Florence, a city ready to explode from the tensions between Blacks and Whites. According to Dino Compagni, Corso's scathing remarks were repeated by jesters, "especially one named Scampolino who exaggerated things when he repeated them, so that the Cerchi would be provoked to brawl with the Donati."[45] The Venetians, those

42. Siena 1427, I, 243.

43. Ibid., I, 246–47. "O Roma, come se' capitata male! Chi n'è stata cagione? Pure la mala lingua. Ella è generatrice di contumelie. O Patrimonio, come se' disfatto! Ella ha sempre generato contenzioni fra città e città. O Lombardia, quanti ne so' morti per cagione de la mala lingua. Ella ha fatto disfare molte terre e molte città. Ella ha fatti fare molti incendii; ella ha fatti fare molti omicidii; ella ha fatti fare molti patricidi . . . ella è stata disperatrice della speranza; ella è stata nimica di tutte le virtù."

44. Paton notes that other Sienese preachers also linked the sin of calumny to homicide; *Preaching Friars*, 151–63.

45. Dino Compagni, *Chronicle of Florence*, 23–24.

paragons of social order, had an understandable terror of "speech-crimes" and believed that evil words could spread sedition; the state acted swiftly and mercilessly towards those who murmured against it.[46]

This fear of words and their potentially lethal impact upon society places Bernardino firmly within more general preoccupations of late-medieval culture. From the thirteenth century onwards many religious and secular writers were concerned with both ethical codes and practical advice, aimed at precisely delineating human behavior. Confessors' manuals, *fiori di virtù*, lives of the saints, and miracle stories often confront the same underlying issues as family diaries, *novelle*, and secular guidebooks. While many of these works discuss the problem of living well in this world in order to get on to the next, their predominant concern remains with this life, and with the achievement of personal success through the manipulation of the divine and the nurturing of careful social relations. This traditional advice literature is in fact an ancestor—though not always a recognizable one—of the sophisticated *Courtier*. Although Renaissance historians have often noted the fundamental changes which took place in the transformation from merchant to gentleman, the persistent interest which Italians took in these "advice books" suggest that the demands of urban life were slow to change. What unites all these writings, secular and sacred, is a consuming interest in human relations and how to define oneself within them.[47]

But what emerges is very far from an optimistic confidence in the world around the self. On the contrary, the anxiety lying just beneath the surface of even the most self-confident humanist displays a corro-

---

46. Guido Ruggiero, *Violence in Early Renaissance Venice* (New Brunswick, NJ: Rutgers University Press, 1980), 125–26, 142. See Muir, *Mad Blood Stirring*, for Friulian laws against verbal abuse, 71–72. For another example of "speech-crime," see the "Constitutiones Egidiane," trans. in Ephraim Emerton, ed., *Humanism and Tyranny: Studies in the Italian Trecento* (Gloucester, MA: P. Smith, 1964), 249.

47. The classic statement on Renaissance manners is Norbert Elias, *The Civilizing Process*, trans. Edmund Jephcott (New York: Urizen Books, 1978). A more recent analysis by a social historian is Marvin Becker, *Civility and Society in Western Europe, 1300–1600* (Bloomington: Indiana University Press, 1988).

sive fear of potential disaster. In the neurotically detailed advice given by the householders in Alberti's *Della famiglia,* not only fortune but other men are presented as obstacles to one's fragile security and peace of mind. Just as the sleek courtier hides a paranoia of the knife in the back, much of the advice literature depicts a world where others can never be trusted.[48] This pervasive distrust of one's fellows is especially apparent in the advice about speech. Although many late-medieval writers had high praise for the art of rhetoric and understood the positive uses of speech in society, they also spent a remarkable amount of time instructing people when *not* to talk. As one proverb tartly says: *Chi molto parla spesso falla* (He who talks too much often fails).[49] Variants of this basic folk wisdom can be found in a wide range of sources. The thirteenth-century judge and moralist Albertano da Brescia, for instance, entitled chapters "When to speak and when to remain silent" and "How to restrain speech and tongue." The main lesson is how to "tame" one's speech by never permitting even one word to escape unless it is carefully measured for effect. Albertano provides a highly anxious list of what speech should be: "true and efficacious, not vain; not dirty or bad; neither harmful nor dubious, sophistic nor injurious; not seditious or full of treachery; not scornful or deceptive or proud or lazy."[50] Little wonder, then, that it was often better not to

48. See Leon Battista Alberti, *Della Famiglia,* trans. as *The Family in Renaissance Florence* by Renee Neu Watkins (Columbia: University of South Carolina Press, 1964). The most obsessive testament to this pervasive distrust and anxiety is the diary of Giovanni di Pagolo Morelli; see *Mercanti scrittori: Ricordi tra medioevo e rinascimento,* ed. Vittore Branca (Milan: Rusconi, 1986), 101–339. Also see William Bouwsma, "Anxiety and the Formation of Early Modern Culture," in *After the Reformation: Essays in Honor of J. H. Hexter,* ed. Barbara C. Malament (Philadelphia: University of Pennsylvania Press, 1980), 215–46. Particularly helpful is Bouwsma's point about the anxiety produced by "the erosion of boundaries" in the late Middle Ages and how "self-control and vigilance both kept the individual within the boundaries of his self-definition and guarded them against infringement by others . . . ," 230 and 237.

49. Siena Biblioteca, MS. I. VI. 5, 83r. From a list of *dicerie* entitled "Detti e insegnamenti di savi huomini."

50. Albertano da Brescia, *Dei trattati morali,* ed. Francesco Selmi (Bologna: G. Romagnoli, 1873), 18. Also see James M. Powell, *Albertanus of Brescia: The Pursuit of Happiness*

speak at all. More than a century later, Franco Sacchetti ended his account of a spiteful verbal exchange between two enemies with the following advice: "Many are wounded by talk, but silence never hurt anyone" (*A molti è già nociuto il favellare; il tacere mai non noque ad alcuno*).[51]

Some of the most nervous warnings about how to *frenare la boca*, "rein in the mouth," are found in the aphorisms collected by Paolo da Certaldo in the mid-fourteenth century. Paolo cautions his readers to avoid gossip, flattery, and the revelation of personal secrets. "The tongue," he insists, "can go in a place where the knife cannot." Whispers at a dinner table give rise to suspicion and offense, while flattery is nothing but poison. Like Bernardino, he especially worries about the inflammatory nature of speech: a "small flame makes a big fire so guard yourself against instigators and hearsayers." In his suspicious world, words possess an almost palpable weight: "The spoken word is like the thrown rock." The frequent result of untamed speech, then, is physical violence, and Paolo warns that even excessive joking could result in brawls. The tongue as a knife, gossip as wildfire, words as poison: all are frightening metaphors which pair slander and civil disturbance. This disquieting association haunted Bernardino decades after Paolo, suggesting that his ideas on gossip and faction are powerful not because of their originality but because of their deep roots in popular fears about the perils of the word.[52]

---

in the Early Thirteenth Century (Philadelphia: University of Pennsylvania Press, 1992), 56–70. For a thorough overview of the categories of "speech sin," see Carla Casagrande and Silvana Vecchio, *I peccati della lingua: Disciplina ed etica della parola nella cultura medievale* (Rome: Instituto della Enciclopedia Italiana Fondata da Giovanni Treccani, 1987), esp. 331–51, for detraction. Useful as a general introduction to the power of words in traditional cultures: Walter Ong, *The Presence of the Word: Some Prolegomena for Cultural and Religious History* (New Haven: Yale University Press, 1967).

51. Franco Sacchetti, *Il trecentonovelle*, ed. Antonio Lanza (Florence: Sansoni, 1984), Novella CLXXX, 405–6.

52. Paolo da Certaldo, *Il libro di buoni costumi*, ed. Alfredo Schiaffini (Florence: F. Le Monnier, 1945), 279, 137, 66, 192, 225. Similar fears about the tongue as a weapon occur among the Mombasa Swahili. Unlike Mediterranean peoples, who are accustomed to blatant gossip in everyday street life, the Swahili are far more close-mouthed about

Although the caution surrounding speech was partly meant to dissuade good Christians from harming their neighbors, its original impulse was not charitable at all. Guarding one's tongue was in reality self-defense, a kind of armor against a dangerous world. The basic message delivered by Paolo is, Don't cause trouble and trouble won't come to you. Most of his *Libro di buoni costumi* is constructed around a desire to defend oneself against every danger, verbal and otherwise. For example, he gives detailed instructions about avoiding bushes, trees, and dark alleys where one's secrets might be overheard. A prudent cunning could ward off disaster: if a man intended to travel to Lucca, he should declare that he was off to Siena, in the opposite direction, in order not to be waylaid en route. The epitome of this ethic of self-protection is the good household manager who keeps a rope in his room in case of fire, but forbids access to servants and even family members, since they might want to use it for an evil purpose.[53]

This fanatically suspicious state of mind is symbolized by the house locked by a key which only the master carries; like the *boca frenata*, nothing goes in or out except to his personal advantage. In essence, Paolo's is a self-serving morality. Although he warns against speaking too much, his ideal man is always on the alert: "Keep your mouth shut and your eyes open." This is akin to the cryptic message in another advice list, which notes, "There is greater security in listening to gossip than in gossiping yourself."[54] In other words, despite an ostensibly Christian belief that gossip was a sin, it sometimes paid to listen. This double message encouraged exploiting others' weaknesses while avoid-

---

both their own doings and those of others; they worry about reputation, however, and possess an active fear of harmful words and their capacity to inflict shame. Three Swahili proverbs: "Forty tongues [are] forty spears"; "The tongue wounds [worse] than the teeth"; "Where there are many chickens don't spill millet." For a discussion of Swahili notions of shame and reputation, see Marc J. Swartz, *The Way the World Is: Cultural Processes and Social Relations among the Mombasa Swahili* (Berkeley and Los Angeles: University of California Press, 1991), esp. 177–208.

53. Paolo da Certaldo, *Il libro di buoni costumi*, 81, 90.

54. Ibid., 64; Siena Biblioteca, MS I.VI.5, 81r.

ing the same. Paolo is most explicit in his cynical advice not to take bribes if you are a judge, but to win over rectors and *signori* with them yourself.[55]

The morality literature helps us to survey the Italians' psychological landscape from their own vantage point, however inconsistent that landscape may seem to us. It developed in response to a world where people spent most of their time with others and where extensive obligations towards family, friends, and neighbors created a tight network, with the urban landscape itself seeming to echo the dense social world. Clifford Geertz, in a discussion of cultural personality, defines Moroccans, with their own close streets and social bonds, as "contextualized persons":

> The selves that bump and jostle each other in the alleys of Sefrou gain their definition from associative relations they are imputed to have with the society that surrounds them.[56]

To some extent, we might similarly characterize late-medieval Italians: the selves that jostled each other in narrow *vicoli* were also defined by their membership in a lineage, or confraternity, or faction. This is perhaps true for every society—we are all to some extent what we are assumed to be—but resistance to being engulfed by these bonds lies at the very heart of Italian culture and helps to explain its dynamism as well as its tensions.[57] One is reminded here of Renaissance artists and

55. Paolo da Certaldo, *Il libro di buoni costumi*, 33–34.

56. Clifford Geertz, "From the Native's Point of View: On the Nature of Anthropological Understanding," in *Local Knowledge: Further Essays in Interpretative Anthropology* (New York: Basic Books, 1983), 66. For a summary of Geertz's ideas, see Yme B. Kuiper, "The Concept of Person in American Anthropology: The Cultural Perspective of Clifford Geertz," in *Concepts of Person in Religion and Thought*, ed. Hans G. Kippenberg, Yme B. Kuiper, and Andy F. Sanders (Berlin and New York: Mouton de Gruyter, 1990), 35–49.

57. Ron Weissman stresses the "impression management" and "verbal gamesmanship" needed to survive in the competitive world of Florence, where a complicated network of social relationships often meant conflicting obligations and a corresponding "ambiguity" in personal behavior; "The Importance of Being Ambiguous: Social

their competitive, if fraternal, relationships, their marvelous exchange of ideas always heightened by rough-edged competition. And, as we have seen among writers, one of the most consistent links between "high" and "middlebrow" culture, along with anxiety about words, is an acute consciousness of the dangers of sociability. Even desirable social relationships were often seen to carry the risk of betrayal.

The problem was that, in a worst-case scenario, the self may be defined and then defeated by others. A painful example of the shifting boundaries of the self occurs in a famous fifteenth-century novella attributed to Antonio Manetti and supposedly based on a true incident. Brunelleschi, Donatello, and some other clever fellows decide to play a trick on a slow-witted artisan friend, Grasso Legnaiuolo (literally "Fatty the Woodworker"), who has offended them by not showing up for a group dinner. They enlist what seems to be half of Florence in order to pretend that Grasso is not Grasso, but someone else instead. The unfortunate protagonist lands in debtors' prison, is confused and abused by the jokesters around him, and is even persuaded that, indeed, he is not Grasso at all! When the trick is revealed—to the enormous delight of Brunelleschi and cohorts—the victim is covered in shame and retreats to Hungary for many years before he feels ready to return home and finally enjoy the joke himself.[58]

Beneath its amiable veneer and the author's admiration for the genius of Brunelleschi lies a profoundly disturbing tale of psychological alienation. The clever do not hesitate to exploit vulnerability (in Grasso's case, a kind of heavy slow-wittedness); on the contrary, they delight in exposing a naked and undefended psyche, and making its em-

---

Relations, Individualism, and Identity in the Renaissance," in *Urban Life in the Renaissance*, ed. Susan Zimmerman and Ronald F. E. Weissman (Newark, NJ: Associated University Press, 1988), 269–80. Also note the importance of guarding one's speech, 273–75. For examples of the complex relationships within a single Florentine neighborhood, see D. V. and F. W. Kent, *Neighbors and Neighborhood: The District of the Red Lion in the Fifteenth Century* (New York: J. J. Augustin, 1982), esp. 48–74.

58. Antonio Manetti, "Novella del Grasso Legnaiuolo," in *Novelle Italiane: Il Quattrocento*, ed. Gioachino Chiarini (Milan: Garzanti, 1982), 241–85.

barrassment public. A joke of this nature derives its point from cruelty on the part of "friends" and the shame which Grasso inevitably feels when he realizes everyone in Florence is laughing at him. Brunelleschi happens to be his most trusted friend, and yet he betrays Grasso. The victim would have been wiser to keep his true self under wraps, hidden away with lock and key in the same way that Alberti's householder suggests hiding one's personal papers. What occurs is in essence a theft of the personality itself: in a face-to-face society, it was easy for poor Grasso to be robbed of his identity, since that identity largely consisted of what people said about it. The thick woodworker could only hold out briefly, but one wonders how long even the self-assured Brunelleschi would have lasted if his friends suddenly denied his existence.

Significantly, Brunelleschi and fellows themselves label their prank a "vendetta," while the premises of countless other *novelle* do the same.[59] The *beffe* which delight us in Boccaccio's stories are in fact miniature vendettas, ranging from Giotto's quick response after a friendly insult to the revenge of a spurned lover who makes his lady roast in the summer sun. The less elegant tales of Giovanni Sercambi are much more explicit in their links between humor, vengeance, and brutality. In one story, a bizarre combination of a good trick and obscene cruelty, Ganfo the simpleton gets back at a shoemaker who has been taunting him by urinating on his furs. The comeuppance, appropriate though it may be given the offense, seems excessive: the shoemaker is castrated. In this tale, like so many others in the *novella* tradition, it is masculine identity itself which comes under attack. In Renaissance storytelling, individual selves, either merrily or viciously, assert their male primacy over defeated others.[60]

59. Manetti, "Novella": "conchiusono, così sollazzevolmente, che la vendetta si facessi . . . ," 245. For the relationship between hostility and humor in a modern Italian town, see Sydel Silverman, *Three Bells of Civilization: The Life of an Italian Hilltown* (New York and London: Columbia University Press, 1975), 42–43.

60. Giovanni Sercambi, *Novelle*, ed. Giovanni Sinicropi (Bari: Laterza, 1972), vol. I, 23–25. Poggio Bracciolini also links jokes and grotesque revenge: see the story of a

This is what it really meant to be a "contextualized person" in an aggressive and competitive society like that of Florence. For late-medieval Italians such as Grasso and Paolo, "sociability" did not have the happy associations we alienated moderns attach to it as we reminisce about "the world we have lost." The riches of conviviality and community had a reverse side, for a social network could easily become a "net" in which private lives were trapped and devoured. One aspect of the "individualism" expressed by fourteenth- and fifteenth-century Italians is a heightened and articulated consciousness of society's dangers. The detailed warnings offered by the *Libro di buoni costumi* reflect the profound uneasiness some individuals felt in a suffocating world. Paolo did not perceive himself as a true social creature at all: although he played the game for personal advantage, his cautious life was a solitary tightrope walk. Society was both necessary and dangerous, and the only way to survive in this culture of retaliation was to protect secrets, reputation, and the inner self from the tongues of *amici* and *nemici* alike. His was not a world where men could repose peacefully upon the collective bosom of their fellows.

Not only does a tangled social network provide more occasion for friction, but the mere physical presence of others meant that someone was always around to watch, criticize, and report. In this kind of community, gossip acts as a way of enforcing social mores and limiting individual choice. Word of mouth could move especially fast in an inti-

---

cuckolded husband who revenges himself on the sinful priest by forcing him to eat excrement in public; *Facezie*, 283. Stanley Brandes has found similar associations between humor and male aggression in popular Andalusian skits: see *Metaphors of Masculinity: Sex and Status in Andalusian Folklore* (Philadelphia: University of Pennsylvania Press, 1980), 159–76. Hanna Pitkin notes the pervasive cultural pattern of *furbo* and *fesso*, deceiver and deceived, in her analysis of Machiavelli's "fox" and masculine defensiveness in *Fortune Is a Woman: Gender and Politics in the Thought of Niccolò Machiavelli* (Berkeley and Los Angeles: University of California Press, 1984), 32–51. On an even broader stage, Italians acted out violent insults in the rituals which took place during and after battles between cities. In the late Middle Ages, prostitutes and youths were used to demean the defeated males of an enemy town; see Richard Trexler, "Correre la Terra: Collective Insults in the Late Middle Ages," *Mélange de L'École Francaise de Rome, Moyen Age/Temps Modernes* 96, no. 2 (1984): 845–902.

mate place like Siena. An earlier contemporary of Bernardino provides a useful glimpse of how gossip could be used to spread information and thus compel righteous behavior. The *Assempri morali* of Fra Filippo degli Agazzari, an Augustinian writing in the early fifteenth century, are all supposedly based on "true" stories which happened in Siena's recent past. The moral tales—intended to terrify and convert—are a fantastic mixture of the supernatural and the mundane. Everyday sins like vanity are punished in gruesome detail by a vengeful deity with the devil as his instrument. In one story, a demon poses as a maidservant and gives a conceited lady some "beauty creme" which destroys her face (she dies in agony); in another, a young monk masturbates and is then raped by the devil (he dies in agony).

Although Fra Filippo's point is to show how even minor sins are punished by an angry God, the stories, vicious and fanciful as they are, inadvertently tell us much about the world of Siena, real or perceived. Filippo often gives the date, place, and social identity of the person who saw everything happen and then reported the story to the friar or others. In this community of narrow streets and open windows, there is always a servant or old woman who is conveniently present and who of course edifies the neighbors. This adds to the surrealistic quality of the tales since it is Everyman or Everywoman who witnesses the supernatural event. In 1400, for example, a man lost at *zara*, became angry, and hurled a stone at an image of the Virgin. Filippo has the gambler's fate on the authority of

> an old and venerable woman of holy life who was coming out of a church when she saw him swell up like a jug [*botticello*]. She was his neighbor and the next morning she saw him dead.[61]

61. Fra Filippo degli Agazzari, *Gli assempri*, ed. Piero Misciatelli (Siena: Cantagalli, 1973), 208: ". . . mi disse una antica e venerabile donna e di santa virtù, la quale esciva allora de la chiesa, e vidde aventar la pietra e viddelo enfiare come un botticello, e poi la mattina el vedde morto, però che era suo vicino." For a discussion of gossip and the supernatural in Filippo, see Cynthia Polecritti, "Watchful Eyes: Gossip, Retribution, and the Devil in Filippo degli Agazzari's *Moral Tales*," in *Self and Society in Renaissance Eu-*

In another case, the chain of witnesses stretches farther back. A man who sold himself to the devil was lifted high in the air and then abruptly dropped to the earth; the story was related to Filippo by a man who heard it from a friar who confessed the wife who saw it all! The point is not merely that Filippo was overly credulous. His stories operate through a double principle of terror: both God and vigilant neighbors work to keep one on the straight and narrow. Fra Filippo's Siena, like Paolo's Florence, has corners and shadows where someone waits and watches and lives to tell the tale. Even intimate sins become public knowledge. For Filippo, easy gossip thus provides social benefits. Yet the darker side of the failure to *frenare la boca* is occasionally sensed by even this doctrinaire friar. He seems to contradict the spirit of his own work when he warns readers not to believe people who stand around all day with companions

> laughing and chattering away, and speaking vain and lazy words the whole day long, murmuring and destroying the doings of others . . .[62]

Apparently a sober Christian would be able to distinguish between useless and constructive murmuring.

Bernardino was less optimistic about his listeners' judgment. He realized that listening to vicious talk could be pleasurable: "Oh! tell it another time!" he mimics the avid bystander.[63] But he hoped to prevent the ripple effect of slander by having the good Christian humiliate the speaker: openly register your contempt for the gossip, he advises, by holding your nose and exclaiming, "Oh, it stinks!" (Typically, he demonstrates himself and then repeats the message for the children in the audience.)[64] Like his advice to call detractors "cockroaches," these

---

rope, ed. William Connell (Berkeley and Los Angeles: University of California Press, forthcoming).

62. Filippo degli Agazzari, *Gli assempri*, 179–80: ". . . con compagni a ridare et a cianciare, e tutto dì parlare oziose e vane, e disutili; e tutto dì mormorando e detruendo e' fatti altrui . . ."

63. Siena 1427, I, 270.

64. Ibid., I, 241.

instructions might have caused more trouble than they prevented. More useful, perhaps, was his order that confessors must refuse pardon to the slanderer . . . or else go to hell themselves.[65] Ideally, the good neighbor would also do his part by first reproving the gossip in private, then bringing along a few trusted neighbors sworn to secrecy, and finally reporting the matter to the church.[66]

But the destructive power of words was not necessarily bound to the falsely spoken. In this Bernardino completely differed from Fra Filippo's black-and-white morality. Like Paolo da Certaldo, he understood the grave implications of the unleashed word and thought it best to avoid careless speech of all kinds. But he goes beyond Paolo in his insistence that Christian love should be the determining factor in what is spoken. The direct connection between heart and mouth meant that you should ideally feel nothing but *"amore, amore, amore,"* and all speech should reflect this charitable feeling. The tongue, Bernardino explains, is like a spoon. A person eating good lasagna would prefer a silver spoon to one made with a shoe sole; similarly, a man with inner charity would only use a tongue made of silver or gold.[67] For Bernardino, the great propagator of *carità*, "not every true thing is well said." As usual, he made the point with a telling example drawn from real life:

> . . . if you saw a man entering a woman's house at night and she opened the door for him, you couldn't judge it to be anything but evil. But if you go tell it to your neighbors—"I saw such and such"—then you are committing a mortal sin.[68]

Bernardino was trying to force his listeners to resist the easy social commentary bred by close-knit communities. The true but uncharita-

65. Ibid., I, 273–74.
66. Ibid., I, 266.
67. Ibid., I, 311–12.
68. Florence 1424, I, 332. ". . . se vedessi di notte tempo entrare uno uomo in casa a una femmina, e ch'ella aprisse, non ne puoi istificare altro che male. Asempro, se lo vai a dire alla vicina o al vicino: 'io vidi così e così,' è peccato mortale . . ."

ble word was as vicious as the outright lie because it slashed the bonds of *carità*.

The preacher tells this particular story during a sermon on restitution. Here he compares words with more tangible goods, such as money gained from usury. As with usurious profits, it was always necessary to restore the *buona fama* stolen from another.[69] Even if what was said was true, the offender had to ask pardon for the damage which he had inflicted on the victim's reputation. And if the injury was done in public, the detractor had the additional responsibility of giving public satisfaction.[70] Naturally, Bernardino felt that the sermon provided the perfect setting for an apology. He urged the detractor to stand up before the crowd and announce: "I have done an evil thing and I want to tell the truth openly so that I don't remain tied up in the hands of the devil."[71] Whether such events ever took place within the context of actual peacemakings is recorded neither by the preacher nor by witnesses to his sermons, but it is unlikely that many people would have risked such public humiliation. The only incident which Bernardino mentions involved not laymen, but rival preachers. A jealous cleric lied about one of Bernardino's Franciscan colleagues, claiming that the friar had preached false doctrine—that baptisms were invalid unless performed in the name of Jesus. The bad cleric was forced to retract his slander—Bernardino does not say by what means—but he made sure to do it on an occasion when few people were present at the sermon.[72] The pressure to save face would have been enormous, even if the gossiper's conscience tormented him.

Although Bernardino's primary target was the slanderer, he also assigned a large measure of responsibility to the victim, at least in terms

---

69. Siena 1427, I, 225.

70. Elsewhere, Bernardino points out that confession is not enough if you have injured someone with words. Instead, you are obliged to ask the victim for forgiveness; Florence 1424, I, 329.

71. Siena 1427, I, 274.

72. Ibid., I, 256–57.

of preventing the next dangerous step once vicious words were unleashed. Even if the social world was constructed so that it bred antag-
onism between watchful neighbors, he thought that a good person
could learn to shield himself from the worst consequences. Thus, if
the preacher's injunctions against *detrazione* failed, the victim needed to
have some emotional recourse other than retaliation. Keen (if unlikely)
self-examination was one way of keeping all gossip in perspective.
Look inside your own conscience, Bernardino advises; if someone mis-
takenly says something good about you,

> . . . alas, alas, alas! "Oh, I'm held to be good, and I'm not; alas, how bad
> this is! God won't judge me according to how I'm perceived, but accord-
> ing to how I am . . ." And so I say to you, if something bad is said about
> you, and you haven't done it, don't worry about it. Even if you've heard it,
> do you know what to do? Jump up and say: "I didn't commit this sin,"
> and in this way you'll make the dragon die. What stupidity is yours if you
> haven't done something bad, nor wanted to do it, that you'd believe the
> words of an evil person![73]

You should also have compassion for someone who is consumed by
envy (*sempre in sè arde*), just as you would if his physical body was being
consumed.[74] And simple resignation to the ways of the world can
work, too. Bernardino tells his audience about an abbot, young monk,
and ass who were journeying together; no matter how they arranged
the trip, intrusive onlookers found something negative to say. If the
old man rode, they would remark how terrible it was for the boy (and
vice versa), while if the ass bore both, someone else would cry out in

73. Ibid., I, 283–84. ". . . oimè, oimè, oimè! 'Oh io so' tenuto buono, e non so';
oimè, quanto va male questa cosa! Imperò che Idio non mi giudica sicondo ch'io so'
tenuto, ma sicondo ch'io so'." Così, dico, se è detto male di te, e tu non hai fatto tal
male, fa' che mai tu non te ne curi. Se pure tu l'udissi, sai che fa'? Da' un salto e di':
'Questo peccato non feci io mai'; e in questo modo farai crepare il dracone. Che scioc-
chezza sarà la tua, se non hai fatto il male, né hai voglio di farlo, che tu te ne curi per
le parole d'un gattivo!"
74. Ibid., I, 289.

pity for the animal, at the same time as others thought it strange if the two humans had an ass and chose *not* to ride. Apparently, there was no pleasing everyone so it was best not to worry about idle talk at all.[75]

Much of the practical advice Bernardino offers, however, resembles that of Paolo da Certaldo, even if the preacher claims that self-knowledge and *carità* are essential. Hostile neighbors should be blockaded with a hedge of protective devices. Be circumspect, he warns, and take care to hide your possessions so that they do not arouse envious tongues. Make sure that even your good works are hidden from jealous eyes. Keep to the *mezza via* "according to the state in which God has placed you . . . and don't announce your affairs in the piazza."[76] Lurking behind these injunctions, perhaps, is a superstitious fear of the evil eye: the slanderer resembles one who has "*l'occhio torbo e pieno di malore.*"[77] Bernardino's listener was faced with the paradox of living in a close and watchful world while striving to distance oneself from it. Potential victimization by others (and by the evil eye) could be avoided through an emotional, as well as verbal, withdrawal. Trust only in God, the preacher advises, and not in the broken ship (*barca rotta*) of this world. Go your own way and let neighbors say what they will. Try to realize that God balances the flattering things said about you with some nasty gossip. Remember how much Christ himself was villainized despite his perfection. Finally, know that it is ultimately God, and not this world, who will judge you.[78] These ideas, though psychologically astute, were not original and must have been quite familiar to Bernardino's listeners. Several generations before, Catherine of Siena also believed that social violence had its roots in the untamed word and she gave her followers similar advice. Murmurers, she said, were sent by God to test us, so it was necessary to stifle pride and recognize one's own sins. Discussion with a spiritual advisor could help, and it was also possible to counteract evil words with good ones. Silence provid-

75. Ibid., I, 259–61.

76. Florence 1424, II, 35.

77. Siena 1427, I, 293.

78. Ibid., I, 193–94.

ed a final solution to violent speech, she claimed, advocating complete social withdrawal when necessary.[79]

Protective measures, as well as Christian acceptance, were intended to keep the victim from becoming enmeshed in a situation which could destroy him, either spiritually or physically. Bernardino seems to have hoped that these would eliminate the need for a future peacemaking (which necessarily took place after even greater damage had been done). By placing some of the moral responsibility upon the shoulders of the victim, he optimistically tried to abort the unhappy progression from word to fist to sword to civil discord.

There is, however, an underlying desperation in Bernardino's long list of suggestions, just as there is in Paolo's fanatically detailed advice about avoiding trouble. Both were attempts to construct an airtight space where people could enjoy an uneasy peace, the only kind available to them in this world. Bernardino's disciplined soul might hope to create the spiritual equivalent of Paolo's locked doors, but it was unlikely that the average person could achieve such taut emotional control in a society which encouraged the free expression of anger. The preacher's strong reaction to the *mormoratori* who plagued his own mission shows how difficult it could be to practice forgiveness and emotional detachment. He proudly uses himself as an example of how to despise the world and its biting words: "Don't worry"("*Non ti curare*"), he advises, as he carefully explains his own sane reaction when taunted by the malicious:

> Whoever castigates me sends me above and whoever praises me sends me below. And because I've gotten around quite a bit, I've heard what is said about me. When I want to go to one place or another, they say there: "O, O, O! Frate Bernardino is coming!" And if I find one who says good things there are a hundred others who say bad. And there is nothing I

79. Karen Scott, "Not Only with Words but with Deeds: The Role of Speech in Catherine of Siena's Understanding of Her Mission" (Ph.D diss., Berkeley, 1989). Scott says Catherine believed that ". . . for proper relations with other people to be possible, it is necessary to develop at least an inner attitude of suspicion and detachment from them," 487.

fear more than someone who says good about me: I know who I am . . . and because I know myself, I am always afraid. Hence it's always more useful when someone blames me rather than praises me.[80]

Bernardino, with his strong sense of personal identity and confidence in his mission, may be speaking the truth when he claims not to be threatened by gossip; indeed, he supposedly welcomes it, since it strengthens his character. Unfortunately, despite the elevated tone of this passage, he did not always practice what he preached.

Beneath the soothing words and forgiving message was a very defensive man on the lookout for whisperers. As the object of envy and jeers as well as uncritical adulation, Bernardino sometimes felt victimized himself. In fact, the closest he ever came to losing control in the sermons is when he complained about how malicious people have gossiped about him, apparently because of his alleged heresy. Few though these unguarded moments are, they highlight the difficulty of anyone practicing complete patience when taunted by slanderers. Bernardino bitterly comments at one point that no matter how much good a man tries to do, there is always somebody ready to twist it in another direction:

> Even if he is a religious person preaching the word of God as he ought to do, an evil tongue says: "Oh, that one there is searching for some bishopric!"[81]

This to the Sienese just a few short months after he had been offered a bishopric in their city. Apparently, gossip was circulating even as he preached, for later in the same sermon he pleads with his audience not

---

80. Siena 1427, I, 292. "Chi mi detrae, mi manda in su, e chi mi loda, mi manda in giù. E perché io so' andato gran pezzo atorno, io ho udito di me quello che se n'è detto. Quando io so' voluto andare da uno luogo a un altro, elli si dice in quello luogo dove io voglio ire: 'Oooh! Che è! Che è! Oh, oh! Frate Bernardino viene!' e tale è che ne dice bene, e tale ne dice male. E non è niuna cosa che facci temere me più di me, che uno dica bene di me; e io cognosco quello che io so'. . . . e perchè io mi cognosco, sempre temo. Unde più mi fa utile chi mi biasima, che chi mi loda."

81. Ibid., I, 259: "E se è pure religioso, elli va predicando la parola di Dio puramente come deba fare; e la maladetta lingua dice: 'Oh, costui cerca qualche vescovado!'"

to listen to evil tales which will be told once he has left Siena: his true friends should walk out of any sermon where there is backbiting.[82] Denigrating religious professionals was a popular sport, and Bernardino resented it on behalf of his colleagues as well as himself. Some slanderers attacked preachers, he said, by adding evil words to good ones, or by substituting bitter words for sweet; they are like the Pharisees who persecuted Christ.[83] His control temporarily collapses during his August 21 sermon when he remembers how priests and nuns are slandered; thanks to the recorder, we can almost hear the preacher sputter in rage as he recalls a mysterious piece of gossip which he recently heard in Siena: "Ooooh! I've heard such things in this land during the Lenten season that I'd like, I'd like . . . I don't know what, and certainly I don't believe it . . ."[84]

Bernardino's personal grievance towards *mormoratori* thus partly explains his agitated descriptions of them as beasts, as snakes, as cockroaches. He contemptuously labels them frogs: "They croak 'qua, qua, qua' but flee when you approach them; you hear 'qua, qua, qua' and see nothing at all."[85] The preacher claims he wants his audience to ignore these insidious creatures, and to resist any desire to avenge one's good name:

> That one says: "I want to purge myself of this infamy!" And I answer: "The more you purge yourself, the more the infamy soils you. Doh! Stop going around purging yourself!"[86]

82. Ibid., I, 276.

83. Ibid., I, 273.

84. Ibid., I, 267–78. The disjointed passage is worth quoting in its entirety: "Ooooh! Io sento alcune cose in questa terra, in questa quaresima, che vorrei, che vorrei . . . no so che, e per certo io nol credo; e èssene sparta una voce a Siena . . . 'Fu così e così; e per questo si dice tanto' *et cetera*. Io ti dico che fusse bene stato vero, che nol credo; un'altra volta, che se fusse stato vero, tu facesti un grande male a palesarlo. Vuo'lo vedere? Guarda quello che hai fatto: tu hai messo in bocca a genti tal cosa, che . . . per ora lassiamol andare!"

85. Ibid., I, 273.

86. Ibid., I, 297: "'io voglio purgare la mia infamia'. E, io dico, 'quanto più la purga, più la 'mbratta. Doh, non andate più purgando!'"

Yet that impulse to "purge oneself," to retaliate in some way which would reclaim personal honor, was sometimes overwhelming, even for Bernardino, and his plea to ignore and forgive one's detractors is undercut by his own ambivalence. Immediately after telling his listeners not to purge themselves, he urges them all to spit: "Now spit with love!" (*Or sputavi su con buona carità!*) He then tells them to notice how the spit is yellow in color, like love, but the action itself is clearly contemptuous, just as it was when Bernardino ordered his audiences to "spit on the fire of sodomy." Like the sodomite, the witch, and, of course, the partisan, slanderers were placed outside the boundary of the human, as beasts and insects who were only worthy of contempt. Despite his avowed belief that it was possible for the victim to retreat into some haven of inner peace, Bernardino's anger oversteps the boundaries of his own *carità*. His ambivalence illustrates the immense difficulty of ignoring attacks and removing one's beleaguered self from a world which exerted pressure to gossip, take offense, and retaliate.

III. Forgiveness and the Vendetta

In a society where words encouraged violence, spread discord, and threatened the self, preaching forgiveness was no easy task. Like other preaching peacemakers and mediating friends, Bernardino performed a valuable service for his listeners, probing tender areas of the psyche and trying to dispel the cloud of anxiety which hovered around the solitary person who felt vulnerable to aggressive others. But he also recognized the dangers of a self-regard which always cried out "Mio! Mio! Mio!"[87] and so he struggled to build fraternal unity even as he acknowledged the problems the individual faced in begging or granting pardon. The preacher's dilemma was that of maintaining a tenuous balance between healing the soul and permitting people to wear an honorable face in a very public world.

Towards the end of his 1425 visit to Siena, Bernardino preached a sermon on concord which illustrates the delicate issues involved in the

87. Siena 1425, II, 33.

internal peacemaking. This sermon must have culminated in a public ritual since he gives specific directions on how to conduct the *pace di fuore:*

> ... as a sign of wanting to pardon, go to the Duomo, to the altar, and then when you find your adversary, make peace with him, and pardon one another. And you women, all of you go to the church of San Martino, and there enter by one way and then exit through another, in sign that you pardon everyone.[88]

Note that Bernardino is careful to designate these actions as "signs," external markers of an interior process; his intention is not to get his listeners to move from the piazza into a church, but to move their hearts towards authentic forgiveness. The sermon begins with a plea that the audience see itself as an undivided whole, each person filled with good will towards the others. Individual circumstances should not preclude union: if one person has children and another does not, then the fortunate one should comfort the childless; the healthy should succor the sick; the strong must give aid to his crippled fellow. Husbands and wives should be of one will. Naturally, concord and *carità* also consist in "never believing him who wishes to put *scandolo* between you." Thus envy and gossip, which give rise to rancor and hatred, are set up as opposites of union and brotherly love. Predictably, Bernardino has high praise for that one group of citizens which he believes possesses an ideal unity:

> O Venice! How much glory you have! How do you maintain yourself so well? O my fellow citizens, do you know the principal reason? It is nothing if not the concord between them; everything is for unity.[89]

---

88. Ibid., II, 263. "... vada, in segno di volere perdonare, al Duomo, a l'altare, e poi, quando trovarà el suo avversario, facci pace co' lui e perdoni l'uno a l'altro. E a voi, donne, tutte andate costì a la chiesa di santo Martino, e intrate dall'una parte e uscite da l'altra in segno che voi perdoniate a ogni persona."

89. Ibid., II, 255–56. "O Venegia, quanta gloria ài in te! Come ti mantieni tu bene? O cittadini miei, quale credete che sia la principal cagione? Non è se no' la concordia che ànno fra loro; tutto è per la unità."

Two years later, when he once again preached to the factious Sienese, he would develop the theme of the divided city, the opposite of his happy vision of Venice. For now, however, he chooses to establish merely that social union is an ideal before he moves on to the social reality: stubborn individuals who are unable to forgive and who tear their community apart. *Duro con duro si rompe*, he claims. "The obstinate with the obstinate break each other."

Bernardino's challenge in this sermon was to convince his audience that self-restraint and a willingness to forgive are not only possible, but desirable. But his Christian ethos confronted an alternative code that was impossible to ignore. For just as the tightly woven social world encouraged both gossip and feelings of alienation, so did it paradoxically trap people within a tangled web of obligations to kin, *amici*, and one's personal sense of honor. Public forgiveness might work in the abstract, but it also could mean a loss of face before society's ever-present spectators. In 1427, the preacher advised his audience to ignore slanderers who nastily remarked that someone who forgave an injury was "a big sheep" (*pecorone*) and "without feeling."[90] He who refused to retaliate after an insult would be labeled *vile*, and there were also mighty pressures from one's own family. Bernardino was aware of the dilemma, and acknowledges that "many will say: 'It is shameful to pardon!' or 'Our house has never been accustomed to forgive!'"[91] Nevertheless, this attitude that pardoning was a shameful sign of weakness exasperated the preacher:

> Are you ashamed to do well? If you are ashamed to do well, how ought you to do? Badly? I believe that you have already conceded to me that it is good to have love and concord with one another [this must indicate that his opening statement had been well-received]. If you conceded this and yet you are not in this state, why isn't it good to return to it?[92]

90. Siena 1427, I, 29.

91. Siena 1425, II, 261.

92. Ibid, II, 257. "Vergogniti tu di far bene? Se ti vergogni di far bene, che debbi tu fare? Male? Io credo che tu già mi concedi che è bene avere carità e concordia l'uno co' l'altro. Se tu mel concedi, e tu se' fuore di questo stato, come non è bene a tornarci?"

His goal was to make them see the contradiction between their enthusiastic agreement that peace was the proper state, and their behavior in
actual situations. But he understood that it would have been extraordinarily difficult for some proud listeners to "return" to a state of forgiveness, even when as earnest Christians they were caught up in the
flow of a powerful sermon and conceded that it was the right thing
to do.

Even if most fifteenth-century Tuscans did not pursue enmities
with formal vendettas, many of Bernardino's listeners were still permeated with inflexible ideas about masculinity, revenge, and public image,
consistent themes in Italian life from the Middle Ages to the present
day (if in diluted form).[93] Note, for example, that the stress fractures
between the Blacks and the Whites, at least as Dino Compagni surveys

---

93. For a general introduction to culture and maleness, see David D. Gilmore,
Manhood in the Making: Cultural Concepts of Masculinity (New Haven: Yale University Press,
1990); for the Mediterranean variety, see Stanley Brandes, *Metaphors of Masculinity*. Anton Blok, in "Rams and Billy-Goats: A Key to the Mediterranean Code of Honor,"
Man 16, no. 3 (September 1981): 427–49, points out that public life is the place for a
real man and he stresses the strong relationship between "honor and the physical person" in the Mediterranean. For a superb analysis of masculinity as public performance, see Michael Herzfeld's work on the aggressive competition involved in Cretan
sheep-thefts, *The Poetics of Manhood: Contest and Identity in a Cretan Mountain Village* (Princeton: Princeton University Press, 1985). Edward Muir, in *Mad Blood Stirring*, esp. 180–81,
closely analyzes the connection between violence and the formation of male identity
in the Italian Renaissance. For the same period, see Peter Burke's discussion of aggression and competitive display through the medium of the sexual insult: "Insult and
Blasphemy," *The Historical Anthropology of Early Modern Italy*, 95–109; and Lyndal Roper,
"Blood and Codpieces: Masculinity in the Early Modern German Town," in *Oedipus
and the Devil: Witchcraft, Sexuality, and Religion in Early Modern Europe* (London and New
York: Routledge, 1994), 107–24. Robert C. Davis shows how Venetian workers literal-
ly fought for status in the *battagliole*, violent competitions held on the city's bridges; see
The War of the Fists: Popular Culture and Public Violence in Late Renaissance Venice (Oxford and
New York: Oxford University Press, 1994), esp. 109–17. James R. Farr examines work-
ingmen's honor and social relations in early modern France in *Hands of Honor: Artisans
and Their World in Dijon, 1550–1650* (Ithaca, NY: Cornell University Press, 1988), 150–95.
A study of modern male identity in a specific Mediterranean locale is Miguel Vale de
Almeida, *The Hegemonic Male: Masculinity in a Portuguese Town* (Providence, RI, and Oxford:
Berghahn Books, 1996).

them, often rupture during public gatherings when young men start brawling.[94] Italian cities, with their narrow streets and stage-set *piazze*, were ideally suited for intense encounters with a ready-made audience. Just as jokes and one-upmanship (like Brunelleschi's tour-de-force victory over Grasso) served as a way of asserting oneself in a competitive social arena, so too did revenge play itself out on the public stage as one way of vaunting masculinity, in essence a form of ritual display rather than true "self-help."

Bernardino was acutely sensitive to the loss of honor in its myriad variations. Early in his visit in 1425, he tried to get the Sienese to imagine their shame when they realized the entire population of heaven, including all the saints and angels, were able to see their hidden sins (he compares it to the intense shame everyone would feel if a naked woman were standing in the middle of the Piazza del Campo).[95] It is doubtful, however, that exposure before God and the Heavenly Court was as shame-inducing as the critical gaze of one's fellows. To a certain degree, Bernardino unconsciously sympathized with contemporary ideas about honor, shame, and manhood: as we have seen, his own as-

94. For example, the neighborhood dance where youths from the Donati faction attack their Cerchi counterparts; Dino Compagni, *Chronicle of Florence*, 25. Carol Lansing makes the same point in her analysis of the Compagni incidents and the violent behavior of youthful males; *The Florentine Magnates: Lineage and Faction in a Medieval Commune* (Princeton: Princeton University Press, 1994), 184–91. Bette S. Denich says that males in traditional Balkan societies are apt to become violent at public festivities such as weddings; "Sex and Power in the Balkans," in *Women, Culture, and Society*, ed. Michelle Zimbalist Rosaldo and Louise Lamphere (Stanford: Stanford University Press, 1974), 250. Similarly, in Appalachia, another feuding, face-to-face society, boisterous men often defended their masculinity at public gatherings: on Election Day of August 1882, Ellison Hatfield was stabbed and shot by the McCoys in a public quarrel (at one point during the fight he shouted, "I'm the best goddamn man on Earth!"); Altina L. Waller, *Feud: Hatfields, McCoys, and Social Change in Appalachia*, 71–72.

95. Siena 1425, I, 29. Bernardino assumes that his audience understands what "shame" feels like. For a precise discussion of the physiological and psychological aspects of shame, written by a sixteenth-century physician, see Werner L. Gundersheimer, "Renaissance Concepts of Shame and Pocaterra's 'Dialoghi Della Vergogna,'" *Renaissance Quarterly* 47, no. 1 (Spring 1994): 34–56.

sertive projection of masculinity in his role as preacher-warrior was played out in the very public arena of the sermon, and he disliked being openly criticized. His line of attack does not attempt to do away with the code of honor itself; instead, he wants to convince his listeners that true masculinity is best equated with magnanimity. Throughout the sermon on concord, he tries to bend the received wisdom about male honor into a new configuration, arguing that true *dis*honor lies in taking revenge. The implication is that forgiveness can also be acceptable in worldly terms: at one point, he asks his audience who is more *gagliardo* (in this context best translated as "manly"), "one who conquers his own heart, or one who conquers a city with his own arm, through the force of his sword?" He praises those two famous *gagliardi*, Alexander and Julius Caesar, not for their conquests but for their generosity towards enemies. A lion does not stop to chase mice, nor an eagle bother to catch flies. In other words, taking vengeance cannot confer nobility of soul; the most *gagliardo* of all is he who is *signore* of himself.[96]

Given his attempt to re-channel beliefs about male honor, it is ironic to remember that the majority of Bernardino's listeners were women. How did they fit into this culture of retaliation and male display? What practical meaning would his words have had for them? At first glance, it seems as if so fixed was the cultural connection between vengeance and masculinity that, even within a purely fictional realm, it was difficult for women to act in the foreground of the vendetta. In the Second Day, Ninth Tale of the *Decameron*, for instance, a wronged wife, Zinevra, actively retaliates on behalf of her own honor after it has been maligned by Ambrogiuolo, who has made a bet with her husband that she can be seduced and then sets up a cunning trick to provide "proof" of the adultery. Zinevra escapes a murder attempt by her foolish husband, dons male clothing, and begins calling herself "Sicurano." Far from the swaggering boy/honey-tongued lover we meet later in Shakespeare's Viola and Rosalind, Zinevra acts as a real man, ex-

96. Siena 1425, II, 258–59.

ceedingly able in business—she ends up working for the Sultan—and ruthless in her revenge upon the enemy.[97] Once Zinevra's honor is publicly verified at the Sultan's court and her husband's trust restored, the deceiver Ambrogiuolo is smeared with honey and

> subjected to excruciating torments by the mosquitoes, wasps and horse-flies which abound in that country, and not only was he slain, but every morsel of his flesh was devoured.[98]

A manly vengeance indeed, complete with an appreciative audience and the desecration of a corpse. But the problem is that within the narrative itself, Boccaccio begins to refer to "Sicurano" with the personal pronoun "he," as if he could not quite reconcile Zinevra's assertiveness with her female identity. Having daringly placed his creation within masculine territory, he then transforms her, whether consciously or unconsciously, into a real male.

Bernardino's construction of gender was far less ambiguous than Boccaccio's, and there are few hints in the sermons that his ideal female listener, domestic and devout, could play any part in the public game of honor and vengeance. Predictably, he prefers to depict women in terms of their cultural stereotype as peacemakers, whether as brides who reconcile warring clans, or as intermediaries of the sermon itself, relaying the preacher's message to the men at home.[99] But surely he

97. Boccaccio, *Decameron*, trans. McWilliam, 207–20. Note that even the preliminary description of the virtuous Zinevra is a catalogue of both male and female qualities. In addition to listing her domestic gifts, her proud husband compares her to a knight (*cavaliere*) or squire (*donzello*) and says that she can ride and hawk, as well as manage the account books like a merchant, 208. In other words, this paragon already possesses masculine talents, even before she begins to cross-dress. An extraordinary example of real women who were active agents in the vendetta occurred in traditional Albanian society. If all her brothers had been killed, a sister had the right to cross-dress, swear chastity, and permanently assume a male role. And if she herself was killed, she was counted as a male in the procurement of blood money. See Ian Whitaker, "'A Sack for Carrying Things': The Traditional Role of Women in Northern Albanian Society," *Anthropological Quarterly* 54, no. 3 (July 1981): 146–56.

98. Boccaccio, *Decameron*, trans. McWilliam, 220.

99. Florence 1424, I, 420, and Siena 1427, I, 571–72. Bernardino concludes the latter sermon with: "talvolta sarà stata guerra mortale tra uno casato e un altro, tra uno

must have been aware that in reality women could play an active, if still supporting, role in the negative half of the vengeance-peacemaking dichotomy. In their capacities as wives and mothers, Renaissance women were harmed by the repercussions of faction and vendetta. Affective bonds aside, the practical consequences of exile, for example, complicated their own lives and finances, threatening the fabric of their social world when male relatives were absent.[100] And when it came to the expression of culturally sanctioned emotions, hatred included, perhaps gender differences were not so marked as they sometimes appear to be in anthropological discussions of feud, where men are depicted as the sole protagonists in an honorific public drama. Although a woman theoretically lacked a public life and did not possess the hand that raised the sword, she still had heart, mouth, and memory with which to support the battles of her menfolk.[101] Feud feeds

schiattale e un altro, tra uno signore e un altro; e per una fanciulla che si mariti di questa casa in quella, subito fatti parenti con tanta tranquillità e concordia e pace, che è stata una consolazione." For earlier perceptions of woman as peacemaker, see, for example, the role of Prudence in Albertano of Brescia's *Liber Consolationis et Consilii*, a dialogue which argues against vendetta. Prudence is in part an allegorical figure designating the voice of reason, but also the wife of Melibeus, whom she convinces to forgive their enemies; James M. Powell, *Albertanus of Brescia*, 81–85. For real women in thirteenth-century Florence, see Carol Lansing, *The Florentine Magnates*, 125–26: note that the commune itself thoughtfully provided dowries in 1290 when the hostile della Tosa and Lamberti clans intermarried. Marriage unions were still a common part of Corsican peacemaking centuries later, and peacemakers were sometimes known as *maritanti*, or "marryers"; see Stephen Wilson, *Feuding, Conflict, and Banditry*, 262. Of course, such marriages could also provide partisan benefits, if a woman remained faithful to her natal family. For example, in 1402 a plot to murder the two leaders of Crema's Guelph party was discovered by a Guelph woman married to a Ghibelline; see *Historia di Crema*, 29v. Trevor Dean notes that women were the passive catalysts of vendetta if they were sexually violated; see "Marriage and Mutilation," 16–17.

100. Susannah Foster Baxandale discusses the impact of exile on female family members in "Exile in Practice: The Alberti Family in and out of Florence, 1401–1428," *Renaissance Quarterly* 44, no. 4 (Winter 1991): 720–56.

101. And women had their own sense of honor, which is difficult to determine from sources written by men. However, Elizabeth S. Cohen, working with Roman trial records, has found intriguing evidence that even prostitutes "felt that they did have an honor which could be offended," and that women knew how to manipulate the culture of public shame, both in the streets and the courts; see "Honor and Gender in

upon collective memory, which was almost certainly instilled by mothers who had the early responsibility for raising young children. In the *contrada* "factions" of the modern Sienese Palio, mothers and grandmothers socialize toddlers by teaching them traditional enmities towards rival neighborhoods.[102] These later become reinforced through the medium of ritualized folksongs and insults.

Many other traditional cultures provide examples of women as "keepers of the feud." In Icelandic sagas, for instance, women act as "goads" who spur their sometimes reluctant men to carry out vengeance: in the most blatant scenes they ritually bear severed heads and bloodstained garments to kinsmen as graphic reminders of obligation. And well-chosen words could achieve similar results. One of the most striking examples of Icelandic woman as goad takes place in *Njal's Saga*, during the bitter feud between Hallgerd and Bergthora. At one point, when Njal and his sons are seated at the dinner table, Bergthora scornfully reminds her family: "Gifts have been given to you, fathers and sons alike; and you would scarcely be men if you did not repay them." She goes on to inform husband and sons that Hallgerd has dubbed them "Old Beardless" and "Little Dung-Beards," insults which will quickly provoke the rough-tempered Skarp-Hedin into action.[103] Wil-

---

the Streets of Early Modern Rome," *Journal of Interdisciplinary History* 22, no. 4 (Spring 1992): 597–625. Also see the vivid documents and commentaries in Thomas V. Cohen and Elizabeth S. Cohen, *Words and Deeds in Renaissance Rome: Trials before the Papal Magistrates* (Toronto: University of Toronto Press, 1993), esp. 45–101 and 160–87. A concise overview of the intricate webs woven by class and gender is in Sharon Strocchia, "Gender and the Rites of Honor in Italian Renaissance Cities," in *Gender and Society in Renaissance Italy*, ed. Judith C. Brown and Robert C. Davis (London and New York: Addison Wesley Longman Limited, 1998), 39–60.

102. Alan Dundes and Alessandro Falassi, *La Terra in Piazza: An Interpretation of the Palio of Siena* (Berkeley and Los Angeles: University of California Press, 1975), 43–44. The authors observed a two-year-old with his grandmother from the *contrada* of Bruco; when asked what he thought about the Giraffa neighborhood, the traditional enemies of Bruco, the child pinched his nostrils together as a sign that "it stinks." Muir also sees vendetta as "a medium of collective memory"; *Mad Blood Stirring*, 90.

103. *Njal's Saga*, trans. Magnus Magnusson and Hermann Palsson (Harmondsworth: Penguin Books, 1960), 115–16.

liam Ian Miller claims that, during these dramatic scenarios, Icelandic heroines thus not only shame their men but at a crucial moment take at least some part in family decision making.[104] Some Mediterranean societies also made a place for ritualized goading, again involving scornful females, embarrassed males, and dead flesh: one Montenegrin mother, Christopher Boehm discovered, kept showing a container of her husband's blood to their children, thus training them in vengeance. Funeral lamentations could include dirges which were meant to sting male relatives into performing their masculine duty. In nineteenth-century Corsica, for example, mourning women used the dirge (*vocero*) as their opportunity to demand revenge.[105] One notes, incidentally, that in all of these examples there is a close association between ritual gesture, the spoken (or sung), and retaliation.

In early formulations of the supposedly widespread Mediterranean pairing of "male honor" and "female shame," anthropologists assumed passive females whose chastity—a vital sign of family honor—was jealously guarded by male relatives.[106] In the psychological dynamics of

104. William Ian Miller, *Bloodtaking and Peacemaking*, 210–15; also "Choosing the Avenger," esp. 175–85.

105. Christopher Boehm, *Blood-Revenge*, 63; Stephen Wilson, *Feuding, Conflict, and Banditry*, 385–86. Although I have not found similar examples from Bernardino's time, Renaissance Florentines clearly perceived the dangers of unbridled mourning. According to Sharon Strocchia, they understood "the explosive, emotional quality of funerals, which might result in violence, vendetta, or other breaches of civic order and decorum" and, at the end of the fourteenth century, they excluded women from the funeral cortege; see *Death and Ritual in Renaissance Florence* (Baltimore: Johns Hopkins University Press, 1992), 10–12.

106. For classic formulations of the honor/shame dichotomy in Mediterranean cultures, see *Honour and Shame: The Values of Mediterranean Society*, ed. J. G. Peristiany and Julian Pitt-Rivers (London: Weidenfeld and Nicholson, 1966); also Julian Pitt-Rivers, *The Fate of Shechem* (Cambridge and New York: Cambridge University Press, 1977), and Jane Schneider, "Of Vigilance and Virgins," *Ethnology* 10, no. 1 (January 1971): 1–24. Recent studies, however, have begun to modify the generalizations: see, for instance, *Honor and Grace in Anthropology* (Cambridge: Cambridge University Press, 1992), a collection edited by Peristiany and Pitt-Rivers which acknowledges that there can be no simplistic categories based on "guilt" and "shame" and that honor itself should be regarded as a "conceptual field" rather than as a "single constant concept," 4–8. The articles in *Dislocating Masculinity: Comparative Ethnographies*, ed. Andrea Cornwall and Nancy Lindis-

the feud, however, it seems as if women could judge what was appropriate masculine behavior and in certain contexts publicly censure the "unmanly." There are probably few documented cases of this kind of wifely reproach from Italy, since self-conscious Renaissance males were unlikely to record such taunts. But Italian women, too, may have privately goaded their men by pointing out flaws in their manhood. Thomas Kuehn, in his analysis of the Lanfredini family in conflict, quotes a woman who upbraids her husband for unilaterally surrendering the family honor by making peace with an enemy: "O Lanfredino, traitor to yourself, since you have brought such shame to so many sons, because you have made peace that neither they nor I knew about."[107]

---

farne (London and New York: Routledge, 1994), take into account ambiguity and sometimes subversive identities; see esp. Lindisfarne, "Variant Masculinities, Variant Virginities: Rethinking Honour and Shame," 82–96. Also see *Honor and Shame and the Unity of the Mediterranean*, ed. David D. Gilmore (Washington, DC: American Anthropological Association, 1987). Gilmore (in "Honor, Honesty, and Shame: Male Status in Contemporary Andalusia," 90–103) makes a strong case for surveying a range of qualities which define manhood, while Michael Herzfeld ("'As in Your Own House': Hospitality, Ethnography, and the Stereotype of Mediterranean Society," 75–89) focuses on regional variation, in this case hospitality among Greek villagers. In the Italian context, Daniel R. Lesnick shows that, in thirteenth-century Todi, men could lose honor if they were insulted as thieves or liars, thus threatening their reputations in the economic sphere; "Insults and Threats in Medieval Todi," *Journal of Medieval History* 17 (1991): 71–89. Like Herzfeld and Gilmore, Unni Wikan has pursued redefinitions based on contextual analysis: in "Shame and Honor: A Contestable Pair," *Man* 19, no. 4 (1984): 632–52, she notes that even in a most traditional Muslim society such as Oman's, female sexual fidelity is not so rigidly linked to the overall perception of a woman's "honor" as one might expect; other attributes such as hospitality also come into play. Juliet Du Boulay, in *Portrait of a Greek Mountain Village* (Oxford: Oxford University Press, 1974), also recognizes a more flexible connection between female shame and chastity: in practice, stupidity, rather than unchastity, is sometimes regarded as the worse sin (clever women, she claims, can often salvage their tarnished honor), 113–16. One of the most nuanced studies is Carol Delaney's *The Seed and the Soil: Gender and Cosmology in Turkish Village Society* (Berkeley and Los Angeles: University of California Press, 1991), which argues the protection of women's chastity is in fact related to the protection of male seed: "their shamefulness," Delaney says, "is basically a kind of indiscriminate fecundity," 40.

107. Thomas Kuehn, "Honor and Conflict in a Fifteenth-Century Florentine Family," in *Law, Family, and Women*, 129. The peacemaking had exacerbated preexisting ten-

It makes sense that at least some women felt the need for vengeance as keenly as men, and literary sources occasionally allude to this. In Boccaccio's *Elegy of the Lady Fiammetta*, the love-sick heroine is able to convince her husband that her adulterous agony comes from her inability, as a woman, to avenge her slain brother, who (so she lies) has appeared mournfully to her in a dream, and pleaded for justice. Fiammetta tells her husband, "As the gods know, I would have avenged him already if I could bear arms, thereby allowing him to hold his head high among the other spirits, but I cannot do so. Therefore, my dear husband, not without reason do I grieve so miserably." Her solicitous husband is completely convinced, which suggests that it was not unreasonable for real women to be similarly consumed by the emotions aroused by grief and unfulfilled vendetta.[108] In Sacchetti's collection of *novelle*, we have the argument of two partisan women, both married into the family of the Counts Guidi, but still avid to continue their natal families' hostility through the medium of insults. The author wants to make the point that women are apt to speak viciously and that in the good old days (*al buon tempo*) they used to reprove their men for factionalism, but now instead urge them on (*li confortano a combattere per parte*).[109]

The women listening to Bernardino may have lacked the means, but not the heart, to participate actively in avenging kin. The preacher has left us a few telling examples based on his own experience. The

sions between Lanfredino and his son Remigio. Kuehn notes that "honor was part of the symbolic patrimony," 135; this Renaissance mother must have sided with her sons in their mutual anger over the dissipation of family "property."

108. Giovanni Boccaccio, *The Elegy of the Lady Fiammetta*, ed. and trans. Mariangela Causa-Steindler and Thomas Mauch (Chicago: University of Chicago Press, 1990), 106–7. Note, incidentally, the bizarre, non-Christian afterlife where the shade of Fiammetta's brother cannot rest until he is properly avenged: "Dear sister, dispel the shame that makes me walk with furrowed brow and downcast eyes, wailing among other spirits."

109. Franco Sacchetti, *Il Trecentonovelle*, Novella CLXXIX, 404. One woman is the daughter of the mighty Guelph Ugolino della Gherardesca, the other the daughter of the equally famous Ghibelline Buonconte da Montefeltro.

young girl at his sermon in Cremona, who had to be coerced into forgiving her father's killers, may not have been such an anomaly; seized by an overpowering emotion, she had a dramatic nosebleed and decided to make peace only because of supernatural (and public) pressure. In the Sienese sermon on concord, Bernardino gives another example of two feuding women whose blood boils as hotly as their men's: one was able to pardon, but her enemy declared that if Christ himself were to appear and offer her a choice, "I would rather go quickly to hell and not pardon than to pardon and have eternal life."[110] To the Florentines in 1424, he explained the unmanliness of revenge by insisting that, far from restoring honor, it only confers shame: "Your enemy, for the offense he has given you, has become sick, small, and effeminate" (*infermo, piccolino, e femminuccia*). This implies that retaliation is characteristic of women who were supposed to be cowardly by nature. To them, "every injurious word [*paroluzza d'ingiuria*] seems to be a knife."[111] In this context, it is also essential to remember that Bernardino assumed that slander was a vice in which women participated as easily as men. Through both memory and words, they had the capacity to incite violence.[112]

Not surprisingly, Bernardino deftly employs an exemplum to show his listeners that it was possible to renounce vengeance, despite social pressure. A Christian alternative to woman as keeper of the feud and man as its executor is provided as the climax of the concord sermon, in a tale about a vendetta in Piedmont. A woman is pregnant when her husband is killed by an enemy. As a pious Christian, she pardons the murderer, raises her son with good doctrine, and never reveals to the boy what happened to his father. Meanwhile, the killer and the young

110. Siena 1425, II, 260.

111. Florence 1424, II, 234.

112. Although Bernardino does not join the two, some late-medieval Italians also saw a connection between women's vanity and male political disorder. Carol Lansing says that "lawmakers considered women's hems and factional warfare closely linked: a root cause of the lack of order was concupiscence, sensual appetites resistant to rational control"; see "Gender and Civil Authority: Sexual Control in a Medieval Italian Town," in *Journal of Social History* 31, no. 1 (Fall 1997): 33–59.

man become fast friends. One day, however, a wicked murmurer, "trying to place scandal between them," insults the youth by calling him a *ribaldo* who hangs out ("*usì dì e notte*") with the man who killed his father. Stung by the taunt, the boy assaults his former friend with intent to kill. But the older man immediately kneels before him and begs for mercy, praying to God and making the sign of the cross. Moved by this display of humility, the youth consents to humble himself (*s'aumiliò*) by pardoning the killer. God, of course, rewards the boy with a long life in this world and eternal life in the next.[113]

The previous spring, Bernardino had given a more elaborate version of this story to the Florentines, partly in dialogue form and with embellishments which suggest that he was targeting his female listeners. The bereaved wife, he tells his audience, was struck to the heart with grief but nonetheless makes peace with her husband's killer and raises her son—the very image of his father—as a good Christian, loving him with "a tender heart." After the evil gossip challenges her son, she vainly tries to convince the young man to forgo revenge, lest she lose him as she lost his father (here the preacher tells his listeners to "remember how much effort she made to bring him up"). In this version, the angry son ambushes his enemy on Good Friday, but the two reconcile and then go off to hear a sermon together. Bernardino dramatically concludes his story by relating the supernatural event which emphasizes the social miracle of the boy's forgiveness: the two reconciled men are in church when the crucifix is suddenly transformed into a living, bleeding Christ who walks among the crowd until he reaches the pardoner, embracing and kissing him three times before He returns to the cross. It was, Bernardino exclaims to the Florentines, a "stupendous miracle, visible to everyone there!"[114]

113. Siena 1425, II, 272–73. Giacomo delle Marche may have modeled his own sermon, "De Pace et Remissione Iniuriarum," partly on Bernardino's. He uses this peace-making tale, as well as the examples of the magnanimous Caesar and Alexander; *Sermones Dominicales*, vol. 2, 283–85, 292.

114. Florence 1424, II, 244–45. Bernardino's living crucifix is more dramatic than those in William Christian's *Moving Crucifixes in Modern Spain* (Princeton: Princeton

Everyone in this story behaves according to Bernardino's Christian rulebook: the wife forgives, the enemy reforms, the youth restrains his natural impulse and abandons the vendetta, Christ Himself bestows a public *bacio di pace*. Only the man with the *mala lingua* does the expected (although the audience might have been surprised that gossip restrained itself for so long). Like those *paci di fuore* enacted in church and piazza, this individual *pace di dentro*, the softening of the heart towards an enemy, is a tableau of how society can work if it follows Bernardino's sensible advice and reverses its perverted, if entrenched, mores. A real man will not succumb to insults and his wife, guardian of the family memory, has a special duty to break the obsessive chain of vengeance.

But Bernardino himself, even in the act of preaching against vengeance, betrays how deeply ambivalent he and his listeners, both male and female, were towards vendetta and forgiveness. If the recorder in the Siena sermon has properly conveyed the preacher's words, we see that the moment of forgiveness is depicted as a kind of "humiliation." Also, Bernardino occasionally blurs the very idea of revenge as a sin. At several points he talks about God's right to the just vendetta; if people do something evil, God will certainly retaliate.[115] Of course,

---

University Press, 1992), but there are intriguing similarities: both require a large number of witnesses to the miracle, rather than the report of a gifted seer, as is generally the case with apparitions. And just as the modern miracle takes place in a church, hence under the control of the authorities, Bernardino's crucifix comes to life for the benefit of two former enemies as they righteously attend a sermon together. A similar story is told in Florence 1424, II, 242–43. A lord who has killed the son of another begs for forgiveness when his lands are devastated and his people harmed. When his enemy generously pardons him, the two enter a church where a crucifix extends its arms three times, as if to embrace the pardoner.

115. Siena 1425, II, 20. Other Christianized feuding societies similarly blended the impulse for revenge with God's right to legitimate retribution. For example, Frankish and Lombard clerics accepted the concept of *ultio divina*; see Wallace-Hadrill, "The Bloodfeud of the Franks," 127, and Jon N. Sutherland, "The Idea of Revenge in Lombard Society in the Eight and Tenth Centuries: The Cases of Paul the Deacon and Liudprand of Cremona," *Speculum* 50, no. 3 (July 1975): 391–410, esp. 401. Icelandic sagas report blatant accommodations between Christianity and the feud: William Ian Miller

what is wrong for man is not prohibited to God, as he carefully points out in the sermon on concord when he says that men overstep themselves if they try to steal God's right of vendetta, which He alone possesses. Yet moments before making this assertion, Bernardino gave his audience a most peculiar reason to forgive an enemy. The very best vendetta, and one that carries no risk to your own head or soul, is to pardon! Earlier in the sermon course, his terminology is especially revealing: "If you bear hatred, go to the Crucifix and pray for him [your enemy] . . . [your prayers] will be bombards that will go to his heart."[116] And he cleverly poses the argument in terms of both spiritual and worldly benefits. Vengeance automatically means damnation, and so "if you cut with a vendetta, you are wounding your own soul." Why listen to the comments others make when you try to save yourself? If the Palazzo Pubblico suddenly collapsed during the sermon, would it not make more sense to run away than to worry if people laughed at your plight? As usual, Bernardino reminds his listeners of earthly rewards: "God will give you contentments, children, temporal goods, and everything that will give you consolation."[117]

Perhaps he felt that it was more effective not to eradicate the vendetta, but to harness it for good. Was this practicality or an admission of defeat? The best answer may be more complicated than either. Sometimes it seems as if Bernardino unconsciously accepted the very attitude he was fighting against, in the same way as his personal anger towards detractors belied his high-minded advice to ignore their evil tongues. For instance, although he may not approve, he acknowledges the inevitability of revenge (*necessità di vendetta*) in the case of a child

---

notes the blind man in *Njal's Saga* whose sight is temporarily restored by God so that he can take vengeance; *Bloodtaking and Peacemaking*, 190–92. Also see Muir's comments on the "vendetta di Dio" and human ambivalence in *Mad Blood Stirring*, 69–70.

116. Siena 1425, II, 270 for God's right to vendetta; II, 259 for pardoning as the best revenge; II, 222 for prayers as "bombards." In Siena 1427, II, 1154, Bernardino laments those who will never be conceived because their would-be fathers are sodomites: these unborn children scream, "Vendetta, vendetta, vendetta!"

117. Siena 1425, II, 261–65.

who has seen his father abuse his grandsire. When he is grown, the child will naturally beat his own father in turn.[118] Bernardino means to show how parents and children should treat each other with respect, but one moral is that he who misbehaves will be appropriately punished; the implication, too, is that a desire for revenge will be a natural impulse developing in the child. In the most telling example of all, the preacher, carried away by the impetus of a good story, completely forgets that the blood feud is supposed to be wrong. In a sermon against sorcery, he tells about a jealous man who believes his wife is sleeping with a priest. The man foolishly seeks out a witch who confirms his suspicion. After killing his wife, he returns to the witch and triumphantly asks if his spouse is still committing adultery. To his astonishment the witch proclaims that indeed she is! Too late, the man realizes his mistake in trusting the black arts. But instead of ending with a comment about sorcery and damnation, Bernardino adds that the man soon dies in a vendetta carried out by his wife's family. If he added some disclaimer that vendetta was "wrong," the recorder chose not to mention it.[119] Vengeance is presented here as a fact of life, as it surely was to the listeners who heard the story.

As a Franciscan Observant, Bernardino voluntarily removed himself from the constraints of this world, and that removal gave him the authority and the moral stature to reprove those who were enmeshed by society's many demands. But no one, not even a holy man, is free from the cultural imperatives which surround us all. Like the writer of *dicerie* who advocated forgiveness yet also warned that it was unwise to trust an enemy with whom you have made peace, Bernardino and his contemporaries were at the mercy of conflicting patterns of belief.[120] In the course of his preaching, he played with widely divergent ideas about honor, reputation, and the self, using them when he judged

118. Florence 1424, I, 206–7.

119. Siena 1425, II, 197.

120. MS. I. VI. 5, 80r: "Al nemico tuo non credare giamai e sia humile e va inchinato e non fidare di lui."

them to be effective, and remaining silent or ambiguous when he sensed that they would not.

When he preached peace, Bernardino was speaking to an audience for whom, as Paolo da Certaldo claimed, "the first happiness [*allegrezza*] is to carry out a vendetta." Vengeance promised at least as much pleasure as pain.[121] If the *pace di fuore* involved so many motives, not all of them the fruit of *carità*, how much more complicated was the *pace di dentro* in a world of conflicting obligations to self, community, and God? And if one could finally sort out the alternatives, how could one's fellow predator ever be trusted? Paolo da Certaldo praised mutual forgiveness, but prudently remarked:

> And if it happens that you have injured someone, and then afterwards you make peace or a marriage bond with him, don't trust him . . . but always pay attention to his hands, and to his deeds, and to his words, and in every dealing you have with him.[122]

121. Paolo da Certaldo, *Il libro di buoni costumi*, 159. A Greek villager, reporting the intense satisfaction he felt after a series of retaliatory sheep-raids, told anthropologist Michael Herzfeld, "I've never experienced greater pleasure in my life than in this case"; *The Poetics of Manhood*, 179. But Edward Muir reminds us that the obligation of revenge could cause as much pain as pleasure. Renaissance males were sometimes caught in a "double bind," stymied not so much by their Christian consciences as by conflicting social pressures; see "The Double Binds of Manly Revenge in Renaissance Italy," in *Gender Rhetorics: Postures of Dominance and Submission in History*, ed. Richard Trexler (Binghamton, NY: Medieval and Renaissance Texts and Studies, 1994), 65-82.

122. Paolo da Certaldo, *Il libro di buoni costumi*, 85: "E se pur venisse caso ch'avessi disservito uno, e poi facessi pace o parentado co lui, non ti fidare però in tutto di lui, ma sempre gli poni mente a le mani, e ne' fatti e nelle parole e in ciò ch'hai a fare co lui."

CHAPTER FOUR

Peacemaking in Siena, 1427

"Doh, cittadini e voi donne, io ci prego, io vi essorto, io vi comando quanto io posso, che voi aviate e teniate la pace."

As a seasoned peacemaker, Bernardino fully understood the anxieties surrounding reputation and the duties of revenge. He was especially sensitive to the tension between the individual and the collective, and realized, when he arranged large and satisfying public rites, that even when they acted collectively, people were also responding as individuals. The goal of the preacher was to shift back and forth between the two, in some way which would be socially and psychologically convincing to the audiences before him. But the emotional moment of conversion is hard for us to touch, even fleetingly. How did Bernardino reach the shadowy part which few Italians chose to document, obsessed as they were with the public management of the self? How did he make them "convert" and forgive?

All of the contradictions and ambiguities which are part of any real conversion experience come together in the 1427 Siena sermons, where we can watch a peacemaking as it unfolded day by day, from August 15 to October 5. Thanks to the pious and literate cloth cutter Benedetto di maestro Bartolomeo, the sermon course is not merely an approximation of what Bernardino said, but an essentially verbatim account, complete with the preacher's asides and interjections. This means that, unlike other vernacular sermons which are more cursory, with gaps in either the stenographers' understanding or transcription, Benedetto's reverence for each word of Bernardino makes it possible for us to hear him preach, almost as if we were listening to a tape recording made six long centuries ago.[1] The result is not only an entry into the past as intimate as that provided by the most famous Florentine diaries, but also a document which is close to "pure" Bernardino, whose vibrant language makes it one of the masterpieces of colloquial Italian.

The relative precision of Benedetto's recording enables us to study ideology in action as the preacher attempted to convert the Sienese to the ways of forgiveness. Indeed, the peacemaking talk with which Bernardino culminated the visit is arguably his masterwork. Just as the 1427 group as a whole permits us to hear the preacher's voice, the great peace sermon provides access into the inner world of the Sienese. During the six weeks preceding this speech, Bernardino tried to appeal to them both as fellow citizens and as individuals seeking serenity in a troubled world. Finally on September 28, the long-sought conversion

---

1. Even Bernardino's rare moments of hesitation are captured: "Dico che so' molti, molti dico . . . (Che ho io detto? Che ho detto?)"; Siena 1427, I, 290–91. Bernardino, well aware of Benedetto's task, helped the stenographer along. At various points, he interrupted the sermon to address him directly ("doh! odi buona parola o scrittore, scrivela questa!"); Ibid., I, 494–95. For other examples, see Origo, *The World of San Bernardino*, 12–13.

played itself out in the Piazza del Campo. For a brief moment in time community and self merged in the rituals of peace.

I. A Precarious Peace

The Siena 1427 sermons were a response to a specific call for help. Bernardino tells us that he was invited to preach by Pope Martin V and by Cardinal Antonio Casini, the former Bishop of Siena, and that he was eager to return to his *patria* when he realized it needed his aid. On August 7, 1427, the Sienese government wrote to Bernardino asking him to come.[2]

Siena was not openly at arms in the summer of 1427; in fact, Bernardino continually reminded his listeners of their *present* peace and prosperity, and the main threat behind his faction sermons is the potential loss of this happy state. The Republic of Siena was as stable a government as one might hope for in the difficult years of the early fifteenth century, attempting to safeguard its extensive and tempting holdings in southern Tuscany from predatory neighbors during a brief lull between pestilence and war.[3] Even if the memories of its oldest

2. The reference to the pope and Cardinal Casini is in Siena 1427, I, 663: ". . . essendo io a Roma, mi disse il papa che io venissi qua; e anco il vostro vescovo, che è ora cardinale, anco mel disse: che avendo essi sentite divisioni vostre, mi dissero che a ogni modo volevano ch'io ci venisse." For the government's invitation, see Enrico Bulletti, "Per la nomina di s. Bernardino a vescovo di Siena," in *Bullettino di Studi Bernardiniani* 5 (1939): 45. Bernardino says that he decided to come because "io udivo che infra voi era grandissima divisione, e dicevasi anco più che non era"; Siena 1427, I, 524.

3. For political events in fifteenth-century Siena, see Orlando Malavolti, *Historia de' fatti e guerre de' Senesi, così esterne, come civili* (Bologna: Forni, 1968), Part II, Book Ten through Part III, Book Six. General surveys in English are by Ferdinand Schevill, *Siena: The Story of a Medieval Commune* (New York: C. Scribner, 1909), and Langton Douglas, *A History of Siena* (London: J. Murray, 1902); two recent overviews are Judith Hook, *Siena: A City and Its History* (London: H. Hamilton, 1979), and Lando Bortolotti, *Siena* (Rome and Bari: Editori Laterza, 1983), a study of the city's urban fabric. There are few detailed studies of the social and political history of fifteenth-century Siena. See the two articles by David Hicks: "Sienese Society in the Renaissance," *Comparative Studies in Society and History* 2, no. 4 (1960): 412–20, and "The Sienese State in the Renaissance," in *From the Renaissance to the Counter-Reformation: Essays in Honor of Garrett Mattingly*, ed. C. H. Carter (New York: Random House, 1965), 75–94, and, more recently,

citizens reached back to the upheavals of the late Trecento, when a succession of rebellions destroyed the city's peace, the last major political storm had taken place more than two decades before Bernardino's visit. In November of 1403, three of Siena's five factions, or *monti*, purged the government of the Dodici, their former partners. Led by a member of the noble Salimbeni family, the Dodici had started a rebellion which quickly aborted, resulting in many exiles and perpetual exclusion from public office.[4]

"Sources of Wealth in Renaissance Siena: Businessmen and Landowners," *Bulletino Senese di Storia Patria* 93 (1986): 9–42. See Mario Ascheri, *Siena nel Rinascimento: Instituzioni e sistema politico* (Siena: Il Leccio, 1985) and, with Donatella Ciampoli, *Siena e il suo territorio nel Rinascimento* (Siena: Il Leccio, 1986), a collection of edited archival documents. Maria Ginatempo has written a careful demographic analysis of Siena and its *contado*: *Crisi di un territorio: Il popolamento della Toscana Senese alla fine del medioevo* (Florence: L. S. Olschki, 1988). Overviews of magnate relations to the state are in Danilo Marrara, "I magnati e il governo del 1274 alla fine del XIV secolo," in *Studi per Enrico Fiumi* (Pisa: Pacini, 1979), 239–76, and Ann Katherine Isaacs, "Magnati comune e stato a Siena nel Trecento e all'inizio del Quattrocento," in *I ceti dirigenti nella Toscana tardo comunale*, Comitato di studi sulla storia dei ceti dirigenti in Toscana, Atti del III Convegno, 5–7 dicembre 1980 (Monte Oriolo, Florence: Francesco Papafava, 1983), 81–96. Unlike Bernardino, preachers later in the century worried about external threats rather than discord within the city; see Bernadette Paton's discussion of Fra Petrus Paulus Salimbeni and the "San Domenico Preacher" in "'Una Città Faticosa': Dominican Preaching and the Defense of the Republic in Late Medieval Siena," in *City and Countryside in Late Medieval Italy*, ed. Trevor Dean and Chris Wickham, 109–23. By the late Quattrocento, factionalism was apparently less troubling to the consolidated oligarchy which now ruled Siena.

4. By the second half of the Trecento, five institutionalized factions, or *monti*, dominated Sienese politics; political power was parceled out among the descendants of those groups which had held the supreme magistracy in the past. These were the Grandi (or Gentiluomini), the Nove (whose long-standing regime was overthrown in 1355), the Dodici, the Riformatori, and the Popolari. Ascheri says that the *monti* operated through a system of connections; see *Siena e il suo territorio*, 37, and *Siena nel Rinascimento*, 28–31. A discussion of the *monti* in sixteenth-century Siena is in Ann Katherine Chiancone Isaacs, "Popolo e monti nella Siena del primo cinquecento," *Rivista Storica Italiana* 82, no. 1 (1970): 32–80.

The Dodici ruled Siena from 1355 to 1368, but were usually partners in coalition governments until 1403. For the Dodici in the late Trecento, see Valerie Wainwright, "Conflict and Popular Government in Fourteenth-Century Siena: il Monte dei Dodici, 1355–1368," in *I ceti dirigenti nella Toscana tardo comunale*, 57–80, and "The Testing of a

The prelude to Bernardino's visit was new unrest among the *monti*. On December 26, 1426, a member of the Nove faction was beheaded because he had dealings with the exiles, confessing that "he wanted to admit the Dodici back into the *reggimento*." The execution caused anger in the city and the chronicler duly recorded that depressingly familiar phrase found throughout the annals of late-medieval Italy: "*si levò il rumore e ognuno si armò.*"[5] When Bernardino arrived in the summer of 1427, there seems to have been widespread resentment towards a curfew law; the one concrete political result of his preaching would be a reduction in its fine.[6] The government also passed a resolution to work with the preacher in order to achieve "peace," but this was certainly not intended to change the status of the Dodici, who would remain outside the government for most of the century. What the rulers of the city did intend was for their celebrated native son to soothe a city which was threatening to erupt into outright political disorder.

Bernardino completely understood his task, presenting himself as a prophet and healer rather than as a politician. Fiercely proud of his plain speaking, he also had a keen sense of his limitations within the

---

Popular Sienese Regime: The Riformatori and the Insurrections of 1371," in *I Tatti Studies: Essays in the Renaissance*, vol. 2 (Villa I Tatti: The Harvard University Center for Italian Renaissance Studies, 1987), 107–70. The story of their downfall is told in T. Terzani, "Siena dalla morte di Gian Galeazzo Visconti alla morte di Ladislao d'Angiò Durazzo," *Bullettino sanese di storia patria* 66 (1959), 11–15; also see Malavolti, *Historia*, Part II, Book Ten, 193v–194v. Their disenfranchisement and expulsion was followed by a curfew law which stated that members of the Dodici would have their hands or feet cut off if they went out at night after the bell rang. This does not seem to be the same law which was causing problems in the summer of 1427, since the penalty for the latter was strictly monetary.

5. "Aldobrandini Chronicle," Siena Biblioteca, MS. C. IV. I, 277v and 278v.

6. As Maire-Vigueur points out, the reduction of the fine, along with the resolution to achieve peace and concord, were not "resultats bien notables," "S. Bernardino et la vie citadine," 267. Ironically, some of the children who must have heard Bernardino preach peace in 1427 were causing problems as young men in 1439: in that year, two enemy bands of youths, "Chiassa" and "Graffio," were creating civic unrest by insulting each other to the point of armed combat; see Malavolti, *Historia*, Part III, Book Two, 30r.

political sphere. In 1427 he carefully avoided discussing specific problems with the *monti;* his one veiled reference is a humorous play on words which labels partisans as a *monte di pazzi,* or heap of fools. Although some of his words on corrupt government, avarice, and pride must have discomfited the powerful, he never directly assaulted Siena's political structure. Instead, he called for a comprehensive moral reform similar to those he preached elsewhere. Indeed, his sermons on faction are embedded within a broad attack on social sin in general, the usual repertoire of a long visit by a mendicant preacher.[7] The Sienese government wanted a demonstration of unity, one of those morality plays of social concord, while Bernardino desired a peacemaking between souls but also a general conversion from sin.

The fact that the preacher was Sienese meant that his role was slightly different from his peacemaking activity in other towns. Here, he was not technically an "outsider" in civic terms, so he had to emphasize other qualities if he was to be considered an impartial spokesman. Bernardino deftly used his Sienese identity to appeal to his audience. He addressed his countrymen as *"fratelli e sorelle"* or *"figli"* and tried to show his personal concern for their salvation. His listeners undoubtedly felt blessed to hear this homegrown saint, one who was personally familiar to many in the small social world of Siena. An echo of their pride survives in the pious *laude* written after his death in 1444, emphasizing the proprietary relationship between saint and city which was characteristic of urban devotion throughout the Middle Ages. One writer, at the end of a long poem whose conventions are interwoven with a deep pride that Bernardino was Sienese, prays for the heavenly patron's aid in keeping the city united and free:

---

7. It should be noted, however, that the Siena 1427 course may be something of an anomaly. This peacemaking visit took place over a much longer period than several others arranged for specific political situations (for example, Crema 1421 and Belluno 1423), meaning that, instead of giving a few quick sermons, the preacher had time to treat diverse topics at length, reminiscent of the long courses given for Lent and Advent.

... sichè l'un l'altro di charità ardente
come fratelli riamiamo
E divisione lassiamo
che a capo d'ogni mal vituperoso

Dunqua Bernardino padre diletto
e appresso al signiore nostro avvocato
del cuor ci tolga e ciaschuno sia salvato
e tuo città di Siena in buon stato
in libertà mantengha . . .[8]

[. . . so that we as brothers love one another again with ardent charity/And let us leave division which is the head of every vituperous evil/Therefore, Bernardino, beloved father and our advocate near the Lord/Pray Jesus that He take from us each defect of the heart so that everyone is saved/And that He maintain your city of Siena in *buon stato* and liberty . . .]

The new saint's role in heaven is now an extension of his peacemaking on earth, as he continues his intervention for the well-being of Siena.[9]

The devout writers of the *laude* may well have witnessed the earthly Bernardino at work in the same enterprise of peace and salvation. Already in 1427 the Sienese were openly proud of their famed native son. The best evidence for this is their maneuvering in late spring and early summer to get Bernardino as their resident bishop, a move which was clearly intended to make their identification with the great man even stronger. Bernardino adamantly refused, despite pressure from the Curia; the Sienese had to settle for the rector of the Ospedale as their new bishop.[10] Notwithstanding their disappointment, the Sienese may

---

8. "Lauda per San Bernardino," Siena Biblioteca, MS. I. II. 27, 83v.

9. See Diana Webb for the history of Siena's patron saints, *Patrons and Defenders: The Saints in the Italian City States* (London and New York: Tauris Academic Studies, 1996), 249–316.

10. The complete story of the nomination of Bernardino for bishop is in Bulletti, "Per la nomina di S. Bernardino," 27–48.

have been an unusually receptive audience when they faced him in the Campo a month later.

Bernardino might have disagreed. He was exasperated that his grand success in 1425 had apparently dissipated, with his former converts lapsing into old and comfortable sins. He gave a sermon on the evils of backsliding and at several points sarcastically compared the Sienese with the Perugians, whose religious enthusiasm gave him great joy. The preacher, then, had no illusions about the tractability of this audience. The Siena 1427 sermons would be a spiritual duel with the preacher on one side, attacking an ingrained problem of urban life, and the Sienese on the other side, not easily convinced.

In order to understand how Bernardino moved this particular audience, we need to listen to the sermons in context, sensitive to their ebb and flow day by day. He preached forty-five days in a row (except for one morning when he was sick and another when he preached not to the public at large but to a smaller group inside the Palazzo Pubblico), often for several hours at a time. The cumulative effect of so much preaching must have been overwhelming. Although peacemaking was the main reason for his visit, constant repetition of a single theme would have strained even Bernardino's ingenuity: given the number of sermons, there was the danger of either boring or antagonizing people during six weeks of an extended diatribe against faction. The preacher chose to solve this potential problem by alternating the hardest-hitting sermons with moments of repose, either lightening the mood or switching to unrelated vices. He understood the musicality of good preaching, and the texture of each sermon was extraordinarily rich. In his usual fashion, he often wandered delightfully, touching first one subject and then sweeping to another, binding the whole together with snappy exempla, direct dialogues with his audience, and enormous variations in tone. His rhetorical strategy indicates that Bernardino surveyed the road to conversion and then carefully mapped it out, but was confident enough to leave the main path when he chose. This combination of purpose and meandering is evident during the nine days of sermons which preceded his first direct attack on faction. A brief look at his tactics in these opening sermons can help us to decipher his strategy during the entire course.

Bernardino began to preach on Friday, August 15, the Feast of the Assumption, then as now the most important day in the Sienese religious calendar, given the Virgin Mary's status as patroness of the city. The government had requested that he do so, despite the preacher's preference to wait until Sunday (he had only arrived the day before and probably wanted time to rest before starting six weeks of nonstop preaching).[11] The opening sermon is a fairly conventional paean to the Virgin, albeit with lyrical passages praising her depth of understanding and her willingness to help those Sienese who pray to her. The first few minutes of the talk establish Mary's role in the city's salvation, as the *"Avvocata di nostra città,"* but Bernardino also implies that it will be a joint enterprise, with himself and the Sienese as full participants. Another subtext of this sermon and the ones immediately following is the preacher's special relationship with the Sienese, and their inextricable bond to each other. From the very first moments his listeners are addressed as *"cittadini miei"*; throughout the visit he will seek to forge their group identity as citizens rather than as members of warring families or factions. Bernardino himself, as a concerned citizen, will serve as middleman between the Sienese and their Creator: during the third sermon he proclaims that he will bear witness on Judgment Day, prompt to tell God if they responded to his preaching—or if they did not.[12]

His tone is mostly warm and welcoming during these early talks, in marked contrast to his style in the turbulent sermons ahead; perhaps he felt that it was best to begin as gently as possible until he was assured of a sympathetic audience. For example, on the second day he meditates on the Piazza del Campo as a cozy haven of security:

11. Siena 1427, I, 110.
12. Ibid., I, 172–73.

> Think a little about who is having a better time than we are. Here we are
> peaceful with such consolation, without suspicion and without fear: we
> in wealth, we with the peace of the soul in this piazza with such good or-
> der, everyone staying to hear the word of God with good will. Who is it
> who doesn't rejoice in his heart? This is a half-paradise . . .[13]

Oddly coupled with this snug image is an exultant description of the
piazza as a battleground for souls: both guardian angels and devils are
present, protecting or attacking the Sienese. Fortunately, although the
city is under spiritual siege, she is well defended by Mary's prayers, by
warrior angels guarding the gates, and by the Sienese themselves, who
have the free will to choose between good and evil. Throughout his
visit, Bernardino tries to convince his listeners that they have the power and the responsibility to make that choice. People are not victims of
an inflexible destiny; belief in astrological determinism is only an excuse to tread the easy path. It is heresy, he claims, to think that you act
as you do because you were born under a certain star: constellations
have no real power over souls and hence provide no excuse for sin: ". . .
I will show you that you can do the contrary to what you say you are
naturally inclined."[14] This is in fact his entire purpose as a preacher:
conversion is not so much the quick descent of grace as an education-
al process which gradually strengthens the will.

It was important for the preacher-teacher to lay a solid foundation,
since his success depended on the cooperation of his audience. Much
of the third and fourth days are spent teaching the fine art of sermon-
going. Ideally, one carried away lessons which would then be integrat-
ed into the total person. As always, a willingness to learn was essential,
and the lesson took best if people came to a sermon knowing what

---

13. Ibid., I, 128. "Pensa un poco chi è quello che abbi miglior tempo di noi. Noi
siamo qui pacifici con tanta consolazione, senza sospetto e senza paura; noi in divizia,
noi con pace d'animo in su questa piazza con tanto ordine, stando a udire la parola di
Dio tutti con buona volontà. Chi è quello che non si rallegri nel suo cuore? Questo è
uno mezzo paradiso . . ."

14. Ibid., I, 118.

particular sin they needed to amend. For example, some might attend with the guilty thought that they were having trouble forgiving an enemy: "I can't get rid of this hatred" (*io non mi posso levare il tale odio*).[15] Self-knowledge, then, becomes an essential component of true change. Above all, listening to and learning from sermons obliterates the feeble excuse of doing evil through ignorance. On the most practical level, Bernardino sees his preaching as a way of making people think before they act:

> And when you go to make a contract, you will think about it first, asking yourself: "What did Frate Bernardino say? He said such and such to me: this is wrong, I must not do it this way; this is good, this I want to do."[16]

While he tries to convince listeners that change is possible, given the beneficence of the divine and their own free will, Bernardino soon begins to move ominously towards open threats. The early talks depict Siena as the most fortunate of cities, but by the fourth day, the emphasis shifts from cheerful encouragement to the disastrous results of nonrepentance. *Now* is the time for conversion because Siena, fat and content, is a city on the brink of destruction.[17] Bernardino's voice, affable and protective only the day before, suddenly becomes harsh. "*Guarda, guarda, ben guarda!*" is his message now. God is losing His patience, and His anger with Siena, so careless in her prosperity, is now at hand. Satan, too, is watching: a thief who steals the soul, he incites

15. Ibid., I, 187.

16. Ibid., I, 149. "E quando tu andarai a fare uno contratto, tu vi pensarai prima dicendo: 'Che disse frate Bernardino? Elli mi disse così e così: questo è male, non si convien fare: questo è bene, questo vo' fare.'"

17. Bernardino is perhaps exaggerating Siena's great prosperity. While the fifteenth-century city had recovered from the travails of the later Trecento, its wealth was now based on a restricted local economy. David Hicks characterizes Siena's "sound, if circumscribed, economy ... able to attain a natural level of moderate prosperity;" "Sources of Wealth in Renaissance Siena," 11. But even the wealthiest Sienese households could not match the lifestyles of Florentine patricians. Bernardino was speaking mostly to cautious and traditional citizens who were probably anxious to retain their modest assets.

those of the same flesh to kill each other as he spreads hatred among citizens and relatives. In an early reference to faction, the preacher lists shattered relationships:

> The father is the enemy of the son, the son of the father; a brother against brother, friend against friend, companion against companion.[18]

As always, Bernardino wields a double-edged sword: if they do not repent, the Sienese will lose both spiritual and earthly benefits:

> Woe! Put your mind to it: he has already led you to the point where he's made you lose earthly goods, and also spiritual and eternal ones. Doh! Have you understood me? Sì, I'm not talking in French![19]

If his listeners did not understand the message at that point, they certainly did within the next minutes. The warm, protective atmosphere created in the first few days evaporates like mist as Bernardino dramatically ends the sermon with a grisly picture of an unconverted Siena. Humbled by division, its citizens will be tortured by mercenaries who burn, rape, and even slaughter babies. The next morning he asks the audience, "Tell me, how long have you had peace?" God has been patient, waiting and waiting for Siena's repentance, as He did for that of Sodom and Gomorrah.[20] And like Jerusalem before her fall, Siena is beautiful, prosperous, at peace. Like Jerusalem, the city is ripe for punishment.[21] As he preaches in the following weeks, Bernardino will linger over these threats in great detail, deliberately contrasting two radically different Sienas and their fates, forcing his listeners to decide between a peaceful city and one shattered by faction. This tale of two cities, one of the most powerful themes of the course, becomes

18. Siena 1427, I, 199. "El padre nemica el figliuolo; el figliuolo el padre; l'uno fratello l'altro; l'uno consorto l'altro; l'uno amico l'altro; l'uno compagno l'altro."

19. Ibid., I, 200. "Oimè! ponetevi mente, ché elli v'ha già sì condotti, che elli vi fa perdare i beni temporali e anco i beni spirituali e eternali. Doh! Ha' mi tu anco inteso?—Sì—; io non vi parlo in francioso."

20. Ibid., I, 216.

21. Ibid., I, 217–19.

as vivid in Bernardino's preaching as it is in the magnificent frescoes painted by Ambrogio Lorenzetti.

Along with threatening the Sienese, the fifth day's sermon also hints that the preacher felt confident enough to taunt them. He does not regret his decision about the bishopric since he will not go to hell for their sins. And if he had become bishop, "I believe I'd be more than a thousand miles away from here."[22] But neither threats nor sarcasm discouraged people from attending the sermons. In fact, eager devotees were violating the curfew when they rushed to the Campo as early as possible:

> . . . you have such a large and beautiful piazza that if you move at the sound of the bell, there's enough time, and I tell you that you will find a good place [i.e., from which to hear the sermon]. And don't come during the night, in the way that you have; otherwise you will have a bad night and will sleep during the sermon.[23]

In keeping with the city's laws, Bernardino agrees that no one should be out before the bell sounds in the morning. Apparently, complaints were circulating about the curfew and other just laws. In a typical metaphor, he explains why this is wrong: if a person emerges after fifteen days in a dark place beneath the earth, it is the fault of his eyes, rather than the sun, when he is blinded by the light. And so it is with sinners who complain about good laws designed to punish vice. Naturally the lustful complain when they cannot go out at night without paying a fine! The governors of Siena, listening from their dais in the Campo, must have been pleased by this staunch defense of law and order.

Yet even as Bernardino begins to shift to the major theme of the

22. Ibid., I, 207.
23. Ibid., I, 210–11. "Voi avete la piazza grande e tanto bella, che se voi vi movete alla campana, elli è assai per tempo; e dico che ognuna può avere buon lato. E non venite fra la notte, al modo che voi fate; imperò che voi avete la mala notte, e poi quando si predica, e voi dormite."

course, Siena's imminent demise, he also introduces a muted counterpoint which will eventually serve as an alternative strategy of conversion. He threatens his fellow citizens not only with punishment, but with something more elusive and even more inevitable. At several points during the early sermons, he alludes to the passing of time, in order to convince the Sienese to repent immediately. On the second day, when he describes the clash between demons and guardian angels, he notes that the good things of this life—all temptations of the devil—are ephemeral anyway. This is quickly followed by melancholy self-reflection: "O youths, once I was young and now I am old . . ."; it seems to him as if he is already in the grave.[24] So quickly has his life slipped by! He returns to the same theme on the fourth day when he advises his listeners to use each hour well, since it will never return. How terrible it is to waste precious time: think of the fool who tries to reach Rome by walking out the Porta Camollia, which leads to Florence, in the opposite direction! Bernardino's wistful sense of the passing of time and the foolishness of wasting precious moments will be fully developed in the peace sermon at the end of the visit, when he exposes his listeners' fears about old age and death.

For now, however, it will remain a minor key, since the preacher wants to arouse not melancholy but righteous action. The most important theme in the next four days is how to remain calm in the face of gossip. Again, it is free will and self-discipline which are essential. Bernardino keeps arguing that his listeners can control themselves if they want to, by ignoring slander, forgiving the ill-sayer, and accepting the will of God, who sometimes chastises people in mysterious ways. But there are many contradictions within this argument about "controlling" the desire to retaliate. One counsel, in particular, relies on an extremely contrived metaphor, at least to modern ears. When the good soul is maligned by the dragon of slander, it should take black pitch and white tallow, add some hairs, and then mix all together to form pellets (*pallottole*). The pitch and tallow stand for humility and love of

24. Ibid., I, 131–34.

one's neighbors—and Bernardino reminds the audience that black and white are the colors of Siena's heraldic shield—while the hairs signify understanding of self and of God. This densely packed image may be impossible to decode either because it is rhetorically unsuccessful or because we are too far removed from fifteenth-century mentalities.[25] At the very least, it seems bizarre advice on self-control, similar to Bernardino's description of forgiveness as a vendetta against one's enemies. The symbolism of the *pallottole* characterizes love of God and neighbor and understanding of self as *weapons*, albeit defensive ones. In other words, one ignores enemies by attacking them!

The black-and-white imagery also strains the metaphor. A symbol of the collective, it reminds the Sienese that they are part of a civic entity. Throughout his visit Bernardino will link the well-being of the individual with the group, according to the traditional ideology of the *bene comune*,[26] but the awkward pitch-and-tallow image hints that the connection is not quite so simple. The preceding chapter has argued that Italians, despite their tightly woven structures of family and neighborhood, often felt uneasy within this suffocating world. In the 1427 sermons Bernardino addresses both group and individual, but his efforts to weave them together seamlessly often fail, perhaps reflecting uneasiness within the culture at large. And so he shifts between one and the other as he builds up to the great peacemaking. As early as the seventh day, it is clear that his rhetoric, if not his logic, is most effective when it appeals directly to individuals. For example, near the end of the sermon, he begs his listeners:

> And therefore I say to all of you: don't open your hands to works of blood, don't open them, but rather pardon, pardon, pardon. Oh, to

25. Ibid., I, 279–80. Gene Brucker has suggested to me that the recipe might have reminded Bernardino's listeners of a witchcraft formula.

26. Late-medieval political thinkers used Thomist-Aristotelian ideas of the *bonum comunum* in their discussions of man as a social animal. Quentin Skinner, however, makes a convincing argument for the importance of pre-Thomist, pre-humanist treatises (which rely primarily on Roman political writers, especially Cicero and Seneca); see "Ambrogio Lorenzetti: The Artist as Political Philosopher."

whom do I speak? To this one [*colui*] and this one and this one [he is certainly pointing here]. To whom? To that one and that other one, so that you don't suck each other's blood. Don't go against the commandment; each one love his neighbor. And who is this neighbor? We are all neighbors each one to the other.[27]

Bernardino's best preaching is often a dialogue; here, he pleads with people one to one, trying to convince each soul to be responsible for itself. Collectively, they have the power to save Siena. It is perhaps natural that the process of conversion and salvation takes place within a dialogue, since Christianity, although a brotherhood, demands that individuals make their own choices. And Italian society, notwithstanding its dense community structures, can also be seen as a conversation where individual voices are never lost. In his preaching against discord, Bernardino will ask each voice to call out to its true fellows, whether Satan's partisans or the Christian fraternity.

II. The Chain Mail of Faction

After the buildup of the first nine days, with its dramatic shifts in tone and mostly veiled allusions to faction, Bernardino moves to a frontal assault, with a series of sermons which condemn the evil consequences of party strife. There will be little respite until the eighteenth day, when he tries to soothe his audience with a talk on love and forgiveness. In the intervening period he denounces faction on every level, targeting party members, sympathizers, and emblems, and predicting the city's dreadful dissolution. This week is his most concentrated attack on *parzialità*; he prefers a lighter touch in later sermons, especially those which culminate in the healing peacemaking ritual at the end of his visit. But first must come a painful cure.

27. Siena 1427, I, 272. "E però a tutti voi vi dico: non allargate le vostre mani a opera di sangue; non allargate, ma più tosto perdonate, perdonate! O, a chi dico io, perdonate? Io dico a te—A chi?—A te. A chi dico io? A colui e a colui e a colui—A chi?—A quello e quell'altro, e non voliate succhiare el sangue l'uno dell'altro. Non fate contra al comandamento, cioè ognuno ami el prossimo. E chi è il prossimo? Tutti siamo prossimi l'uno dell'altro."

Bernardino's own statement of his method up to the tenth sermon is that "until now in my preaching I have given you some syrups; now I will give you medicines." His words, he claims, can save the city: he reassures the Sienese by boasting of his success in Lombardy where he had been a *mezzano* between warring factions. Nothing he said there was suspect because each side liked him (*me n'ha voluto bene*), thanks to his sound religious doctrine. The results were so positive that "if I hadn't preached, woe to everyone" (*a chinchesia*).[28] Despite the fact that he plans to administer bad-tasting medicine, Bernardino is certain he can cure the disease now, in Siena.

One bitter ingredient is the threat of damnation. The preacher uses his dramatic sense to good effect as he pretends to search for a dead partisan:

> Oh, perhaps he has gone to Paradise? I'm looking, but I don't see him.
> Oh, perhaps he is in Purgatory? I'm looking, but I don't find him there.
> Oh, where can he be? He isn't in this world, he isn't in Paradise, he isn't in
> Purgatory. Oh, where could he be? Do you know where you can find
> him? He's in the house of the devils, in the inferno, and there he will rest
> eternally![29]

Anyone who is a "Guelph" or "Ghibelline"—notice how carefully he avoids labeling the *monti*—will end up in the *casa calda*. All sympathy for faction in thought, word, or deed carries the same penalty, since the preacher wants not just good behavior but a true conversion which will resonate through the soul. Bernardino's closing words tell of a dying man who had been a secret partisan in his heart.[30] His confessor never hears about this, but has a dream after the man's death: as the sinner stands before the judgment seat of God, a devil suddenly ap-

28. Ibid., I, 324–25.

29. Ibid., I, 347. "O forse che egli sarà andato in paradiso? Io miro, anco nol veggo. O forse egli è in purgatorio? Anco miro, e non ve' trovai. O dove sarà costui? Nel mondo non è, nel paradiso non è, nel purgatorio non è. O dove può essare costui? Sai dove il trovarai? Sarà a casa de' diavoli, in inferno, e con loro si riposarà eternamente!"

30. Ibid., I, 348. ". . . ma non ne parlò mai, né mai dè vigore a niuno, ma solo in sé aveva desiderio più dell'una parte che dell'altra."

pears at his side. He demands the man's soul and explains why it is rightfully his. God proclaims: "Render unto Caesar the things that are Caesar's!" and the unfortunate man is carried off to hell.

But Bernardino intends to catch more than just the active or even secret partisan. Throughout this sermon he casts a very wide net, trying to draw in all of his listeners, including those who only passively tolerate the sin or falsely claim to be partisans. Adherence to parties sends more than just the sword bearers to hell. Given that most of his listeners were probably women at this point in his visit, Bernardino needed to convince them that they, too, sinned through the spirit of faction. As always, he understood the social pressure that traps people in sin. Too often, bonds of kinship link them with a doomed relative; unless they renounce the sinner, they, too, will "rest with the devils eternally." Others become partisans through fear, still others for amusement. It is even a mortal sin to falsely declare oneself, given the weight of the spoken word in this culture. Everyone will accept what you have said, just as they believe a woman who stands up during the sermon and declares that tonight she will sleep with a handsome youth! People are far more inclined to believe evil than good, so the false partisan—like the joking woman—has sinned through the statement, even without the act. In the very public world of the fifteenth century, the private self must guard against open scandal, and avoid inciting others.

Naturally, Bernardino also reminds the audience of the connection between faction and gossip: hate slips into the ear with the sly words of the detractor. The preacher's task in Siena is to stop *parzialità* before the process even begins. He asks his listeners if they have ever seen a thorn grow in springtime:

> It is born with a tiny spine [*piccola piccola*] and little by little the spine
> grows and becomes hard. Go, put your foot on it when it is big and hard;
> you'll see how it feels![31]

31. Ibid., I, 328. The passage in its entirety is a good example of how easily Bernardino is diverted by his pleasure in words and images. Before comparing the

Now is the time to eradicate the thorn of *parzialità* before it grows large and tough. The implication is that Siena's problem is in the early stage of growth, still only a tangle of bad feelings and ugly words which, given the chance to flourish, must destroy the city. Bernardino's strategy during this week is to make his audience envision the inevitable future if the thorn of faction is allowed to grow. And hell is not the only threat. Partisans and their sympathizers will surely be damned in the afterlife, but worldly terrors also await them. In fact, these are emphasized to a far greater degree, probably because Bernardino realized what would have the greatest effect on his listeners. What happens in hell is left to their imaginations. Not so the material damage which faction brings. Siena, too, will burn.

A crescendo of brutal images depicts the divided city: the physical destruction of town and countryside; women mercilessly raped before fathers or husbands, killed in their own homes; the murders of their children; the flesh of enemies sold to butchers with the hearts eaten raw (*crudo crudo*). Significantly, the terrifying descriptions are aimed directly at female listeners.[32] Bernardino pauses for a moment to ask, "What do you think about this, women?" (*Che ve ne pare, donne?*). So terrible is partisan hatred that women themselves, who should be gentle by nature, turn vicious in their lust for revenge. The preacher claims that he has even heard of mothers who place a lance in the hands of their little boys, in order that they might carry out the vendetta. An-

---

thorny spine with partisan hatred, he affectionately describes the plant as it blossoms in springtime: "Vedesti mai mai di verno li scardiccioni? Sai, in sur un prato, quando tu guardi d'inverno, tutte l'erbe son secche e senza le foglie; vavi poi a primavera, e tu le vedrai tutte verdicanti; vedrai venirvi i fiori su, vedra' le tutte piacevoli, gittando suavi odori. E così crescono a poco a poco. E come è cresciuto lo scardiccione coll'altre erbe? Egli naque colla spina piccola piccola, e a poco a poco è cresciuta la spina e fatta dura. Quando ell'era giovanella, se tu v'avessi posto suso il piè, tu non ti saresti ponto. Va' ponvi su il piè quando ella è grande e dura; vedrai come tu la sentirai!"

32. Since this sermon was given on a Sunday (August 24), there was probably a large audience, including many men. But the preacher still aims his discourse at the women, probably because he felt that they would be the most receptive to this message.

other was so cruel that she chased a woman on horseback, then killed the victim herself.[33] These stories have added impact because, as Bernardino tells the Sienese, he witnessed factional horrors when he preached in Piacenza, Como, and Bergamo.[34]

Although partisans are predictably described as "rapacious wolves" and as the proud horses of the Apocalypse, ridden by devils, Bernardino uses an unusual metaphor for faction itself. Since he is trying to reach not only the partisans but their sympathizers, he imagines the sin as a cuirass (*panziera*) of hatred, a shirt of chain mail with one link connecting each person to the next. Bernardino, the warrior-preacher, has come to remove it from Siena with a "military" strategy of his own:

> I want to use snares, bombardments, crossbow, lances, and whatever I can so that it is ruined.[35]

This is his most aggressive statement on the power of speech; in the following weeks, his words will become offensive weapons that will blast apart the links which chain partisans together. Bernardino here boldly challenges kinship and clientage, the foremost bonds of Italian life. For the strength of faction is in the way it joins one person to another, in linked social relationships which forge the *panziera*. Earlier in the sermon he had warned his listeners—whether the wife of a partisan husband or the son of a partisan father—that if "you hold with him [*tieni co lui*], you are damned, if you die in that state."[36] Two days later, when he develops the theme further, he sarcastically notes that if

33. Siena 1427, I, 335–56.

34. Ibid., I, 337. "Sì, o patria preziosa, e bella Lombardia, come stai tu per questi parti! Va' prima a Piagenzia, che per queste parti era stata da due mesi che in tutto v'era due preti e tre frati in tutta la città, e non più. A Como, per le parti guasta: quello in tutto non essarvi il quarto delle case dritte: a Bergamo, peggio che peggio. E dicovi che così viddi il suo sterminio come io so' ritto qui, e come io tocco questo luogo."

35. Ibid., I, 343. ". . . e voglio adoperarci trabocchi, bombarde, balestra e lance e ciò ch'io potrò , perch'ella si guasti."

36. Ibid., I, 326.

"Guelphs" or "Ghibellines" want to separate from each other in hell, it will no longer be possible.[37] In other words, in order to save both city and soul, the individual must break away from the tightly linked chain mail, resist the pull of social obligations whenever these violate *carità*. Bernardino, so reticent about attacking political institutions, daringly tries to reconfigure basic elements of social identity, telling listeners that they are first Christians and citizens, rather than members of a faction or a vengeful house defending its honor.

The basic themes introduced in the first faction sermon—the links between partisans and the city's imminent ruin—are developed at length for the rest of the week. Although the general tone of the sermons is harsh, there are subtle variations which demonstrate that the preacher had more than one weapon with which to attack his audience. On Monday, August 25, his speech is basically an appeal to reason, as he tries to make his listeners understand their danger. He begins the sermon with an appeal to the collective: "O Siena," he pleads, "open your eyes."[38] The sermon is interrupted by rain, but Bernardino has time to reaffirm his prediction that a terrible future awaits the city. Peace has made the Sienese careless: "When a people has peace, it's worse than if they had war."[39] By basking in their careless peace, they have ignored God's impatience. The preacher explains that God carries out His vendetta against the ungrateful by sending pestilence and war. Ironically, He does this because He is merciful as well as just; punishment is in fact an instrument of conversion because it makes people understand their sins and repent. Most convincing is a passage near the end of the sermon, when Bernardino presents a list of hypothetical questions. For example: "When someone blasphemes and isn't punished, don't you believe that God wants to punish him? When someone is angry [*si fura*] and isn't punished, do you believe that God won't punish him?"[40] By stressing God's vendetta here and elsewhere in the

37. Ibid., I, 383.
39. Ibid., I, 358.

38. Ibid., I, 350.
40. Ibid., I, 360.

sermons, the preacher was probably able to reach his listeners most effectively. The argument would have made good sense to them, given the widespread belief in "just" revenge. It was natural that God Himself would retaliate when wronged.

Tuesday's talk is more turbulent in mood, dominated by the fiery image of the Four Horsemen of the Apocalypse. The red horse, for example, is the executor of God's justice (*manigoldo*), who brings the locust-mercenaries with him. These have visited Siena before, and Bernardino surely meant to arouse unpleasant memories in his older listeners, who would have remembered the armies which routinely devastated the *contado*, especially during the late fourteenth century when they became one of the major factors in the decline of the state.[41] "Do you know who the locusts are?" he reminds them. "They are the ravaging soldiers [*soldati guastatori*] of everything green; that is, of houses, vineyards, grain, beasts, men, women, children, old, and young: they ravage everything."[42] The preacher's despair for Siena's fate at one point causes him to generalize about the entire peninsula, which is filled with soldiers and riddled by the treachery of her inhabitants. A Frenchman or other foreigner always fears that an Italian will betray him! Bernardino predicts that terrible things will soon befall the Italians whose strong fortifications will not be enough to prevent disaster.[43]

Just as the preacher moves between reason and emotion, so does his tone alternate between despair and hope. The most important message of the faction sermons is that Siena is *still* at peace, even if on the verge of destruction. No matter how imminent the prospect of God's

41. See William Caferro, *Mercenary Companies and the Decline of Siena* (Baltimore and London: Johns Hopkins University Press, 1998). Damage to towns, villages, and farms subject to Siena, along with the cost of fighting or buying off the mercenaries, contributed to a fiscal crisis which accelerated the city's decline from its heyday early in the regime of the Nine. Caferro charts the disastrous correlation of mercenary raids with the imposition of loans, 113–16.

42. Siena 1427, I, 374.

43. Ibid., I, 373.

vengeance, the Sienese, with Bernardino's help, can deflect disaster. During the first few minutes of sermon 12, in a reprimand of those who failed to come because they stayed in bed, he insists that this talk will be so useful that it could save the city. "You won't always have someone who sings as clearly as I sing," he warns them.[44] Ironically, this boast about his forthright preaching is preceded by a homely metaphor which both explains and evades. Bernardino does not want Siena to become like a pot with a flame beneath it:

> You know, when there is noise and everything boils! Doh! I want to be understood without chattering. You can perhaps understand me; so that such a thing is understood, which one cannot say.[45]

What is it that Bernardino "cannot say"? One suspects that this is a broad hint about Siena's internal dissension and rumor mongering, which made her a pot about to boil, but the evasive phrasing makes it difficult to decipher. The preacher was clearly placed in a paradoxical situation: invited to Siena to calm factional unrest, he chose not to make specific accusations which could anger those involved. In one sense, he was "singing clearly," while in another he was curbing his tongue. Admittedly, this is more of a problem for the historian than for Bernardino's listeners. The opaque language severely limits our understanding of what was going on, but those who were gathered in the piazza certainly knew the unmentionable details. And Bernardino's message might have been all the stronger because it was so vague. By not targeting specific groups or incidents, the preacher could make all the Sienese, including his faithful female listeners, collectively responsible for the city's fate.

In fact, it is on this day that Bernardino begins to encourage concrete action on the part of both men and women. In the middle of his

44. Ibid., I, 370.

45. Ibid., I, 369. "Sai, quando si leva il romore, che ogni cosa bolle! Doh! Io vorrei essare inteso senza favellare; tu forse mi puoi intendare; che tal cosa s'intende, che non si può dire."

talk, he informs his listeners that there would be no general sermon on Thursday, August 28, since he will speak inside the government palace; he has heard that some people "want to live well" and so he will address those who are in Siena's *reggimento*.[46] The preacher, however, did not forget the women in his audience. Later, near the end of the sermon, he explains that there are two kinds of peace, one within and the other without. The first peace comes from God, and the second from the world, and he warns his listeners to beware if they cannot find true, inner peace.[47] Clearly, whatever external peacemaking would result from his preaching was secondary to the spiritual peace of God. Bernardino will develop this idea of inner peace in great depth when he preaches his climactic peacemaking sermon a month later. For now, however, he is content to put the *pace di fuore* into motion. He pleads with his female listeners to do their part: "Do what you can with your husbands and sons so that there is peace."[48] The preacher wanted women, who formed the majority of his audience, even for these faction sermons, to exert pressure on their husbands before the restricted (and all-male) talk in the Palazzo, perhaps by repeating his words at home. Apparently he felt that Sienese women, the "silent partners" in factional conflict, should be deeply involved in civic peacemaking, even if they could not legislate change themselves.

In the last few minutes of his speech, the singer-doctor wonders if the audience has truly absorbed his message:

> You have the example of what will happen if you don't search for peace, *popolo sanese*. I see this entire city heading towards extermination. Have you understood what my words were saying this morning? Have you heard and understood?[49]

46. Ibid., I, 378.

47. Ibid., I, 383–84.

48. Ibid., I, 384. "Fate che voi operiate per modo co' vostri mariti e co' vostri figliuoli, che elli ci sia pace: e ingegnatevene quanto v'è possibile."

49. Ibid., I, 387. "Tu hai l'esempio di quello che t'averrà se tu non cerchi pace, popol sanese. Io veggo tutta questa città venire a sterminio. Avete voi inteso quello che vengono a dire queste parole ch'io v'ho detto stamane? Avetelo inteso e udito?"

On the next day, in sermon 13, Bernardino retreats from direct talk of faction, concentrating instead on heavenly judgment and the disasters awaiting Siena. The most striking image in this sermon is the description of God making ready His terrible scythe. The preacher has his audience imagine how God, looking up from the task, decides where He will wreak His vengeance. Everywhere He looks there has been destruction except at Siena, fortunate among cities. But now He "sharpens, sharpens, sharpens" the scythe.[50]

The depiction of an unscathed but soon-to-be-punished Siena gives Bernardino the chance to return to his "inconstancy of the world" theme, which had been briefly introduced during the first week of his visit. In one of his best exempla, he tells about a fox who sees a hen inside a well. Unaware that it is a booby trap set up by villagers, the fox greedily tries to snatch the hen but instead falls into the water, where he saves himself by jumping into a pail. Along comes a wolf who peers inside the well and sees the trapped fox. The cunning fox tells the wolf that there is a hen inside the well, whereupon the wolf jumps into the other pail. This sinks immediately to the bottom, enabling the lighter fox to rise to the top and escape. The wolf in dismay questions the fox about this unhappy turn of events, and the wise animal responds: "Oh, this world is made like steps: one person rises and another goes down."[51] Since the she-wolf was the symbol of Siena, the audience would have immediately understood that the wolf's fate would be their city's, if it failed to repent.

But the most important point here, as always, is that repentance is still possible. Bernardino returns to the image of the fearsome scythe, this time with an avenging angel sharpening the instrument. The angel pauses to lean on the scythe, wondering where he will mow the wheat next. This pause, short as it is, gives the Sienese the time they need. The choice is theirs: God has two granaries, and will store His cut

50. Ibid., I, 398.

51. Ibid., I, 400–401. To emphasize the point, Bernardino immediately follows up the tale with a description of the Wheel of Fortune.

"wheat" in either heaven or hell.[52] The preacher sarcastically tells his listeners that if they want to exterminate Siena, they can continue in their pride and hatred. The double message in sermon 13 sums up one of Bernardino's most persuasive tactics, here and elsewhere in his preaching: punishment now and in the hereafter can always be warded off, even at the last moment, once people decide to repent and convert. Even in the darkest moments of the faction sermons, he provides a lingering hope that people can change.

This tactic resulted in immediate, and gratifying, action on the part of the citizens. We do not have a record of the following day's speech, delivered in the Sala del Consiglio of the communal palace, but its aftermath was a resolution by the government to achieve "pacem et unionem."[53] This may have been more than even the preacher hoped, as he tells his regular audience the morning after his sermon in the Palazzo:

> Doh! I very often find myself deceived by messer Domeneddio [i.e., God] since sometimes, when I am expecting a good thing, he gives a huge harvest of goods. I say this because of what I saw of you through the sermon I gave yesterday.[54]

But Bernardino, despite his pleasure, knew that an official declaration was just the beginning of any real peacemaking. Later in the sermon he notes that yesterday "we made peace in part; thus, with the help of God we'll do the rest, so that nothing remains to be done."[55] Surpris-

52. Ibid., I, 404.

53. Martino Bertagna notes the government's declaration of August 28 in "Vita e Apostolato senese di San Bernardino," *Studi Francescani* 60 (1963): 60–65. It is, however, highly unlikely that city officials were suddenly "inspired" by Bernardino's sermon: since he had been invited to preach against faction (and members of the *reggimento* seem to have attended the general sermons), everything must have been anticipated, if not arranged in detail, before the sermon in the Palazzo.

54. Siena 1427, I, 415. "Doh! io mi truovo spesso spesso ingannato da misser Domenedio, che talvolta, quando io aspetto un bene, e egli mi riesce cor una grandissima brigata di beni. Questo dico per quello ch'io ho veduto di voi per la predica ch'io feci ieri."

55. Ibid., I, 431.

ingly, he does not attempt to arrange a formal peacemaking at this point, as a lesser preacher might. Only two weeks into an extended visit, he seems to feel that his audience is still very far from a true conversion. What Bernardino wants is a deep movement of the soul, a thorough and long-lasting change of heart, rather than an extravagant and short-lived repentance. His task in sermon 14 is not to push his listeners into more action, but to slow them down by tempering their eager enthusiasm. It is a thoughtful and self-disciplined move, one that shows how the preacher could curb his own exultant showmanship when necessary.

His greatest fear, on this successful morning, is that his listeners' desire for change will evaporate into nothing. Pleased as he is with the official response to his preaching, Bernardino uses sermon 14 as a way of calming his listeners and explaining the nature of real change. He prefers the slow route to virtue and has more faith in one who "goes little by little, step by step, from good to better, than in one who jumps suddenly into each big deed."[56] True repentance is persistent, and the preacher compares this steady process to a sword maker who diligently polishes his sword, or a goldsmith who shines his wares.[57] Moving too fast, on the other hand, is counterproductive: a fast horse wears itself out too quickly, while someone who has sinned before is apt to do it again, just as a piece of wood which had once been lit is more likely to burn.[58] The Sienese are reprimanded for the deteriora-

---

56. Ibid., I, 416. "E però dico, che uno che subito comincia cor uno fervore grandissimo a far bene, e mettesi a ogni gran fatto per amor di Cristo; e un altra comincia a fare bene, a poco a poco va crescendo di bene in meglio; io ho più fede in costui che va a poco a poco, a passo a passo di bene in meglio, che in colui che subito saltò in ogni gran fatto."

57. Ibid., I, 432. The metaphor is sealed with a local Sienese reference: "Sapete quando voi passate dalli Spadai, e volete collassù da' Tolomei, coloro che bruniscono l'arme, che hanno un legno e anco hanno una spada, e con essi un poca da polvere, e posta in su l'arme rugginosa, e dalle, dalle, dalle e brunisce, e tanto fa così che la fa bella e pulita e chiara come una bambola."

58. Ibid., I, 417 for the metaphor of the horse, and I, 423 for the inflammable wood.

tion in morals which has occurred since Bernardino's last visit, in the spring of 1425, when they had seemed so responsive to his teaching (and perhaps had "jumped" too quickly towards repentance).[59]

He speaks like a disapproving parent throughout much of the sermon. Bernardino worries that, in other places where he preaches, people might ask why the Sienese, who supposedly love him, refuse to follow his teaching.[60] The Perugians, by contrast, win favor as truly obedient children and he praises them in order to shame his flighty Sienese: "There is as much difference between you and the Perugians as there is between the sky and the earth." He enumerates Perugia's achievements in 1425, which included a great bonfire of vanities and the end of their traditional battle games, dancing in churches, and well-known blasphemy.[61] But, as always in Bernardino's preaching, there is a remedy for obstinate sinners, even the Sienese. Change is possible when you admit your weakness. When a child falls into the mud, he screams, "Mamma, mamma, help me!" And so should a sinner in trouble call out for the Virgin's help.[62]

59. A bit later in the sermon, for example, Bernardino sarcastically notes that he thought the Sienese women had repented (he was probably remembering the bonfire of vanities held two years ago), but he was mistaken: "... io mi credetti che voi perseveraste meglio che donne del mondo, ch'elli vi era una vanità quando io venni l'altra volta, ora ce ne so' sette"; Ibid., I, 420.

60. Ibid., I, 432–33: "Doh! fratelli e padri e figliuoli miei, se voi farete peggio che gli altri popoli, dove io ho predicato o dove io predicarò, elli mi potrebbe essere detto: 'Oh, i tuoi Sanesi, i quali ti portavano tanto amore, come non fanno quello di che tu gli hai amaestrati? Come non s'astengono di tanti vizi, quanto tu lo' predicasti?'"

61. For the 1425 statute forbidding stone-throwing battles (*"prelium lapidum"*), see Fantozzi, *Documenta Perusina*, 125–26. The Perugians were notorious not only for violence, but for blasphemy. According to Bernardino, "El bastemmiare Idio tanto bruttamente e i santi, anco l'hanno levato via, e sapete che quella città di questo era più infetta che niun'altra; e come era più brutta, così è ora più netta, con perseveranzia, però che hanno poste gravissime pene"; Siena 1427, I, 429–30.

62. Siena 1427, I, 434. A few moments later, Bernardino mimes God's warning gesture: "elli zucchea così col capo." Like a mother to her child, God indicates His displeasure when someone fails to act properly by shaking His head and threatening to get up: "... che elli li dice: 's'io mi ci levo ... oh, s'io mi ci levo ...!' e minaccia il figliuolo, e capea, sai"; Ibid., I, 436.

The problem is that God grows tired of waiting for people to change. By the end of the sermon, Bernardino is threatening his listeners once again with an image of an impatient and punishing deity. He compares radiant Siena to a candlestick, whose candle is good government. But he asks the Sienese:

> Do you know when God gives the candlestick a jolt? Do you know when? When divisions among citizens, and battles, and other things enter the city.[63]

The city's fate is the choice of her people:

> Whoever wants justice will have it; whoever wants mercy will have it; whoever wants peace will have it; but if you fall to the earth, you'll be a long time getting up again.[64]

God will till the soil with plague, "so that you'll die like dogs," and He will send famine and war.[65]

Pride and anger are causes of social division and so the next morning, the preacher counsels forbearance in the face of insults. If people say or do something to offend you, they may have a legitimate reason (i.e., if they are motivated by *zelo*, righteous anger, rather than *ira*, a sinful rage) and God may want to punish you, so bear it calmly. However, this advice results in one of Bernardino's least persuasive moments during the entire visit. He tells his audience that once, in Perugia, one man hit another in the piazza for uttering a blasphemy. As soon as he had received the blow, the blasphemer recognized his own sin and requested that the man strike him on the other cheek, too. And when the father of the blasphemer ran to the piazza and heard the story, he requested that his son be struck yet another time for his sin![66] The

---

63. Ibid., I, 438. "Sai quando Idio dà al candeliere lo scrullo? Sai quando? Quando elli viene nella città fra i cittadini divisioni e battaglie o altro."

64. Ibid., I, 438. "Chi vorrà giustizia, l'arà; chi vorrà misericordia, l'arà; chi vorrà pace, l'arà; ma se tu caschi in terra, tardi ti rilevarai."

65. Ibid., I, 440.

66. Ibid., I, 451.

recorded sermon does not indicate an audience response, but it must have been difficult for the Sienese to imagine this incident in their own piazza, with an adult male passively submitting to a public insult. This particular narrative seems profoundly unconvincing in the context of urban life. Bernardino, usually alert to the nuances of *buona fama*, adheres to a highly idealistic view of Christian restraint, one which few fathers and sons could have followed with dignity.

Much more effective than this pious advice is the imagery with which Bernardino closes the sermon. In a vivid description of Siena and other Italian towns as vessels upon the sea, he reminds his audience that the fleet will be safe as long as it remains united. He asks his listeners if they have ever seen the harbor at Venice, and goes on to describe that splendid scene, with its multitude of ships of all kinds.[67] Again, there is no recorded reaction to this passage, but it was undoubtedly more pleasing to his audience than the well-worn Christian maxims in the rest of the talk. Bernardino always tried to balance the two strategies, but his greatest skill was evoking visual images through narrative and metaphor. The memories which probably lingered after his preaching were striking and simple pictures, like the angry angel sharpening his scythe or the locust-mercenaries closing in on the city.

So important was the power of the visual that Bernardino scheduled a sermon exclusively on party symbols on a Sunday (August 21), when he would have expected a substantial audience. Although he uses the Guelph lily and Ghibelline eagle as his paradigm, he notes at the beginning of the sermon that he is not speaking "only of the Guelph and Ghibelline parties,"[68] and so his listeners are implicitly invited to

67. Ibid., I, 459. "Fusti tu mai a Vinegia? Se tu vi se' stato, tu sai che in mare vi so' di molte ragioni navi: quale grande, quale piccola, quale mezzana. Elli vi so' in mare galee, elli vi so' galeazze; elli vi so' cocche, sovi barche, sovi barchette, sovi gondole, sovi scafe, quale ha trecento banchi, quale trecentocinquanta. Sovi de' brigantini di vinti o di vintidue banchi; sovi navicelle piccole; èvi di quelle che vanno in qua, quale in là; chi ha uno essercizio, chi n'ha un altro; chi remica, chi aconcia canape, chi vela, chi fa questo e chi quello, né mai non hanno posa."

68. Ibid., I, 464.

substitute Siena's own factions for these labels (he is careful to point out, however, that he is not condemning other signs such as family coats of arms, or those which represent the city and the *popolo*).[69] His concern is the malevolent party signs which use images to focus misplaced loyalty. Satan and his horde, once worshipped in the guise of pagan statues, were defeated by the coming of Christ. But the demons cleverly devised to maintain their status as idols. Now embodied in the animal imagery of party emblems, they are the objects of a secret religion. Drawing upon his personal experience, as he does throughout the sermons on faction, the preacher remembers that when he saw those emblems in other cities, he'd say to himself: "Oh, there is a great devil!"[70]

A Christian's duty is to love God and neighbor, but a partisan's soul is given to these infernal symbols. Bernardino emphasizes the irrationality of partisan devil worshippers. Their already tenacious honor code is transferred from persons to objects. These provoke a fierce loyalty: if an emblem is thrown into filth or cut with a sword, a partisan is willing to die for the supposed slight, "for the honor of that sign; so dear does he hold its honor! And you don't care anything about God, and would not undergo one slap [*sosterresti un buffetto*] for him!"[71] The proud fanatics who adore the signs will murder those who defile them, and even cut to pieces someone who refuses to join their party. The Christian response is to preserve true faith by retorting, "I'd rather be an ass." And the preacher assures his audience that someone who is killed because of a "Viva Idio!" is a martyr for God. Like the tale of the patient Perugian who begged to be slapped, this impractical advice must have left some skeptical listeners shaking their heads in disbelief.

The mere sight of party emblems triggers a response, and Bernardino, great lover of words, admits that the visual is a stronger sense than the aural. He employs an attention-getting image of his own in order to reinforce the point. If a woman suddenly stood up during the sermon and took her clothes off, wouldn't the mere sight of her bring temptation, especially if she were beautiful? And so it is with insignia, the implication being that banners, too, are beautiful and arousing sights. Bernardino is especially scandalized by their flagrant display in churches, where the connection between emblem and idolatry is most obvious.[72] Whenever he sees a crucifix with a party sign above it, he thinks to himself: "O Lord God, you have the devil above you, so that one could say he is pissing on Your head!"[73] This earthy comment apparently made an impression on his listeners, since the preacher's next recorded words are "Enough, enough!" as he tried to hush a laughing audience.

But the ultimate fate of partisans, the descendants who follow them, and the artisans who paint emblems is no laughing matter. Bernardino tells his audience that he wants to say a prayer for the souls of his own dead relatives. That prayer is a peculiar one indeed. He prays that, if his father or mother or other relatives died with the sin of *parzialità* on their souls, any prayer or mass he has ever said for them will be worthless. If they died as unconfessed partisans, he hopes that a "thousand devils will have their souls and that there will never be redemption for them."[74] This bitter "prayer" both emphasizes his complete independence from the city's factions, despite his birthright as a Sienese aristocrat, and encourages his listeners to do the same by renouncing their own partisan relatives in death, as well as in life. He then ends his "prayer" with his one open reference to the *monti*:

72. One can only imagine Bernardino's reaction if he could see the decoration of neighborhood chapels during Palio season, when the spirit of faction still lives in twentieth-century Siena. The chapels are hung with the colorful flags of *contrade*, and on the day of the race, the holy space itself is desecrated by the horse, a symbol of faction to both Bernardino and the modern Sienese. Blessed by a "partisan" *contrada* priest, the animal is supposed to defecate for good luck in the race. Ironically, ritualized faction is a way of preserving Siena's traditional identity in the modern world.

73. Siena 1427, I, 475.

74. Ibid., I, 478.

. . . And this prayer has been made for their souls. What parties, what Guelphs, what crazy men are these? O, O, O, do you know what Monte it is? A *monte dei pazzi* [i.e., a heap of fools]. I won't say anything else.[75]

Bernardino preferred not to say anything more specific, here or anywhere else, but he did feel free to criticize the government in general terms. In sermon 17 he continues to attack faction as he discusses the role of officials in the exercise of *buon governo*. This sermon is appropriate for the circumstances, he says, because the new Signori had just begun their term of office (and were apparently present at the sermon).[76] He encourages them to take an active hand in suppressing discord: whenever they hear of some hatred, they should try to make peace (Bernardino declines to say whether the means will be persuasion or force).[77] His most practical counsel, though, is aimed at the audience as a whole. Slander, once again, is targeted as the root of faction, and he warns his fellow citizens to end their litany of recriminations and stop believing "every word that is spoken." He mimics the conversations circulating in the city: "He did or said this to me; he slandered me; he said I did such and such!" Cut off all these useless words, Bernardino says, and forget the past when you forgive.[78]

Apparently words were also circulating about the curfew law, and Bernardino was assailed by complaints:

> I've heard so much from people who want to say what's happening, that my ears have rotted from so much listening, and I would have preferred not to hear so much.[79]

75. Ibid., I, 478. "E questa orazione è fatta per l'anime loro. Che parti, che guelfi, che pazzie so' queste? Oooh! Monte sai ch'è? Uno monte di pazzi. Non ti dico altro."

76. Ibid., I, 482.

77. Ibid., I, 486. ". . . che ladove tu truovi alcuna inimicizia o odio o rancore, sempre t'ingegna di spegnarle e di mettarvi ogni pace, ogni concordia che tu puoi. Così dico de' Signori i quali so' il capo di tutta la città: che se vogliono avere o usare di quello di Dio, che sapendo una inimicizia, subito mandare per loro, e a giusta loro possa far lo' far pace."

78. Ibid., I, 487.

79. Ibid., I, 497. The complete passage is as follows: "Ora a casa, per non pagare

It is not clear whether the Sienese were angry about the law itself, or its indecorous results as people went in and out of each other's homes at night, since they were afraid to stay in the streets. The preacher's response to all these complaints is a general exhortation: "Castigate, castigate the bad person, and aid the good." By punishing evildoers, you will discourage others, just as every dog flees if you break just one dog's leg. True to the spirit of this sermon and to his overall approach to political topics, Bernardino's reference to the curfew is quickly turned into a wider and safer moralizing.

He prefers to linger on stories rather than on practical political counsel. In sermon 17 he tells two of his best exempla, which permit him to be more scathing than in his direct advice. The first is a clear favorite of Bernardino's ("Oh, how much salt [i.e., "flavor," "bite"] there is in this story!"). The lion, king of beasts, was sitting in judgment over his subjects. When the wolf and the fox, great scoundrels and oppressors of the weak, come before him, the unjust ruler lets them off with praise. But when the gentle ass and sheep are brought in for judgment, the lion has them beaten. If the officials in the audience missed the point, Bernardino made sure to state the moral outright: "O, you who rule, don't beat the ass and the sheep for a small thing, and don't commend the wolf and the fox for a great fault." In other words, don't abuse power by failing to protect weak subjects, while showing favoritism to the mighty. The preacher acidly notes that "if the sheep or the goat—that is, the widow or orphan or poor person— says or does something minor, it's 'kill, kill!'"[80] Later in the sermon, Bernardino uses another pointed exemplum, this time based on Sienese history. Pier Pettinaio, one of the city's Franciscan holy men (d. 1289), was on his way to Pisa when there was a revolt in Siena. Be-

---

cinque soldi, ché non gli ho da pagare. Dico che in luogo so' stato, che chi v'andava, stava di fuore a parlare con loro; poi per li ordini, come so' gionti, subito entrano dentro. Io ho tanto udito da chi m'ha voluto dire di quello che si fa, ch'io ho sì fracide l'orecchie del tanto udire, ch'io non vorrei avere udito tanto."

80. Ibid., I, 489–92.

lieving Pier to be a prophet, fleeing exiles asked him when they would return to their homes (at this point, Bernardino briefly interrupts the tale with a directive to the recorder: "Doh! Listen to the good word, o writer; put it down"). Pier's wise answer to the exiles is that they will return when their sins are purged and those of the other party have multiplied . . . but they will be thrown out again when the cycle repeats itself.[81] The story of Pier Pettinaio and the partisans encapsulates the tragic politics of Italy, with its cycle of violence and each faction's dizzying ride on the Wheel of Fortune. Bernardino asks his listeners: have they "understood?" They must rule their city with justice and punish those who do wrong.

The general moralizing of the justice sermon culminates in the next day's speech on unity and forgiveness. It serves as a kind of pre-peacemaking before the formal one, which will not take place for several weeks. The eight talks which led up to sermon 18 covered *parzialità* and its moral and material damage, the dangers of delaying repentance, party emblems, the necessity of justice. Now Bernardino continues to widen his discussion by treating civil discord as just one part of a larger problem. Near the beginning of the sermon he announces that the next few days will show how people ought to love each other as husbands, wives, and friends, as well as fellow citizens. His emphasis, surprising after the preceding week's buildup, is not narrowly aimed at pacifying faction, but in providing a much broader definition of Christian love. Despite his earlier statement that a patient needed to take specific medicine for a specific ailment, Bernardino's preaching on *carità* was meant to heal various social ills, from family disputes to political disharmony. He firmly believed that most social sins were connected: women's vanity was a catalyst for sodomy, for example, and slander led directly to faction. Conversely, healing one ailment soothed another. In sermon 18, he implies that the ideal city is rooted in a peaceful household, the smaller unit a microcosm of the larger one:

81. Ibid., I, 494–95.

God has everyone of one custom and one will live without contradiction
in the same house; that is, fathers with wives and sons and brothers, all
orderly in wanting to live well and in peace and concord. One can also
understand the same thing of a city, of all the citizens that live there,
great and small, rich and poor, desirous to live well. Oh, one can say how
blessed is that house and that city, arranged so well to the glory of God![82]

The preacher then urges the Sienese to throw off any discord which
arises between them. His portrayal of sin as contagion, of *parzialità* as
chain mail composed of many links, and of *carità* as both civic and
spiritual peace show his need to define all human interaction as part of
a tightly bound whole. Division of any kind was profoundly distaste-
ful to him. There is always the anxious sense in Bernardino's preaching
that division in one sphere leads to discord in another, just as the ill-
spoken word inexorably provokes citywide conflict.

Once again, he tries to make people understand that discord is
senseless and unnatural. The four elements have contrary properties,
for example, but God has ordered them to work together in order to
make the earth fruitful. The human being is also composed of different elements, including nerves, flesh, bone, and blood, but there is
concord between them. And animals understand their natural fellowship: unlike human beings, birds, cattle, and pigs become upset when
one of their kind is endangered. Haven't the butchers in the audience
noticed a cow's tears of compassion when watching another get
slaughtered? The preacher begs his listeners to pardon one another:
everyone is a sinner and God, too, will pardon, if they do.[83] Bernardino's plea for compassion gives him a chance to speak up for society's
unprotected widows, orphans, and prisoners. He wants the Sienese to
feel guilty, and uses his familiar tactic of comparing them to others:

82. Ibid., I, 510. " 'Idio il quale fa abitare in una casa tutti coloro che vi sono in uno
costumo, in un volere, senza niuna contradizione,' cioè padre con donna e con figliuoli
e con fratelli, tutti ordinati in volere bene vivare e in pace e in concordia. Anco si può
similmente intendare d'una città, tutti i cittadini che v'habitano, grandi e piccoli, ric-
chi e povari, tutti volontarii a ben vivare. Oh, quanto si può dire beata quella casa e
quella città, così bene ordinata a gloria di Dio!"

83. Ibid., I, 512.

I don't know what you do here, you [the second "you" is contemptuous].
I know well what they do in Rome: they gathered so much money that
about thirty prisons were emptied. Oh! what a pious thing! Alas, what
I've heard of you![84]

Charity, like a harmonious household, is a sign of fellowship to Bernardino, another part of the ideal and undivided city.

Thus, after a week of virulent preaching against faction, Bernardino gentles his tone and tries to relate civic harmony to other elements
of social life. He realized that hammering the audience on one point
could only yield diminishing returns. In the next four sermons (September 3 to 6), he completely abandons all talk of factionalism and
switches to a discussion of good marital relations and widowhood.
These sermons, like many others in the course, show that Benardino
felt overall moral reform was indispensable to peace, its bedrock foundation. And the domestic subject matter—placed between the concord talk and a final faction sermon—may have been a subtle way of
telling his female listeners that their private concerns were part of the
civic world.

But the breathing space provided by sermons 17 to 22 is suddenly
interrupted by one last, powerful talk directly aimed at factionalism. A
summary of the major points discussed two weeks before, it was delivered on a Sunday (September 7), which ensured that anyone who
missed an earlier sermon on the topic had another chance to hear, particularly some of the men who may have avoided the weekday preaching. Bernardino's argument is by now familiar to his listeners: *parzialità*
is a kind of devil worship, and baptized Christians who worship insignia have renounced their faith; rabid dogs and lepers, partisans in-
fect everyone else with their sin; slander and suspicion are key elements in the spread of discord. The preacher is hopeful that this sermon will have a positive effect, telling his audience, "If you stay to

84. Ibid., I, 515. "Io non so come voi vi fate, voi: io so bene come si fece a Roma,
che furono racolti tanti denari, che ne furono tratti da trenta prigioni o circa. Oh,
quanto fu piatosa cosa! Oimè, che ho io udito di voi!"

hear me, I believe that these parties of yours will begin to stink" (*vi verrà puzza delle vostre parti*).[85]

Ridicule, rather than threat, is Bernardino's most potent weapon, as he stresses the irrationality of partisan loyalties. Factionalism is an incredibly stupid sin, since it provides neither utility nor pleasure, unlike the sins of theft, lust, or gluttony.[86] Each party has its peculiar customs, and even slicing garlic or fruit in the wrong way can be dangerous for someone on the other side.[87] Frenzied partisans are worse than wolves or dogs, sometimes killing their own family members (animals, on the other hand, do not devour their own kind).[88] And their behavior is idiotic: a partisan is like a fool with a club who tries to fight his shadow and then breaks his own head in the scuffle! At this point in the sermon, the preacher becomes so upset that he stumbles over his words:

> Great big fool, that he breaks his head for such craziness, and also everyone else's! For certain, if I were emperor . . . Doh! I know well . . . but I lack the rod. Oh! I'd make them go without eating! Oh! I'd make them get rid of this sin . . .[89]

This is one of the few places where Bernardino admits frustration with his own political limits. He realized that sometimes even the greatest preaching had little effect. A few minutes before the shadow simile, he told his audience about one especially dismal failure. In another place where he preached peace, a partisan father and son approached him, "trembling," after the sermon. Yet despite their fear and Bernardino's efforts both during the sermon and in private, he could not get these basically good men to believe that their devil-worship-

---

85. Ibid., I, 655.

86. Ibid., I, 659.

87. Ibid., I, 659 and 675–76.

88. Ibid., I, 660.

89. Ibid., I, 661. "Pazzarone, che per tal pazzia egli rompe il capo a sé e anco a tutti i suoi! Che per certo se io fussi imperadore . . . Doh! Io so' bene . . . ma elli mi manca la bacchetta. Oh! Io li farei da questo peccato levare . . ."

ping attitude was truly a sin. The man was dead now, Bernardino warned the Sienese, and "I believe that he has gone to the devil's house."[90]

The problem, as always, was the cuirass of hatred, linking partisans with their kin. One man alone does not join a party

> but also the sons which he has, also the sons of sons, so that those [party] insignia are always maintained. O father, where are you going?—To the house of the devil?—And you, his son, where are you going?—Also to the house of the devil.[91]

The links are strong indeed . . . strong enough to drag an entire family off to hell, with the chain of faction snaking throughout successive generations. In a fervent appeal to both logic and sentiment, Bernardino describes the unhappy plight of an infant who is born to a partisan family. Immediately, everyone on the other side hates the innocent child:

> Oh! Oh! What iniquity this is, that a tiny babe [*uno fanciullino così piccolino*] should bring with it such hatred![92]

There can only be one solution for a person whose kinsmen belong to a party. The individual must resolutely choose not to follow his family to hell. In sermon 10, the preacher had warned wives and sons not to hold with partisan husbands and fathers. Both wifely and filial obedience is dissolved under these circumstances since a true Christian must not support a partisan with acts or words or hearts. Now, two weeks later, Bernardino pushes his point even further, by proposing that good people ostracize partisan relatives both in life and after death. Wives must not have Masses said for unrepentant husbands,

---

90. Ibid., I, 658.

91. Ibid., I, 659. ". . . ma anco de' figliuoli ch'egli ha, e anco e figliuoli de' figliuoli; acciò che per quelle insegne sieno sempre mantenuti. O padre, ove vai?—Pure a casa del diavolo.—E tu, suo figliuolo, ove vai? Pure a casa del diavolo."

92. Ibid., I, 662. "Oh! oh! Che iniquità è quella, che a un fanciullino così piccolino gli sia portato tanto odio!"

while priests mortally sin whenever they absolve a partisan, pray for his soul, or bury him in hallowed ground. Unconfessed partisans should be buried in ditches, "along with asses."

Bernardino is deliberately trying to break through society's tightest bonds, including the loyalty families owe to a *paterfamilias*, or the subservience local priests are accustomed to show their patrons. Needless to say, it is difficult to imagine a priest risking his benefice and his skin by tossing a partisan corpse into a ditch. As everyone in the audience knew, the greatest partisans of all were invariably members of the most powerful families. Bernardino argues that these kinds of connections are secondary to the fellowship of Christ. But the wives and priests who walked home after his sermon would have found themselves in a dilemma if they attempted to defy convention.

None of this means that Bernardino was unaware of social reality, of the obligations binding one person to another. In fact, his most radical suggestion of all shows precisely the opposite. He advises his listeners to "shun" partisans:

> Make sure that you don't hold with him, deal with him, touch his hand; don't eat, drink, or sleep with him; don't speak to him . . .[93]

Ironically, such sanctions could only be effective because of the very strength of the social ties condemned by the preacher; to be so utterly cut off was the worse thing which could happen to any Italian, and Bernardino knew it. His solution to the spider's web of *parzialità* was to hack through the threads binding people together, by appealing to individuals to take a moral stand and reject their obligations in favor of a higher loyalty. In the end, however, he needed to rely on those very

---

93. Ibid., I, 668. "Fa' che tu non tenga con lui, non praticare con lui, non li toccare la mano, non bere, né non mangiare con lui, non dormire con lui, non li parlare . . ." A few days before, in sermon 18, Bernardino also proposed "shunning" as a way of avoiding excommunicates and prostitutes (or sexually free women): "Hai in contrada una ribalda la quale non si vuole amendare, e è stata ripresa? Non la favoreggiare, se ella non si ritrae dal peccato suo: non le dare fuoco né acqua né niuna cosa; non le fare motto niuno. E anco se tu la vedi passare per la via, vollele le reni"; Ibid., I, 532–33.

threads if the plan was to work at all. Just as he tried to do with his metaphor of the pitch-and-tallow pellets, he harnessed a negative force in order to combat it: the worst punishment of all was to be severed from the relationships which caused the problem in the first place. Indeed, there were few practical ways that Bernardino or his listeners could ever escape from the bonds, whether oppressive or comforting, of the larger culture.

III. The Peace of the Soul

The sustained attack on discord ends abruptly, in sermon 23, after occupying so much of the first half of the visit. For the several weeks following the last faction sermon, Bernardino again spoke on a wide variety of topics, consistent with his goal of total moral reform. For Siena to be truly at peace, it needed to purge itself of all sins, not just those which led directly to faction. From praise of the Virgin Mary to condemnations of usury, witchcraft, and sodomy, these talks covered the same broad range of subjects as in Lenten or Advent cycles, when preachers also had the opportunity to lead audiences to conversion after many weeks. Bernardino's hold over his audience was subject, as always, to fluctuation. On September 16, for example, he complained about the noisy ball playing near the Campo, and he also needed to urge women to bring their husbands to the next day's talk. When he preached on sodomy on September 25, he was irritated by the low attendance. On the other hand, listeners responded very well to his repeated pleas to help the poor prisoners of the Commune, and he praised their good efforts.[94]

In terms of his peacemaking strategy, Bernardino chose not to discuss faction at length, probably because he was sensitive to the demands he was placing on his listeners' attention; on September 21, he

94. But good evidence for the transitory effect of the 1427 sermons is provided by Samuel Cohn, who found only two testamentary bequests to prisoners during the fifteenth century; see *Death and Property in Siena, 1205–1800* (Baltimore: Johns Hopkins University Press, 1988), 51.

wryly noted that they must be tired of the subject.[95] However, several talks still reinforced his theme of civic unity, particularly another harsh speech on justice and good government (sermon 25, September 9), where he reproves the vices of unjust rulers, including exploitation of the poor. He urges the Sienese to install just officials in both city and *contado* and to prohibit usurers from holding posts.[96] At one point, he condemns the injustice that occurs when a partisan is in power, favoring his friends and humbling his enemies.[97] He also rebukes detractors and their false accusations, which are "enough to ruin a city, a country, a province, especially during a time of suspicion," another muted reference to vicious talk then circulating in Siena.[98] Predictably, he soon adds that in no place has *he* been maligned so much as in Siena![99]

During this time, four sermons form a final, threatening sequence (from Friday, September 19, through the following Monday), emphasizing the city's need for immediate repentance and its forthcoming doom if it ignores the preacher's call. A panoply of sins—pride, sumptuous vanity, witchcraft, sodomy, and faction—will all condemn the Sienese to destruction. Fiercely apocalyptic in tone, the recurrent theme of these four sermons echoes the earlier talks on discord: the devouring mercenary-locusts will teach the proud city a lesson and smash its prosperity and (false) peace. A blunt dialogue in the first of these sermons makes the audience hear its impending doom galloping towards Siena:

95. Siena 1427, II, 1014. "Io ho di questo tanto predicato, che voi ne dovareste essere già stanchi d'udirne più."

96. Ibid., I, 727. But who isn't a usurer? Bernardino laments. Then he slyly suggests, "Uno modo ci è: mieffè! . . . mandaremvi le donne." Of course, some women also practiced the vice, he adds. The belief that preservation of the peace depended upon the justice and good will of officials was a commonplace in Sienese preaching; see Paton's discussion of other Sienese preachers, along with Bernardino, in *Preaching Friars*, 133–63.

97. Siena 1427, I, 717–18.

98. Ibid., I, 720.

99. Ibid., I, 724.

"What is it, what is it?"—"Soldiers."—"And what do they want?"
"Nothing but evil."—"O, where do you want to go?"[Bernardino abruptly shifts into direct dialogue with the mercenaries]—"We want to go into
Sienese territory."—"O, to do what?"—"To enjoy their belongings, their
farms that are so beautiful, to inhabit their houses, where they live in
such ease; to live at their expense, to make up for the bad times we've had:
just as we've had it hard, and they've had it easy, so now we'll take it easy
and they'll have it hard!"[100]

This speech is part of a tirade on women's vanity, and the preacher reminds his listeners that they and their daughters will be raped, or
worse, and that their riches, which they enjoy so much now, will be
seized by soldiers of fortune. For one impassioned moment, he interrupts his terrible description of the gnawing locust-armies to plead
with his audience to live like "upright Christians and children of God;
love each other, hold each other tight" (*ristregnetevi insieme*). If someone
is spreading discord, "don't follow him, don't stay to listen."[101] As always for Bernardino, the premier catalyst of discord is malicious
speech, the premier remedy self-control.

The next day, Bernardino taunts the Sienese, asking if they remember one captain in particular, the scourge of Tuscany during the late
fourteenth century: "Has anyone ever heard of John Hawkwood? . . .
Have you ever heard of the English?"[102] He realizes that some people
do not believe his predictions—"Fra Bernardino, you are dreaming
. . ."—but after he leaves, he will be listening for (bad) news about his
city.[103] Yet even as he blasts the audience one last time throughout
these fearsome talks, he offers an antidote: forgiveness and unity will

---

100. Ibid., II, 951–52. "Che è, che è?—So' soldati.—E che voglion fare?—Voliamo
andare in quel di Siena.—O a che fare?—A godere la loro robba, le loro pocissioni
che so' così belle; ad abitare ne le loro case, dove stanno in tanto agio; a vivare un poco
a le spese loro per ristorare i ma' tempi che noi aviamo auti: come noi siamo stati a'
disagi, e eglino si so' goduti, così ora noi sì godaremo, ellino staranno a disagio."
101. Ibid., II, 955–56.
102. Ibid., II, 1051.
103. Ibid., II, 969.

save Siena. At several points, he advertises the upcoming peace sermon, which will be held on the following Sunday.[104] Receptive and
frightened listeners would have several days to think about his message, and then make preparations to forgive.

The subject matter of the two sermons which immediately preceded the peacemaking also suggests that Bernardino was preparing his
audience in a very deliberate way. In Crema, four years before, he persuaded the citizens to make peace during what was apparently a
mighty hellfire sermon, but this leisurely pace in Siena, his shifting
back and forth from his major themes of discord and its opposite, the
bene comune, demanded a more subtle strategy. On the Friday and Saturday before the peace sermon, he chose to speak on almsgiving, an expression of the *carità* which is necessary for forgiveness. During his
weeks of preaching, he has tried to purge the Sienese of their sins, but
repentance will be incomplete and short-lived if it is only a product of
fear.[105]

Although their mood is relatively calm, these sermons may have
caused a few tense moments for the complacent rich, since Bernardino
valiantly champions the poor. He says that it is a worse sin to deny
charity to a poor thief than for the thief to have robbed in the first
place, and he claims that excess wealth can rightfully belong to the
needy. He also warns people not to display family coats of arms in
chapels, nor to hoard wealth among relatives.[106] And in his pleas for
aid to the city's Ospedale, he describes that institution as a symbol of
Sienese harmony. It is

---

104. Ibid., II, 1040. "Non voglio che m'esca de la memoria che domenica che viene
io vi vorrò dire una predicozza de la pace, ché bene mi credevo che infra voi fusse concordia e pace, ora veggo che non pare ch'e' sia vero; e però fate che voi ci veniate."
Note that Bernardino advertises the peace sermon on a Sunday, when he would have
had a relatively large audience. The next day, he repeats the reminder to come; Ibid., II,
1062.

105. Ibid., II, 1205. "Non mi giovo mai di fare paura là dove non bisogna."

106. Ibid., II, 1188–1200.

. . . one of the eyes of your city, and the other eye is the bishopric: they stand very well next to each other. The right eye is the Vescovado and the left eye is the Ospedale: the nose is the piazza which is in the middle. You see how long it is, just like a nose. Doh, citizens, give to that hospital![107]

Later that morning, he will praise them for improving the city's walls, but then notes that generous alms serve as an even stronger defense. The implicit message of these two sermons is that charity unites citizens and protects them from external danger; individuals must think not of themselves and their family honor, but of the common good. Thus, Bernardino carefully winds down to a calmer mood in sermons 40 and 41, far removed from the strident tone of the previous week. True peace must arise from higher instincts in the soul.

But the peacemaking sermon which he finally delivers on Sunday, September 28, does not follow the rhetorical path we have come to expect. During the previous six weeks, Bernardino alternated between ferocity, fraternal pleading, and his habitual humor in order to make listeners feel, viscerally, the dangers of faction. Attempting to recast their social identities from family or party members to Sienese citizens, he presented a stark picture of the city at war, consumed by locusts and destruction, in contrast to its present, but brittle, prosperity. His softer voice in the sermons on almsgiving began to prepare the audience for a change of tone, but the peacemaking sermon introduces a decisively new mood. After all, Bernardino's deepest beliefs about peace are not primarily civic, but personal. His most powerful sermon tries to reach the individual who is wearied by the burdens of life. Far from being a culmination of his apocalyptic preaching or a development of his ideas about the social good, it is instead a sustained, melancholy reflection on the passing of time and the transience of all worldly pleasure.

---

107. Ibid., II, 1206. ". . . è uno degli occhi de la vostra città, e l'altro occhio è el Vescovado: stanno molto bene a lato l'uno all'altro. L'occhio dritto è el Vescovado, e 'l sinistro è lo Spedale: el naso è la piazza che è in mezzo. Vedi che è longhetta come è il naso. Doh, cittadini, procurate a quello Spedale!"

"*Ecce quam bonum et quam iocundum habitare fratres in unum*" (Psalm 132 [133]: 1). The biblical verse which begins the talk alerts the audience that the point of the sermon will be love and concord. The preacher, however, will take a very long time developing this theme both rhetorically and in the hearts of his listeners. He begins slowly, with a long narrative of how David searched for true peace in this world, but could never find it. These early passages show Bernardino at his most reflective:

> I believe that one of the most contemplative men the Church ever had was David. When I consider it, I'm stupefied. If you speculate upon his gestures, his ways, his words, you will see that everything gave off a sweet odor and flavor. When he was in those most sweet and gentle contemplations, he sometimes tasted eternal life . . .[108]

The preacher's goal will be to persuade his listeners to taste eternal life by embracing each other in love.

Unfortunately, David possessed not only an intellect which led him to the heights of contemplation, but also weak and fragile flesh, like other humans. Bernardino makes David's dilemma accessible by framing it as an inner dialogue the great king has with himself as he goes searching throughout the world, a metaphysical traveler aching to find "solid and invisible things" in place of the "vain and visible things" to which his human flesh has condemned him. Not finding peace within his divided self, David looks outward by examining the honors and delights of this world, from political status to dancing and singing, to see if they in any way resemble eternal life. But both honors and pleasures prove false, and the searcher concludes that "in eternal life there must be sweeter songs, gentler sounds, more delicate dances" than he has found on earth. So David continues his search for peace elsewhere.

108. Ibid., II, 1231–32. "Io mi credo che de' più contemplativi omini che mai avesse la Chiesa di Dio, si fusse David. Quando il considaro, io stupisco. Se tu vai speculando ne' gesti, ne' modi, ne' le parole sue, tu vedrai che d'ogni cosa cavava odore e sapore. Quando elli era in quelle dolcissime e suavissime contemplazioni, elli gustava talvolta vita eterna."

But when he goes on to contemplate wealth, he realizes that its accumulation and possession is only veiled in sadness: "With labor to attain it, with effort to hold it, with sadness to let it go."[109] Attachment to earthly goods only brings pain. Bernardino pauses to exhort his audience to follow David as he searches for paradise, just as Dante followed Virgil through the inferno. (But at least one person in the piazza was following neither David nor the sermon, since the preacher snaps: "O you who are sleeping, stay awake and learn this morning, so that it doesn't turn out badly for you, and instead of paradise, you end up with hell!")[110]

Bernardino then addresses the audience as a whole, in a sudden outburst for foolish and weary humans:

> Oooh! When I think about how much effort I see in this gathering and gaining of earthly possessions! I see so much fatigue and sweat, I see vigils and anguish, I see so many [heavy] thoughts and sufferings! I know so many who gather and are hungry, endure thirst, suffer cold and immeasurable heat. You go sometimes here and sometimes there, sometimes by land and sometimes by sea. In rainy weather, through snow and winds, you never stay in your own house. At the farms, in the vineyards, you are in every place, and there you entangle yourself with the greatest suffering. Alas, what dolor . . . never are you satisfied.[111]

Neither acquisition nor possession brings peace of mind; some accident of fate always assails the weary worker. Bernardino wants to know

109. Ibid., II, 1234.

110. Ibid., II, 1234. "O tu che dormi, impara stamane e sta' desto, acciò che tu non capiti male, credendoti avere il paradiso, e forse arai l'inferno!"

111. Ibid., II, 1235. "Oooh! quand'io ci penso, quanta fatiga ci veggo in ragunare e guadagnare questa robba! Io ci veggo molta fatiga e molto sudore: io ci veggo vigilie, io ci veggo angosce, io ci veggo dimolti pensieri e dimolti afanni: io ci cognosco molte volte colui che raguna avere fame, patire sete, sofferire freddo e caldo smisurato. Tu vai quando qua e quando là; tu vai quando per mare, e quando per terra; tu per tempi piovatichi, tu a nievi, tu a venti, tu ne la propria tua casa mai non ti ristai; tu a le pocissioni, tu a le vigne, tu in ogni luogo, e in ciò che tu t'impacci, afanno grandissimo! Eimmè, che dolore è egli. Al fine di riposo sempre afanno! Mai non ti vedi sazio . . ."

if anyone in the audience feels secure in his wealth; he asks them to lift a finger. Predictably,

> O, O, there is not one person who raises a finger! What a great mercy, that you see I'm speaking the truth![112]

How could this audience of worried wives and anxious merchants, shopkeepers, and landowners not agree that the pursuit of wealth caused distress? Like Alberti's depiction of the tense merchants in *Della famiglia*, Bernardino's eloquent portrait of human restlessness shows the gnawing anxiety which results from the pursuit of wealth and status in this world. The preacher emphasizes the futility of placing one's hope in worldly goods with the example of an old miser who hides money here and there, and then laments because he has forgotten where it is! Such dolor to part from worldly possessions . . . and yet how much worse to lose them irretrievably through death.[113]

The poignant theme of the peacemaking sermon is that there is nothing stable, nothing permanent. Every happiness disappoints, and even life's greatest moments have only emptiness at their core. A sharp thorn always hides beneath the flower. The sermon reaches its first rhetorical climax with a long passage about a happy young bride, garlands in her hair and shining with gold, riding to the home of her new husband. Bernardino's vivid description of the bride going to the groom with music in the air and flowers in the streets makes the inevitable debacle all the more striking. At first the newlyweds are enamored of each other and at the very pinnacle of worldly happiness, but trouble soon follows. Beauty causes jealousy: in a short time (*pochi pochi dì*), the bride is so unhappy that she can barely eat a mouthful "which

112. Ibid., II, 1236. "Oh, oh! e' non ci è persona che alzi il dito? Gramercè, che tu vedi ch'io il vero!"

113. Ibid., II, 1237. The miser nervously moves his money around, just as a cat does with her kittens: ". . . faceva de' suoi denari come fa la gatta de' suoi gattucini: polli oggi qua, domane colà. Così faceva lui: quando gli poneva sotto el letto; quando gli sotterrava ne la stalla, quando fra 'l panico, quando fra 'l grano, quando fra le fave; e tante volte gli aveva rimossi qua e quando là, che infine non si ricordava dove gli aveva posti, e andavagli cercando e piagneva."

seems good to her."[114] Stepchildren can bring woe, a daughter-in-law likewise. And

> if there is a mother-in-law, I don't want to say anything to you about it! You know how that goes! Little peace: little will that good time last![115]

Everything carries pain and discontent, whether the lack of money or good family or fertility. And even those with riches, an honorable lineage, and children can lack political power.[116]

With one of the homeliest of all his metaphors, Bernardino makes the point that no one can ever be perfectly content: if you have a good lasagne, you can't even enjoy it because "a fly has fallen in!"[117] Whatever your condition in life, you will lack one thing or another, ruining your peace of mind. He follows this up with concrete dialogues which show how there is always "a fly in the lasagne." A woman asks her husband for a long, heavy train and then complains because her shoulders ache; she moves on to another new fashion, which also fails to please her. A young man wants a beautiful wife. The preacher asks him:

> "Now go ahead; you have her. Are you content?"—"No."—"O what would you like?"—"I'd like other things, too."—"What?"—"I'd like to live sumptuously. I want dainty food: partridges, pheasants, capons, and every kind of good meat."—"Go ahead, you have it. Do you lack anything else?"—"O, now I'd like to drink the very best wines (you know, that one from Maciareto) and supply myself in abundance: to take a bellyful every time!"[118]

114. Bernardino's humorous description of the anxious spouse is reminiscent of Paolo da Certaldo's frantic efforts to guard his home: "O elli n'è geloso, perché ella è bella, giovana; e anco lei, che come sente uno bussarello per casa, pur de la gatta, subito entra el suspetto; e se egli è nel letto, si leva e cerca la casa tutta quanta, e va a vedere l'uscio se è serrato, e talvolta per suspetto vi semina la cennare per vedere se persona v'entra. Tale suggella l'uscio per gelosia"; Ibid., II, 1242.

115. Ibid., II, 1241. ". . . se v'è la suociara, non te ne vo' dire nulla: tu tel sai in ogni modo! Poca pace: poco ti durò quello bel tempo!"

116. This is perhaps an indirect address to some members of the Dodici, bearers of high social status, but excluded from government.

117. Siena 1427, II, 1242.

118. Ibid., II, 1243–44. "Or oltre; e tu l'abbi. Se' contento?"—"No."—"O che vor-

But once his thirst is satisfied, he cries for something else, whether soft feather beds or silken clothes. "Are you content?" Bernardino asks. The young man's answer is inevitably "No."

If youth's desires are insatiable, then the longings of old age are even worse. Bernardino addresses his aging listeners and turns the knife slowly as he asks them: tell me, you old people,

> you who were once young, and who did so many things, all of them displeasing to God. What is left of your youth? Nothing.[119]

He forces them to go through their store of memories, recalling their former beauty, vigor, and vanity. Now all has vanished forever, like smoke. The fresh and happy time of their youth lasts only until thirty, and then begins the slow, inexorable twilight. Bernardino's caricature of old age is both humorous and pathetic: he mimics an elder's trembling head, and describes how he dribbles soup on his chin. And if the old person has lived a vicious life, neither his family nor God and His saints will show him compassion.[120]

Bitter memories of the flesh can bring David no peace, so he continues his search. But high social status carries its own burdens. The preacher pauses to empathize with his female listeners:

> Oooh! I've even seen the wives of great lords live in such tribulation and suffering that they are worse off than a serving woman. This one because

---

resti?"—"Vorrei anco altro."—"O che?"—"Io vorrei vivare splendidamente, io vorrei de' cibi dilicati: vorrei starne, fagiani, pernici, capponi ed ogni buona carne."—"Or oltre, e tu l'abbi: mancati altro?"—"Oh, mo' io vorrei da bere perfettissimi vini, sai di quello da Maciareto, e fornirmene in abondanza: ogni volta pigliarne una corpacciata."

119. Ibid., II, 1244. "... che già fuste giovani, e faceste dimolte cose ne le vostre gioventù, che tutte dispiacqueno a Dio: che hai tu de la tua gioventudine? Nulla."

120. Ibid., II, 1245–47. Bernardino's melancholy reflections on age may have been particularly disturbing to his female listeners. If the city's demographic profile resembled that of Florence, there were many elderly widows in his audience. For old age in Florence, see David Herlihy, "Growing Old in the Quattrocento," and Richard C. Trexler, "A Widow's Asylum of the Renaissance: The Orbatello of Florence," in *Old Age in Preindustrial Society*, ed. Peter Stearns (New York: Holmes & Meier, 1982), 104–18 and 119–49.

of jealousy, that one because she can't have children: she thus sees her husband possess other women. You believe that this is sadness, eh?[121]

Meanwhile, their powerful husbands are consumed by fear. If they are served by a defeated enemy, he longs to cut them to pieces. Lords worry about being poisoned, even by a brother or mother or son; they can trust nobody (*non si fida di criatura*). Whenever they sleep or ride or perform ordinary tasks, their minds are devoured by suspicion. No need to search ancient books, Bernardino says, if you want examples of how the mighty are ruined; just look at the history of Lombardy to see how lords have lost their states.[122] Implied in this passage is the book of memory that the Sienese could examine for themselves, while remembering the tumultuous past of their own city, with the rise of one faction and the fall of another.[123] In the course of his attack the preacher twice stops to ask his audience: "Have you understood how many worries there are in worldly honors?" and "Do you see how many dangers there are in this world?" In both cases the answer is "Yes."[124]

Everywhere David has searched, he has found nothing but pain and fear. But the search was not in vain. Suddenly Bernardino concludes that David at last finds true happiness. He finds it in a united city, where he sees

> a people completely united in one will, in charity, in concord, and he
> then says, "Now have I found the shadow of Paradise, which I have been

---

121. Ibid., II, 1250. "Oooh! che ho io veduto pur io essare state donne di grandi signori vivare in tanti affanni e tante tribulazioni, che so' state tenute da meno che una fantesca, chi per gelosia, chi perché non può avere figliuoli, vede il suo marito tenere altre femine. Credi che lo' sia dolore, eh?"

122. And the mighty aren't even immune to the contempt of the *popolo minuto*. Bernardino has a wry understanding of the true state of relations behind gestures of deference: ". . . quanti credi che sieno negli onori, a' quali l'è fatto di capuccio, e poi quando e' è passato, si fanno maggior beffe di lui, che d'una bestia, dicendo molte volte, quando elli va in mezzo accompagnato: 'Egli è l'asino fra le ceste'"; Ibid., II, 1250–51.

123. Ibid., II, 1251–52.

124. Ibid., II, 1250 and 1251.

searching for so long!" And seeing such sweetness, he then says these words: "*Ecce quam bonum et quam iocundum habitare fratres in unum!* Oh, how good and how joyful for brothers to live together as one!" And he recognizes this as true peace and true calm.[125]

Now, the preacher triumphantly adds, "let us make peace in such a way that nothing remains to be done." The moment of conversion has arrived.

During the course of the sermon, Bernardino has relentlessly exposed the deepest fears of his listeners. Rhetorically, his barrage of questions, use of the dialogue format, and repetition of the familiar "*tu*" all force a direct confrontation with the individual, attempting to probe the soul and overcome any inner resistance. Susan Harding has pointed out, in her work on fundamentalist rhetoric in America, that conversion can be seen "as a process of acquiring a specific religious language." As Harding discovered after an interview with a powerful Baptist preacher (who took for granted that she was ripe for conversion), her anthropologist's stance was momentarily displaced by his religious vision, as his language and personal revelations sought to draw her into his world. But, as she describes it, it was precisely the "space between belief and disbelief, or rather the paradoxical overlap," which enabled her to feel how the rhetoric of conversion worked.[126] In order to understand the conversion to peacemaking, we should not be dismayed by the gap between the preacher's Christian ethos and the honor code of his audience, nor by his wavering between the civic and per-

125. Ibid., II, 1252. ". . . uno popolo tutto unito insieme in uno volere, in una carità, in una concordia, e elli dissi allora: 'Ora ho io trovata l'ombra del paradiso, ch'io so' tanto tempo andato cercando!' E vedendovi tanta dolcezza, allora disse queste parole! 'Ecce quam bonum et quam iocundum habitare fratres in unum! Oh, quanto è buono e quanto è giocondo abitare e frategli in uno volere!' E qui conobbe essare la vera pace e la vera quietare!"

126. Susan F. Harding, "Convicted by the Holy Spirit: The Rhetoric of Baptist Conversion," *American Ethnologist* 14, no. 1 (February 1987), 167–85. In Harding's case, the emotional "hook" was the preacher's sudden revelation that he had accidentally killed his own son.

sonal. The bridge between the two worlds is not logic, but language and emotion. By listening to Bernardino's speech patterns, his rhythmic use of words and rhetorical questions, and his absolute assurance that we, the audience, are in complete agreement, we can intuit, if not logically understand, the *pace di dentro*.

By the middle of the peace sermon Bernardino "has" his audience. After reaching the climactic moment of the united city, he pauses to warn the audience to carry out an orderly ritual and he announces his final three sermons. The women, he jokes, have caught him like a thrush in lime, so that he cannot leave Siena.[127] This pause, which seems to break the emotional flow of the sermon, perhaps gave listeners a chance to collect themselves before the *pace di fuore*.

The tone in the second half of the sermon abruptly shifts from melancholy to forcefulness, the theme from troubled souls to positive action. Bernardino proceeds not through a tightly structured argument, but by the sheer force of language and storytelling, using example after example to sweep his audience towards the kiss of peace. He starts with the pleasure of the word, as sound:

> This peace is such a useful thing! Even the word is so sweet—*pace*—that it gives sweetness to the lips! Look at its opposite, to say *guerra!* It's such a rough thing, it gives so much roughness, that it makes your mouth bitter.[128]

He then quickly moves to the visual, in this case the frescoes of Lorenzetti in the Palazzo behind him. The "Peace" scene is happiness to look upon, while "War" is all darkness (*scurità*). And, he continues,

127. Siena 1427, II, 1253. "Egli è il tempo che si suole pigliare de' tordi al fischio co la pania. A me mi pare che queste donne m'abbino impaniato, ch'io non mi posso partire da voi, che mi conviene predicare domane, che sarà la predica delli angioli, cosa molto gentilissima."

128. Ibid., II, 1254. "Ella è tanto utile cosa questa pace! Ella è tanto dolce cosa pur questa parola 'pace' che dà una dolcezza a le labra! Guarda el suo opposito, a dire 'guerra!' è una cosa ruida tanto, che dà una rustichezza tanto grande, che fa inasprire la bocca."

think about Noah's ark and how the dove with the olive branch was a sign that God had ended his war with humans, thanks to Noah's humility—and so no one should be too proud to forgive. This series of loosely connected images naturally culminates in a story. A boy was planning to go to the university to learn science and virtue. His father wants him to promise not to quarrel with anyone, but the proud son will only swear that he won't *start* a fight. The wise father makes him stay home, since the boy refuses to forgo retaliation, even in theory. Bernardino, the wise *padre*, implores his audience: swallow insults, don't save words in your mouth, be like a goose with a long throat. Don't search for quarrels, but for the peace of your city.[129] It takes about five minutes for the preacher to leap from the sweet sound of "peace" to a goose's throat and the peace of Siena; he has abandoned his script and is now improvising, with words and images tumbling one after another.

The peacemaking ritual is almost at hand. Bernardino has been provided with a list of names of those involved in quarrels, indicating that part of the "conversion" has taken place even before the peace sermon.[130] But the preacher makes his own task clear:

> However, I will not do the individual reconciliations, but we'll talk about general ones, and you can understand both from my speech.[131]

He then reveals his technique to the audience, explaining the method he has followed throughout the previous weeks. He has taken so long because it was necessary to show them their sins and God's punishment if they failed to amend. His goal was to "move hearts and lead them to bend towards those who have injured them, and to have them

129. Ibid., II, 1255–56.

130. Ibid., II, 1257–58. "Io ho un tela grandissima di genti che sono in guerra, di moglie con marito e di marito con mogli; e simile, anco di molte altre persone, ché credo avere uno fascio di scritte, di memorie, di questioni che sono fra cittadini, l'uno contra l'altro."

131. Ibid., II, 1258. "E però se io non potrò fare fare le paci particulari, parleremo de le generali, e potrai nel mio dire comprendare per l'una e per l'altra."

make peace."[132] In other words, souls become pliable only after they acknowledge their sins and the vanity of the world. To make peace with each other, they first must make peace with God.

In the remaining minutes, Christ is shown to be the model of love and forgiveness, a foil to the Sienese who must learn to reject their own sins and forgive those of their enemies. Bernardino follows this up with a list of questions: "Do you love God?" "Do you want peace?" (Benedetto dutifully recorded the obedient *"Si"* which follows each question.) The preacher briefly refers to the tenacious honor code: some people think they lower themselves by pardoning an enemy. Does God lower Himself (*Era vile Dio*)? Instead, God's judgment awaits those who will not pardon. In passing, Bernardino even suggests that there should be a law exiling anyone who refuses to make peace (or interferes with one).[133] Typically, he chooses not to develop this particular idea.

At the end of the sermon, the preacher instructs the women to walk to San Martino, leaving the piazza by way of Via Porrione; they should take care so that pregnant women are not jostled in the crowd. As for the men, they should offer their peace to the Virgin in the cathedral. Both groups are to make peace in such a way "that nothing remains to be done."[134] Yet before the crowd leaves, Bernardino cannot resist detaining them with a final story, which he claims is *"fresco fresco,"* since it took place so recently, in 1419. In this final tale of an obstinate sinner, too vindictive to forgive, he targets the elderly women in the audience, emphasizing for one last time that even they play their part in vendetta and peacemaking.[135] An old pilgrim woman on her way to Jerusalem has her foot trampled by a youth. Although the injury is minor and the boy repeatedly begs pardon, the woman refuses to make

132. Ibid., II, 1258–59.

133. Ibid., II, 1264.

134. Ibid., II, 1265–66.

135. Since Bernardino chooses not to end with the example of a male partisan, it may be that women predominate, even now, at the very climax of his visit.

peace. Because of her stubbornness, she is set upon by devils who stuff her in a cistern, where she disappears![136] The story is hardly a lofty end to the sermon, and the preacher seems to have miscalculated: whether bored by the long-winded tale or eager to be off to San Martino, the women become restless. An agitated Bernardino orders them to remain still (*"state salde, donne: non vi partite"*):

> and so my peacemaking was broken that other time! I'd give three pounds of blood so that my talk isn't interrupted![137]

But, in the last moments, he ends the sermon in a more fitting manner, imploring the Sienese to follow Christ's example, and forgive. He also acknowledges his own exhaustion after these many weeks of preaching, begging them to "help me with the labor that I have borne with such delight and love . . ."[138] And finally Bernardino sends them off to church and their mutual embraces, there to find both civic and spiritual peace.

136. Siena 1427, II, 1266–68. The story occupies two printed pages in the Delcorno edition; despite Bernardino's enthusiastic rendition ("Oooh! Oh, che orribile cosa fu questa! O giudicio di Dio grande!"), the tale seems a bit tiresome at the end of a long sermon.

137. Ibid., II, 1268. "Così mi fu anco rotta la predica l'altra volta. Io vorrei che mi costasse tre lire di sangue, e questo mio parlare non mi fusse stato rotto!"

138. Ibid., II, 1270. The complete concluding passage is as follows: "Doh, cittadini e voi donne, io vi prego che voi m'aitate a la fatiga ch'io ho portata con tanto diletta e amore per la vostra pace. Chi può aitare a nulla, mettisi a far fare ogni pace e concordia l'uno coll'altro. Che se così sarete rapacificati insieme, voi arete la pace qui in terra, e di là l'arete poi in gloria; la quale io prego che ve la concordia per la grazia e per la sua misericordia *in secula seculorum. Amen.* (Donne, valentemente per Porrione; e voi valenti uomini, in Vescovado.)"

Conclusion: The Buon Cavalcatore

Bernardino ended his preaching in Siena on October 5, only a week after he had achieved the goal he set for himself and his city.[1] Once he persuaded the Sienese to exchange the *bacio di pace*, little remained to be done. His final efforts consisted of miscellaneous advice concerning the *bene vivere*, and a winding down from the powerful emotions aroused by the peace sermon. In the two talks preceding his closing speech, he spoke on the angels and on Saint Francis, themes which reinforced the tranquil mood he had established on September 28. The concluding sermon begins with a poignant farewell as he says good-bye to his fellow citizens: ". . . and perhaps this will be the last sermon I preach to you, so that perhaps we won't ever see each other again."

1. The preacher gave both himself and his audience a rest once the peacemaking was accomplished. After a sermon on the next day (Monday, September 29), Bernardino did not preach again until the following Saturday, October 4; his final sermon was on Sunday.

Then he sums up the lessons of peace and salvation. Bernardino ends with a plea to his fellow citizens that they pray for him; he, in turn, will ask God to lead them to heavenly glory. As for the peacemaking, the preacher firmly disengages himself from further responsibility:

> I pray you to excuse me, and I believe that you will accept my excuse. You must understand that I am busy attending to preaching. I pray the Lord, or others, that they work in such a way that no peace remains to be done. Deh! For the love of God, love one another! Oimmè! Don't you see what will come of it if you love to destroy one another?[2]

And so Bernardino left Siena believing that he had accomplished his mission, at least in part. Given his heroic self-image and his conviction that God spoke through his words, this was probably the usual case when he saw the response of enthusiastic audiences. The farewell speech, for example, contains one last mention of the dutiful Perugians and their eagerness to turn towards the good, displayed in the peace which they made because of his visit.[3] Of course, like most mass peacemakings, this did not affect the long-term politics of Perugia, just as the 1427 peacemaking would be no more than a happy interlude for Siena.[4] Bernardino must have been aware that, for most people, peace and conversion were temporary experiences, but the sermons rarely betray a sense of frustration. At one point, he snapped at the Florentines: "Every year to preach and preach, to start again and again,

2. Siena 1427, II, 1375. "... egli ci è rimasto a fare molte paci; pregovi che m'aviate per iscusato, e così credo che voi accettiate la mia scusa. Voi dovete considerare ch'io ho auta molta faccenda attendare a le predicazioni. Priego il Signore o altri, che aoperino per tal modo che niuna pace ci rimanga a fare. Deh! per lo amore di Dio amatevi insieme. Oimmè! o non vedete voi che se voi amate la distruzione l'uno dell'altro, quello che ve ne seguita?" It's not entirely clear from Benedetto's recording whether "il Signore" refers to God or to one of the members of the regime.

3. Ibid., II, 1371. Earlier in the course, Bernardino pointed out that the Sienese, too, had changeable characters, which meant that they were as quick to do good as they were to do evil: "... voi sete molto mobili; e come sete mobili al male, così ritornate tosto al bene"; Ibid., I, 725.

4. See Bornstein, *Bianchi of 1399*, for the equally transitory effect of the Bianchi peacemakings, 196–97.

and it's worth so little!"[5] In general, however, he and his contemporaries preferred to remember not the short duration of repentance, but its spectacular results: weeping, exorcisms, bonfires, and peacemakings,

Yet despite the flamboyant and transient aspects of his preaching, Bernardino's idea of conversion was far more complex. He accepted that, for most people, the classic Christian narrative of deep and sudden change was rare.[6] There were many strata involved in mass conversion, and great preachers could mine them all. Peacemakings, lightning flashes illuminating a dark terrain of distrust and vengeance, could still generate power over the long term. Eyewitnesses and chroniclers celebrated these brief moments of unity because they provided hope and blessed memories of success.

Bernardino was not deterred by either the brevity of repentance or the ebb and flow of conversion. As we have seen in the Siena sermons, he often tempered quick enthusiasm, even as he appreciated those gains which could be made in leaps and bounds. At its core, his preaching was a slow process of education, designed as a step-by-step course in how to live well. During the farewell sermon in 1427, he urged his audience to hold God's lessons in mind, even while enmeshed in the activities and pleasures of the world: "He is our A, B, C. If you keep your mind on Him, you'll learn every virtue," just as children learn when the master gives them an example, or as the painter learns when he holds up an image to copy.[7] Bernardino's preaching, with its righteous examples and sweeping narrative of peace and redemption, served as God's lesson book. In 1425 he told the Florentines that his goal, by Easter, was to make them "all wise and full of knowledge and the learning of God, in order to acquire holy Paradise, illuminated by virtue and science, having cast out ignorance, that evil

5. Florence 1424, I, 54. "Ogni anno predica, predica, riprendi, riprendi, e poco giova!" In this context, *riprendere* could mean "reprove" as well as "start again."

6. Of course, an unusually sensitive soul could undergo that profound transformation as she listened to sermons: Clare of Assisi was converted to a new way of life through the preaching of Francis.

7. Siena 1427, II, 1348–49.

beast."[8] The beginning of doing good was to know one's evil, confound it, and repent. Implicit in this view was the preacher's firm belief that people could change, thanks to the power of free will. In 1427, he repeatedly told the Sienese that it was almost too late to save themselves and their city, but the choice was still theirs. The idea of conversion as education thus left room for mistakes and backsliding on the part of his listeners. At several points, he encouraged them with the image of the *buon cavalcatore*, the horseman who keeps falling from his steed while he learns to ride. God, in His compassion, waits patiently while the sinner climbs on the horse yet another time.[9] Bernardino understood that preachers also needed patience, and that the deepest conversion was usually an ongoing process, rather than a one-time event. Real conversions were volatile, often hampered by fluctuations and missteps. But the possibility for change was always available, and the sinner could try again, tomorrow or years hence. There is no simple explanation for Bernardino's success as a preacher, but surely this essential optimism must have played its part.

His great popularity was also due to the way in which he deftly combined both progressive and traditional aspects of fifteenth-century culture. Just as his saintly image was versatile—he was by turns ascetic, swordsman, *padre dolce*—so too was his preaching style and the nature of his advice. His faith in education and rhetoric, bolstered by his confidence in free will, was similar to ideas current among intellectuals. But Bernardino also drew deeply from the well of everyday life, and his preaching reflected a vivid appreciation of both the natural and the social worlds. At times, his pleasure in the concrete—a flower blooming in springtime, the colorful ships floating in Venice's har-

8. Florence 1425, I, 327–28.

9. Florence 1425, I, 17, and Siena 1427, II, 1365. The latter passage includes another telling metaphor directed at children and young students: "O fanciulli, sapete voi, quando voi imparate bene a scrivare quando e' si fanno de li scalambroni? Né tu che impari la gramatica, mai non impararai se tu non fai prima de' latini gattivi; così dico d'uno che vogli cavalcare: mai non impararai a cavalcare se tu non cadi qualche volta."

bor—makes him sound like Boccaccio. On the other hand, he never abandoned the mainstays of charismatic preaching, repelling less populist preachers such as Andrea Biglia, and making potent use of violent threats. Not infrequently, he managed to do all of these things within a single sermon. His preaching always united diverse aspects of elite and popular culture.

In the act of conversing with his listeners from the pulpit, Bernardino engaged in what can be characterized as simultaneous discourses. For example, his reward system appealed to both the soul's salvation and material gain: he accommodated his mercantile listeners by telling them that good behavior earned worldly benefits, including wealth and long life.[10] Punishment, too, had a double edge, with the loss of goods as sharp as the pain of hell. A great propagator of almsgiving, this strict ascetic only asked that people give what they could: God did not want you to "skin yourself" for others. His words on forgiveness and peacemaking had the same duality. Bernardino's preaching against vendetta was countered by a recognition of the masculine honor code, which saw retaliation as both natural and desirable. While he advised Christian forbearance, his own response to slander was anger and virile counterattack, revealing an unconscious absorption in secular values.[11]

The greatest irony of Bernardino's peacemaking was that his social message—that citizens live harmoniously united in an ideal city—was never fully reconciled with his appeal to the individual. He induced his listeners to participate in a collective rite meant to symbolize civic unity, but his understanding of conversion was strongly personal, rather than social. His peacemaking sermons reflect the tension between

10. Even in his farewell sermon to the Sienese, when he tries to convince them that spiritual goods are superior to worldly ones, Bernardino soothes the righteous rich: ". . . usa questa prosperità per modo che tu n'acquisti vita etterna"; Siena 1427, II, 1358.

11. Empathy with listeners' values was typical of late-medieval preachers. Many of the Sienese clerics described by Bernadette Paton in *Preaching Friars and the Civic Ethos* seem relatively tolerant, even when they deal with knotty social issues.

public and private identities, a tension which is perhaps characteristic of traditional Mediterranean Catholicism, which stresses external states in the form of ritual and public display.[12] He praised the *pace de fuore* as a visible manifestation of the *bene comune*, but Bernardino was most moving when his words echoed the fears of the vulnerable self in an aggressive world. The peace sermon worked because it appealed to the individual's frustrated desire for inner peace, a peace that could never be found on earth, even if a united town served as a temporary facsimile. In other words, the great sermon undercuts the civic message of the rest of the course. The many ambiguities in Bernardino's sermons are never logically resolved within his aesthetic achievement.

The final irony is that, over the centuries, Bernardino's complex self has condensed, or congealed, into a stereotypical image of the "saint." Paintings produced after the Quattrocento usually depict him as a typical miracle worker or generic preacher, bleached of his strong individuality and robbed of the messages he preached to fifteenth-century audiences. In the civic profile of twentieth-century Siena, he has been reduced to playing second string behind Saint Catherine and, of course, the Madonna, Queen not only of Heaven but, more importantly, of the Palio, the ritual which defines modern Sienese identity. On the private devotional level, he is not even as honored as Saint Anthony, who still has altars in Siena and elsewhere, thickly clustered with ex-votos. Bernardino's listeners have vanished and the mighty voice has been silenced. His quiet fate shows us how vibrant personalities are transformed during the saint-making process and how even the greatest among them can fade as devotional patterns change over time. What remains alive are the sermons, which still connect us to that living audience which heard him speak.

The picture Bernardino drew of his world was convincing because

---

12. Jill Dubisch, in *In a Different Place: Pilgrimage, Gender, and Politics at a Greek Island Shrine* (Princeton: Princeton University Press, 1995), characterizes Mediterranean religiosity as placing "importance on the public act or performance through which inner states are made visible," 74.

it was directed at the individual and tried to capture the truth of the inner landscape, with all of its contradictions. His preaching did not mirror social reality, but it did identify pervasive cultural patterns and the hopes and fears which surrounded them. His ephemeral peace-makings were a way of reminding people that change was possible, if only for one beautiful moment. Bernardino the peacemaker was brother to the Quattrocento artist who used perspective to create images which were "real" and yet idealized deceptions, outlining a world which could never be.

Bibliography

Primary Sources

Albertano da Brescia. *Dei trattati morali.* Edited by Francesco Selmi. Bologna: G. Romagnoli, 1873.

Alberti, Leon Battista. *Della famiglia.* Translated as *The Family in Renaissance Florence* by Renee Neu Watkins. Columbia, SC: University of South Carolina Press, 1969.

"Aldobrandini Chronicle." Siena Biblioteca, MS. C.IV.1.

Anonymous Friar. "Vie inédite de S. Bernardino de Sienne par un frère mineur, son contemporain." Edited by Francois van Ortroy. *Analecta Bollandiana* 25 (1906): 304–38.

Ascheri, Mario, and Donatella Ciampoli, eds. *Siena e il suo territorio nel Rinascimento.* Siena: Il Leccio, 1986.

Barnabò da Siena. "Vita sancti Bernardini senensis." In *Acta Sanctorum*, Maii tomus V, die vigesima. Paris and Rome: V. Palme, 1866.

Bellonci, Goffredo, ed. *Novelle Italiane: Dalle origini al Cinquecento.* Rome: Lucarini Editore, 1986.

Benvoglienti, Leonardo. "Vie de Saint Bernardin par Léonard Benvoglienti." Edited by Francois van Ortroy. *Analecta Bollandiana* 21 (1902): 53–80.

Bernardino da Siena. *Le prediche volgari.* Edited by Ciro Cannarozzi. 2 vols. Pistoia: Pacinotti, 1934.

———. *Le prediche volgari.* Edited by Ciro Cannarozzi. 3 vols. Florence: Libreria Editrice Fiorentina, 1940.

———. *Le prediche volgari.* Edited by Ciro Cannarozzi. 2 vols. Florence: Rinaldi, 1958.

————. *Prediche volgari sul Campo di Siena 1427.* Edited by Carlo Delcorno. 2 vols. Milan: Rusconi, 1989.

————. *Opera Omnia.* 9 vols. Quaracchi: Collegio San Bonaventura, 1950–65.

Boccaccio, Giovanni. *The Decameron.* Translated by G. H. McWilliam. London: Penguin, 1972.

————. *The Elegy of the Lady Fiammetta.* Edited and translated by Mariangela Causa-Steindler and Thomas Mauch. Chicago: University of Chicago Press, 1990.

Bracciolini, Poggio. "On Avarice." Translated by Benjamin G. Kohl and Elizabeth B. Welles. In *The Earthly Republic: Italian Humanists on Government in Society,* edited by Benjamin G. Kohl and Ronald G. Witt with Elizabeth B. Welles, 241–89. Philadelphia: University of Pennsylvania Press, 1978.

————. *Facezie.* Edited by Marcello Ciccuto. Milan: Biblioteca Universale Rizzoli, 1983.

Branca, Vittore, ed. *Mercanti scrittori: Ricordi tra medioevo e rinascimento.* Milan: Rusconi, 1986.

Brucker, Gene, ed. *The Society of Renaissance Florence: A Documentary Study.* New York: Harper and Row, 1971.

————. *Two Memoirs of Renaissance Florence.* Translated by Julia Martines. New York: Waveland Press, 1967.

Capestrano, Giovanni da. "Sermo S. Iohannis de Capistrano, O.F.M. ineditus de S. Bernardino Senensi O.F.M." Edited by Ferdinando Doelle. *AFH* 6 (1913): 76–90.

Certaldo, Paolo da. *Il libro di buoni costumi.* Edited by Alfredo Schiaffini. Florence: F. Le Monnier, 1945.

Compagni, Dino. *The Chronicle of Dino Compagni.* Translated by Daniel E. Bornstein. Philadelphia: University of Pennsylvania Press, 1974.

Cronaca della Città di Perugia dal 1309–1491, nota col nome di Diario del Graziani. Edited by F. Boniani, A. Fabretti, and F. L. Polidori. *Archivio Storico Italiano* 16 (1850): 53–750.

Dante. *Purgatorio.* Translated by John D. Sinclair. New York: Mentor, 1961.

"Detti e insegnamenti di savi huomini." Siena Biblioteca, MS. I.VI.5.

Dominici, Ser Luca. *Cronache.* 2 vols. Pistoia: A. Pacinotti, 1933.

Emerton, Ephraim, ed. "Constitutiones Egidiane." In *Humanism and Tyranny: Studies in the Italian Trecento,* 197–251. Gloucester, MA: P. Smith, 1964.

Fantozzi, Antonio, ed. "Documenta Perusina de S. Bernardino Senesi." *AFH* 15 (1922): 103–54 and 406–75.

I fioretti di San Francesco. Edited by Cesare Segre, notes by Luigina Marini. Milan: Rizzoli Editore, 1979.

Giacomo delle Marche (Jacopus de Marchia). *Sermones Dominicales.* Edited by Renato Lioi. 4 vols. Ancona: Biblioteca Francescana, 1978.

Historia di Crema, raccolta da gli annali di M. Pietro Terni per A. Fino. Venice: Domenico Farri, 1571; reprint, Crema, 1988.

Humbert of Romans. "Treatise on the Formation of Preachers." In *Early Domini-cans: Selected Writings*, edited by Simon Tugwell, 184–370. Ramsey, NJ: Paulist Press, 1982.

Landucci, Luca. *A Florentine Diary*. Translated by Alice de Rosen Jervis. London: J. M. Dent and Sons, 1927.

"Lauda per San Bernardino." Siena Biblioteca, MS. I.II.27.

The Life of Cola di Rienzo. Translated by John Wright. Toronto: Pontifical Institute of Medieval Studies, 1975.

Livi, Ridolfo, ed. "San Bernardino e le sue prediche secondo un suo ascoltatore pratese del 1424." *Bullettino Senese di Storia Patria* 20 (1913): 458–69.

Malavolti, Orlando. *Historia de' fatti e guerre de'Senesi, cosi esterne, come civili*. Part II, Book Ten through Part III, Book Six. Bologna: Forni, 1968.

Manetti, Antonio. "Novella del Grasso Legnaiuolo." In *Novelle Italiane: Il Quattro-cento*, edited by Gioachino Chiarini, 241–85. Milan: Garzanti, 1982.

Masi, Gino, ed. *Chartum Pacis Privatae Medii Aevii ad Regionem Tusciae Pertinentium*. Milan: Società Editrice Vita e Pensiero, 1943.

Meditations on the Life of Christ: An Illustrated Manuscript of the Fourteenth Century. Edited and translated by Isa Ragusa and Rosalie B. Green. Princeton: Princeton University Press, 1961.

Milanesi, Gaetano, ed. *Documenti per la storia dell'arte Senese*. Siena: Onorato Porri, 1854–56.

Njal's Saga. Translated by Magnus Magnusson and Hermann Palsson. Harmondsworth: Penguin Books, 1960.

Piana, Celestino, ed. "I processi di canonizzazione su la vita di S. Bernardino di Siena." *AFH* 44 (1951): 87–160 and 383–435.

"The Poetical Life of San Bernardino" ("Vita di S. Bernardino"). Siena Biblioteca, MS. I.II.34.

Raymond of Capua. *The Life of St. Catherine of Siena*. Translated by George Lamb. London: Harvill Press, 1960.

Sacchetti, Franco. *Il Trecentonovelle*. Edited by Antonio Lanza. Florence: Sansoni, 1984.

Salimbene de Adam. *Chronicle*. Translated by Joseph L. Baird with Giuseppe Baglini and John Robert Kane. Binghamton, NY: Medieval and Renaissance Texts and Studies, 1986.

"La Sconfitta di Montaperti." Siena Biblioteca, MS. A.IV.5.

Scripta Leonis, Rufini et Angeli, Sociorum S. Francisci. Edited and translated by Rosalind B. Brooke. Oxford: Clarendon Press, 1970.

Sercambi, Giovanni. *Le cronache di Giovanni Sercambi, Lucchese*. Edited by Salvatore Bongi. Lucca: Tipografia Giusti, 1892.

———. *Novelle*. Edited by Giovanni Sinicropi. 2 vols. Bari: Laterza, 1972.

Tosti, Salvatore, ed. "De Praedicatione S. Bernardini Senensis in patria civitate, anno 1425." *AFH* 8 (1915): 678–80.

Vegio, Maffeo. "Vita sancti Bernardini senensis." In *Acta Sanctorum*, Maii tomus V, die vigesima. Paris and Rome: V. Palme, 1866.

Velluti, Donato. *La cronica domestica di messer Donato Velluti.* Edited by Isidoro del Lungo and Guglielmo Volpi. Florence: G. C. Sansoni, 1914.

Vespasiano da Bisticci. *Vite dei uomini illustri del secolo XV.* Edited by Paolo D'Ancona and Erhard Aeschlimann. Milan: Ulrico Hoepli, 1951.

Secondary Sources

Alessio, Felice. *Storia di San Bernardino da Siena e del suo tempo.* Mondovi: Tipografia B. Graziano, 1899.

Almeida, Miguel Vale de. *The Hegemonic Male: Masculinity in a Portuguese Town.* Providence, RI, and Oxford: Berghahn Books, 1996.

Amore, Agostino. "Matteo d'Agrigento a Barcelona e Valenza." *AFH* 49 (1956): 255–335.

Amos, Thomas L., Eugene A. Green, and Beverly Mayne Kienzle, eds. *De Ore Domini: Preacher and the Word in the Middle Ages.* Kalamazoo, MI: Medieval Institute Publications, 1989.

Arasse, Daniel. "Fervebat Pietate Populus: Art, devotion, et societé autour de la glorification de S. Bernardin de Sienne." *Mélanges de l'École Française de Rome (Moyen-Age et Tempe Modernes)* 89, no. 1 (1977): 189–233.

———. "Andre Biglia contre Saint Bernardin de Sienne: L'Humanisme et la fonction de l'image religieuse." In *Acta Conventus Neo-Latini Turonensis, Troisième Congrès International D'Etudes Néo-Latines, Tours,* edited by Jean-Claude Margolin, vol. 1, 417–37. Paris: J. Vrin, 1980.

———. "Saint Bernardin ressemblant: La Figure sous la portrait." In *Cateriniano-Bernardiniano,* 311–32.

Ascheri, Mario. *Siena nel Rinascimento: Instituzioni e sistema politico.* Siena: Il Leccio, 1985.

Baxandale, Susannah Foster. "Exile in Practice: The Alberti Family in and out of Florence, 1401–1428." *Renaissance Quarterly* 44, no. 1 (Winter 1991): 720–56.

Baxandall, Michael. *Painting and Experience in Fifteenth-Century Italy.* Oxford: Oxford University Press, 1972.

Becker, Marvin. "Changing Patterns of Violence and Justice in 14th and 15th-Century Florence." *Comparative Studies in Society and History* 18, no. 3 (July 1976): 281–96.

———. *Civility and Society in Western Europe, 1300–1600.* Bloomington: Indiana University Press, 1988.

Bertagna, Matino. "Frater Silvester Senensis, O.F.M.—Concionatur Saeculi XV." *AFH* 45 (1952): 152–70.

———. "Vita e apostolato senese di San Bernardino." *Studi Francescani* 60 (1963): 20–98.

Biller, Peter. "The Common Woman in the Western Church in the Thirteenth and Early Fourteenth Centuries." In *Women in the Church,* edited by W. J. Shields and Diana Wood, 127–57. Oxford: Basil Blackwell, 1990.

Bitel, Lisa M. *Isle of the Saints: Monastic Settlement and Christian Community in Early Ireland*. Ithaca, NY: Cornell University Press, 1990.

Black, Christopher F. *Italian Confraternities in the Sixteenth Century*. Cambridge: Cambridge University Press, 1989.

Black-Michaud, Jacob. *Cohesive Force: Feud in the Mediterranean and Middle East*. Oxford: Basil Blackwell, 1975.

Blanshei, Sarah Rubin. "Criminal Law and Politics in Medieval Bologna." *Criminal Justice History* 2 (1981): 1–30.

Blok, Anton. "Rams and Billy-Goats: A Key to the Mediterranean Code of Honor." *Man* 16, no. 3 (September 1981): 427–49.

Boehm, Christopher. *Blood Revenge: The Anthropology of Feuding in Montenegro and Other Tribal Societies*. Lawrence, KS: University Press of Kansas, 1984.

Bornstein, Daniel. *The Bianchi of 1399: Popular Devotion in Late Medieval Italy*. Ithaca, NY: Cornell University Press, 1993.

Bortolotti, Lando. *Siena*. Rome and Bari: Editori Laterza, 1983.

Bouwsma, William. "Anxiety and the Formation of Early Modern Culture." In *After the Reformation: Essays in Honor of J. H. Hexter*, edited by Barbara C. Malament, 215–46. Philadelphia: University of Pennsylvania Press, 1980.

Bowsky, William. *Henry VII of Italy: The Conflict of Empire and City-State, 1310–1313*. Lincoln, NE: University of Nebraska Press, 1960.

———. "The Medieval Commune and Internal Violence: Police Power and Public Safety in Siena, 1287–1355." *American Historical Review* 73, no. 1 (October 1973): 1–17.

———. *A Medieval Italian Commune: Siena Under the Nine, 1287–1355*. Berkeley and Los Angeles: University of California Press, 1981.

Brandes, Stanley. *Metaphors of Masculinity: Sex and Status in Andalusian Folklore*. Philadelphia: University of Pennsylvania Press, 1980.

Brown, Keith M. *Bloodfeud in Scotland*. Edinburgh: J. Donald, 1986.

Brown, Peter. "The Rise and Function of the Holy Man in Late Antiquity." *Journal of Roman Studies* 61 (1971): 80–101.

Brucker, Gene. *Florentine Politics and Society, 1343–1378*. Princeton: Princeton University Press, 1962.

———. *Civic Life in Renaissance Florence*. Princeton: Princeton University Press, 1977.

Burke, Peter. *The Historical Anthropology of Early Modern Italy: Essays on Perception and Communication*. Cambridge: Cambridge University Press, 1987.

Caferro, William. *Mercenary Companies and the Decline of Siena*. Baltimore and London: Johns Hopkins University Press, 1998.

Cantini, Gustavo. "I compagni missionari o socii de S.B. da Siena." *Studi Francescani* (1945): 262–77.

Cardinali, Claudia. "Il santo e la norma: Bernardino da Siena e gli statuti perugini del 1425." In *Gioco e giustizia nell'Italia di Comune*, edited by Gherardo Ortalli, 182–91. Treviso: Fondazione Benetton, and Rome: Viella, 1993.

Casagrande, Carla and Silvana Vecchio. *I peccati della lingua: Disciplina ed etica della parola nella cultura medievale.* Rome: Instituto della Enciclopedia Italiana Fondata da Giovanni Treccani, 1987.

Christian, William. *Person and God in a Spanish Valley.* New York: Seminar Press, 1972.

—. *Moving Crucifixes in Modern Spain.* Princeton: Princeton University Press, 1992.

—. "Provoked Religious Weeping in Early Modern Spain." In *Religious Organization and Religious Experience,* edited by J. Davis, 97–114. London: Academic Press, 1982.

—. "Tapping and Defining New Power: The First Month of Visions at Ezquioga, July 1931." *American Ethnologist* 14, no. 1 (February 1987): 140–66.

—. *Visionaries: The Spanish Republic and the Reign of Christ.* Berkeley and Los Angeles: University of California Press, 1996.

Cohen, Elizabeth S. "Honor and Gender in the Streets of Early Modern Rome." *Journal of Interdisciplinary History* 22, no. 4 (Spring 1992): 597–625.

Cohen, Thomas V. and Elizabeth S. Cohen. *Words and Deeds in Renaissance Rome: Trials before the Papal Magistrates.* Toronto: University of Toronto Press, 1993.

Cohn, Samuel. *Death and Property in Siena, 1205–1800.* Baltimore: Johns Hopkins University Press, 1988.

—. *Women in the Streets: Essays on Sex and Power in Renaissance Italy.* Baltimore and London: Johns Hopkins University Press, 1996.

Connerton, Paul. *How Societies Remember.* Cambridge: Cambridge University Press, 1989.

Darnton, Robert. "A Bourgeois Puts His World in Order: The City as a Text." In *The Great Cat Massacre and Other Episodes in Cultural History,* 107–143. New York: Basic Books, 1984.

Davies, R. R. "The Survival of the Bloodfeud in Medieval Wales." *History* 14, no. 182 (October 1969): 338–57.

Davis, Natalie Z. "The Sacred and the Body Social in Lyon." *Past and Present* 90 (February 1981): 40–70.

Davis, Robert C. *The War of the Fists: Popular Culture and Public Violence in Late Renaissance Venice.* Oxford and New York: Oxford University Press, 1994.

D'Avray, D. L. *The Preaching of the Friars: Sermons Diffused from Paris before 1300.* Oxford: Oxford University Press, 1985.

de Gaiffier, Boudouin. "Le Memoire d'Andre Biglia sur la predication de S. Bernardin de Sienne." *Analecta Bollandiana* 53 (1935): 308–58.

Dean, Trevor. "Marriage and Mutilation: Vendetta in Late Medieval Italy." *Past and Present* 157 (November 1997): 3–36.

Delaney, Carol. *The Seed and the Soil: Gender and Cosmology in Turkish Village Society.* Berkeley and Los Angeles: University of California Press, 1991.

Delcorno, Carlo. "L' 'ars praedicandi' di Bernardino da Siena." In *Cateriniano-Bernardiniano,* 419–49.

—. "L' 'exemplum' nella predicazione di Bernardino da Siena." In *Bernardino predicatore nella societa del suo tempo,* Centro di Studi Sulla Spiritualità del Suo Tempo, 71–107. Todi: l'Accademia Tudertina, 1976.

———. *Giordano da Pisa e l'antica predicazione volgare.* Florence: L. S. Olschki, 1975.

———. *La predicazione nell'età comunale.* Florence: Sansoni, 1974.

Denich, Bette S. "Sex and Power in the Balkans." In *Women, Culture, and Society,* edited by Michelle Zimbalist Rosaldo and Louise Lamphere, 243–62. Stanford: Stanford University Press, 1974.

Douglas, Langton. *A History of Siena.* London: J. Murray, 1902.

Du Boulay, Juliet. *Portrait of a Greek Mountain Village.* Oxford: Oxford University Press, 1974.

Dubisch, Jill. *In a Different Place: Pilgrimage, Gender, and Politics at a Greek Island Shrine.* Princeton: Princeton University Press, 1995.

Dundes, Alan and Alessandro Falassi. *La Terra in Piazza: An Interpretation of the Palio of Siena.* Berkeley and Los Angeles: University of California Press, 1975.

Elias, Norbert. *The Civilizing Process.* Translated by Edmond Jephcott. New York: Urizen Books, 1978.

Enriquez, Anna Maria. "La vendetta nella vita e nella legislazione fiorentina." *Archivio Storico Italiano* 19 (1933): 85–146 and 181–223.

Farr, James R. *Hands of Honor: Artisans and Their World in Dijon, 1550–1650.* Ithaca, NY: Cornell University Press, 1988.

Ferrers-Howell, A. G. *San Bernardino of Siena.* London: Methuen, 1913.

Fisher, Arthur. "The Franciscan Observants in Quattrocento Tuscany." Ph.D. dissertation, University of California, Berkeley, 1978.

Fontaine, Michelle Marie. "Urban Culture and the Good Bishop in Sixteenth-Century Italy." Ph.D. dissertation, University of California, Berkeley, 1992.

Frugoni, Arsenio. "La devozione dei Bianchi del 1399." In *L'attesa dell'età nuova nella spiritualità della fine del medioevo,* 232–40. Todi: l'Accademia Tudertina, 1962.

Galletti, Alfredo. *L'eloquenza dalle origini al XVI secolo.* Milan: Casa editrice dottor Francesco Vallardi, 1938.

Geertz, Clifford. "From the Native's Point of View: On the Nature of Anthropological Understanding." In *Local Knowledge: Further Essays in Interpretive Anthropology,* 55–70. New York: Basic Books, 1983.

Ghinato, Alberto. "Apostolato religioso e sociale di Giacomo della Marca in Terni." *AFH* 49 (January and April 1956): 106–142 and 352–390.

Gilmore, David D. "Honor, Honesty, and Shame: Male Status in Contemporary Andalusia." In *Honor and Shame and the Unity of the Mediterranean,* edited by David D. Gilmore, 90–103. Washington, DC: American Anthropological Association, 1987.

———. *Manhood in the Making: Cultural Concepts of Masculinity.* New Haven: Yale University Press, 1990.

Ginatempo, Maria. *Crisi di un territorio: Il popolamento della Toscana Senese alla fine del medioevo.* Florence: L. S. Olschki, 1988.

Gluckman, Max. "The Peace in the Feud." *Past and Present* 8 (November 1955): 1–14.

Greenstein, Jack M. "The Vision of Peace: Meaning and Representation in Ambrogio Lorenzetti's *Sala Della Pace* Cityscapes." *Art History* 2, no. 4 (December 1988): 492–510.

Gundersheimer, Werner L. "Renaissance Concepts of Shame and Pocaterra's 'Dialoghi Della Vergogna.'" *Renaissance Quarterly* 47, no. 1 (Spring 1984): 34–56.

Hanawalt, Barbara. *Of Good and Ill Repute: Gender and Social Control in Medieval England.* New York and Oxford: Oxford University Press, 1998.

Harding, Susan F. "Convicted by the Holy Spirit: The Rhetoric of Baptist Conversion." *American Ethnologist* 14, no. 1 (February 1987): 167–85.

Heers, Jacques. *Parties and Political Life in the Medieval West.* Translated by David Nicholas. Amsterdam: North Holland Publishing Company, 1977.

Henderson, John. "The Flagellant Movement and Flagellant Confraternities in Central Italy, 1260–1400." In *Religious Motivation: Biographical and Sociological Problems for the Church Historian.* Papers read at the Sixteenth Summer Meeting and the Seventeenth Winter Meeting of the Ecclesiastical History Society. Edited by Derek Baker, 147–60. Oxford: Published for the Ecclesiastical History Society by Basil Blackwell, 1978.

Herlihy, David. "Growing Old in the Quattrocento." In *Old Age in Preindustrial Society*, edited by Peter Stearns, 104–18. New York: Holmes & Meier, 1982.

Herzfeld, Michael. "'As in Your Own House': Hospitality, Ethnography, and the Stereotype of Mediterranean Society." In *Honor and Shame and the Unity of the Mediterranean*, edited by David D. Gilmore, 75–89. Washington, DC: American Anthropological Association, 1987.

———. *The Poetics of Manhood: Contest and Identity in a Cretan Mountain Village.* Princeton: Princeton University Press, 1985.

Hicks, David. "Sienese Society in the Renaissance." *Comparative Studies in Society and History* 2, no. 4 (1960): 412–20.

———. "The Sienese State in the Renaissance." In *From the Renaissance to the Counter-Reformation: Essays in Honor of Garrett Mattingly*, edited by C. H. Carter, 75–94. New York: Random House, 1965.

———. "Sources of Wealth in Renaissance Siena: Businessmen and Landowners." *Bulletino Senese di Storia Patria* 93 (1986): 9–42.

Hook, Judith. *Siena: A City and its History.* London: H. Hamilton, 1979.

Howard, Peter Francis. *Beyond the Written Word: Preaching and Theology in the Florence of Archbishop Antoninus, 1427–1459.* Florence: L. S. Olschki, 1995.

Hughes, Diane Owen. "Distinguishing Signs: Ear-Rings, Jews, and Franciscan Rhetoric in the Italian Renaissance." *Past and Present* 112 (August 1986): 3–59.

———. "Sumptuary Law and Social Relations in Renaissance Italy." In *Disputes and Settlements: Law and Human Relations in the West*, edited by John Bossy, 69–99. Cambridge: Cambridge University Press, 1983.

Hyde, J. K. "Contemporary Views on Faction." In *Violence and Civil Disorder in Italian Cities, 1200–1500*, edited by Lauro Martines, 273–307. Berkeley and Los Angeles: University of California Press, 1972.

Isaacs, Ann Katherine. "Popolo e monti nella Siena del primo Cinquecento." *Rivista Storica Italiana* 82, no. 1 (1970): 32–80.

————. "Magnati comune e stato a Siena nel Trecento e all'inizio del Quattrocento." In *I ceti dirigenti nella Toscana tardo comunale: atti del III Convegno, Firenze, 5–7 dicembre 1980*. Comitato di studi sulla storia dei ceti dirigenti in Toscana, 81–96. Monte Oriolo, Florence: Francesco Papafava, 1983.

Izbicki, Thomas M. "Pyres of Vanities: Mendicant Preaching on the Vanity of Women and Its Lay Audience." In *De Ore Domini: Preacher and the Word in the Middle Ages*, edited by Thomas L. Amos, Eugene A. Green, and Beverly Mayne Kienzle, 211–34. Kalamazoo, MI: Medieval Institute Publications, 1989.

James, Mervyn. "Ritual Drama and Social Body in the Late Medieval English Town." *Past and Present* 98 (February 1983): 3–29.

Jamous, Raymond. "From the Death of Men to the Peace of God: Violence and Peacemaking in the Rif." In *Honor and Grace in Anthropology*, edited by J. G. Peristiany and Julian Pitt-Rivers, 167–91. Cambridge and New York: Cambridge University Press, 1992.

Jorgensen, Kenneth. " 'Love Conquers All': The Conversion, Asceticism, and Altruism of St. Catherine of Genoa." In *Renaissance Society and Culture: Essays in Honor of Eugene F. Rice, Jr.*, edited by John Monfasani and Ronald G. Musto, 87–106. New York: Italica Press, 1991.

Kent, Dale. *The Rise of the Medici: Faction in Florence, 1426–1434*. Oxford: Oxford University Press, 1978.

———— and F. W. Kent. *Neighbors and Neighborhood: The District of the Red Lion in the Fifteenth Century*. New York: J. J. Augustin, 1982.

Keyes, Charles F. "Charisma: From Social Life to Sacred Biography." *Journal of the American Academy of Religious Studies* 48 (1982): 1–22.

Kieckhefer, Richard. "Holiness and the Culture of Devotion: Remarks on Some Late Medieval Male Saints." In *Images of Sainthood in Medieval Europe*, edited by Renate Blumenfeld-Kosinski and Timea Szell, 288–305. Ithaca, NY: Cornell University Press, 1991.

————. *Unquiet Souls: Fourteenth-Century Saints and Their Religious Milieu*. Chicago: University of Chicago Press, 1984.

Klein, Benjamin. " 'Between the Bums and the Bellies of the Multitude': Civic Pageantry and the Problem of the Audience in Late Stuart London." *London Journal* 17, no. 1 (1992): 18–26.

Kleinberg, Aviad. *Prophets in Their Own Country: Living Saints and the Making of Sainthood in the Later Middle Ages*. Chicago: University of Chicago Press, 1992.

Koch, Klaus-Friedrick, Soraya Altorki, Andrew Arno, and Letitia Hickson. "Ritual Reconciliation and the Obviation of Grievances: A Comparative Study in the Ethnography of Law." *Ethnology* 16, no. 3 (July 1977): 269–83.

Koziol, Geoffrey. "Monks, Feuds, and the Making of Peace in Eleventh-Century Flanders." In *The Peace of God: Social Violence and Religious Response in France around the Year 1000*, edited by Thomas Head and Richard Landes, 239–58. Ithaca, NY: Cornell University Press, 1992.

Kuehn, Thomas. *Law, Family, and Women: Towards a Legal Anthropology of Renaissance Italy*. Chicago: University of Chicago Press, 1991.

Kuiper, Yme B. "The Concept of Person in American Anthropology: The Cultural Perspective of Clifford Geertz." In *Concepts of Person in Religion and Thought*, edited by Hans G. Kippenberg, Yme B. Kuiper, and Andy F. Sanders, 35–49. Berlin and New York: Mouton de Gruyter, 1990.

Lansing, Carol. *The Florentine Magnates: Lineage and Faction in a Medieval Commune*. Princeton: Princeton University Press, 1994.

———. "Gender and Civil Authority: Sexual Control in a Medieval Italian Town." *Journal of Social History* 31, no. 1 (Fall 1997): 33–59.

Larner, John. *Culture and Society in Italy, 1290–1420*. New York: Scribner, 1971.

———. "Order and Disorder in the Romagna, 1450–1500." In *Violence and Disorder in Italian Cities*, edited by Lauro Martines, 38–71. Berkeley and Los Angeles: University of California Press, 1972.

Le Goff, Jacques. "The Symbolic Ritual of Vassalage." In *Time, Work, and Culture in the Middle Ages*, translated by Arthur Goldhammer, 237–87. Chicago: University of Chicago Press, 1980.

Lesnick, Daniel. "Dominican Preaching and the Creation of Capitalist Ideology in Late Medieval Florence." *Memorie Domenicane* 8–9 (1977–8): 221–37.

———. "Insults and Threats in Medieval Todi." *Journal of Medieval History* 17 (1991), 71–89.

———. *Preaching in Medieval Florence: The Social World of Franciscan and Dominican Spirituality*. Athens, GA: University of Georgia Press, 1989.

Liberati, A. "Le vicende sulla canonizzazione di S. Bernardino." *Bullettino di Studi Bernardiniani* 2 (1936): 91–108.

———. "Le prime manifestazioni di devozione dopo la morte di S. Bernardino." *Bullettino Sanese di Storia Patria* 2 (1936): 149–61.

Lindisfarne, Nancy. "Variant Masculinities, Variant Virginities: Rethinking Honour and Shame." In *Dislocating Masculinity: Comparative Ethnographies*, edited by Andrea Cornwall and Nancy Lindisfarne, 82–96. London and New York: Routledge, 1994.

Longpré, Ephrem. "S. Bernardin de Sienne e le nom de Jesus." *AFH* 29 (1936): 142–68, 443–77 and 30 (1937): 170–92.

Lovati, Guido. "La predicazione del B. Alberto da Sarteano a Brescia (1444–1449)." *Miscellanea Francescana* 37 (1937): 55–76.

Luria, Keith. "Rituals of Conversion: Catholics and Protestants in Seventeenth-Century Poitou." In *Culture and Identity in Early Modern Europe, 1500–1800: Essays in Honor of Natalie Davis*, edited by Barbara B. Diefendorf and Carla Hesse: 65–81. Ann Arbor, MI: University of Michigan Press, 1993.

Magli, Ida. "L'Etica familiare e la donna in S. Bernardino." In *Atti del convegno storico Bernardiniano in occasione del sesto centenario della nascita di S. Bernardino da Siena*, 111–25. L'Aquila: Comitato aquilano del sesto centenario della nascita di S. Bernardino da Siena, 1980.

————. *Gli uomini della penitenza: Lineamenti antropologici del medioevo Italiano*. Milan: Garzanti, 1977.

Maire-Vigeur, Jean-Claude. "Bernardino e la vie citadine." In *Bernardino Predicatore nella Società del Suo Tempo*, Centro di Studi Sulla Spiritualità del Suo Tempo, 251–82. Todi: L'Accademia Tudertina, 1976.

Marrara, Danilo. "I magnati e il governo del 1274 alla fine del XIV secolo." In *Studi per Enrico Fiumi*, 239–76. Pisa: Pacini, 1979.

Mayr-Harting, H. "Functions of a Twelfth-Century Recluse." *History* 60, no. 200 (October 1975): 337–52.

McAodha, Loman. "The Holy Name of Jesus in the Preaching of Bernardino of Siena." *Franciscan Studies* 29 (1969): 37–65.

McClure, George W. "Healing Eloquence: Petrarch, Salutati, and the Physicians." *Journal of Medieval and Renaissance Studies* 15, no. 12 (Fall 1985): 317–46.

————. *Sorrow and Consolation in Italian Humanism*. Princeton: Princeton University Press, 1991.

McCreery, John. "Potential and Meaning in Therapeutic Ritual." *Culture, Medicine, and Psychiatry* 3, no. 1 (March 1979): 53–72.

McGinness, Frederick. *Right Thinking and Sacred Oratory in Counter-Reformation Rome*. Princeton: Princeton University Press, 1995.

McGuire, Meredith B. *Pentecostal Catholics: Power, Charisma and Order in a Religious Movement*. Philadelphia: Temple University Press, 1982.

McLaughlin, Eleanor Commo. "Equality of Souls, Inequality of Sexes: Woman in Medieval Theology." In *Religion and Sexism: Images of Woman in the Jewish and Christian Traditions*, edited by Rosemary Radford Ruether, 213–66. New York: Simon and Schuster, 1974.

Melli, Grazia Fioravanti. "Bernardino da Siena: I quaresimali Fiorentini del 1424–5." *Rassegna della Letteratura Italiana* 77, no. 3 (September–December 1973): 565–84.

Miller, William Ian. *Bloodtaking and Peacemaking: Feud, Society and Law in Saga Iceland*. Chicago: University of Chicago Press, 1990.

————. "Choosing the Avenger: Some Aspects of the Bloodfeud in Medieval Iceland." *Law and History Review* 1, no. 2 (Fall 1983): 159–204.

Misciatelli, Piero. "Cassoni Senesi." *La Diana* 4, no. 2 (1929): 117–26.

Moorman, John. *A History of the Franciscan Order from Its Origins to the Year 1517*. Oxford: Clarendon Press, 1968.

Morisi, Anna. "Andrea Biglia e Bernardino da Siena." In *Bernardino predicatore nella societa del suo tempo*, Centro di Studi Sulla Spiritualità del Suo Tempo, 337–59. Todi: l'Accademia Tudertina, 1976.

Mormando, Franco. "Bernardino of Siena: 'Great Defender' or 'Merciless Betrayer' of Women?" *Italica* 75, no. 1 (Spring 1998): 22–40.

————. *The Preacher's Demons: Bernardino of Siena and the Social Underworld of Renaissance Italy*. Chicago: University of Chicago Press, 1999.

————. "Signs of the Apocalypse in Late Medieval Italy: The Popular Preaching of Bernardino of Siena." In *Medievalia et Humanistica: Studies in Medieval and Renais-*

sance Culture 23, edited by Paul M. Clogan, 95–122. Lanham, MD: Rowman and Littlefield, 1997.

———. "The Vernacular Sermons of San Bernardino da Siena: A Literary Analysis." Ph.D. dissertation, Harvard University, 1983.

Muir, Edward. "The Cannibals of Renaissance Italy." *Syracuse Scholar* 5, no. 2 (Fall 1984): 5–14.

———. *Civic Ritual in Renaissance Venice.* Princeton: Princeton University Press, 1981.

———. *Mad Blood Stirring: Faction and Vendetta in the Friuli.* Baltimore: Johns Hopkins University Press, 1993.

———. *Ritual in Early Modern Europe.* Cambridge and New York: Cambridge University Press, 1997.

——— and Ronald F. E. Weissman. "Social and Symbolic Places in Renaissance Venice and Florence." In *The Power of Place: Bringing Together Geographical and Sociological Imaginations,* edited by John A. Agnew and James S. Duncan, 81–103. Boston: Unwin Hyman, 1989.

Mulchahey, Marian. "Dominican Education and the Dominican Ministry in the Thirteenth and Fourteenth Centuries: Fra Jacopo Passavanti and the Florentine Convent of Santa Maria Novella." Ph.D. dissertation, University of Toronto, 1989.

Mullett, Michael. *Popular Culture and Popular Protest in Late Medieval and Early Modern Europe.* London: Croom Helm, 1987.

Myerhoff, Barbara. "A Death in Due Time: Construction of Self and Culture in Ritual Drama." In *Rite, Drama, Festival, Spectacle: Rehearsals Towards a Theory of Cultural Performance,* edited by John J. MacAloon, 149–78. Philadelphia: Institute for the Study of Human Issues, 1984.

Niccoli, Ottavia. *Prophecy and People in Renaissance Italy.* Princeton: Princeton University Press, 1990.

Nicholas, David. "Crime and Punishment in Fourteenth-Century Ghent." *Revue belge de philologie et d'histoire* 48, nos. 2 and 4 (1970): 298–334 and 1141–76.

———. *Medieval Flanders.* New York: Longman, 1992.

Nobile, Bernardo. "Romiti e vita religiosa nella cronachistica italiana fra '400 e '500." In *Christianesimo nella storia: ricerche storiche esegetiche* 5: 303–40. Bologna, 1985.

O'Malley, John. *Praise and Blame in Renaissance Rome: Rhetoric, Doctrine, and Reform in the Sacred College.* Durham, NC: Duke University Press, 1979.

Ong, Walter. *The Presence of the Word: Some Prolegomena for Cultural and Religious History.* New Haven: Yale University Press, 1967.

Origo, Iris. *The Merchant of Prato.* London: J. Cape, 1957.

———. *The World of San Bernardino.* New York: Harcourt, Brace and World, 1962.

Orsi, Robert Anthony. *The Madonna of 115th Street: Faith and Community in Italian Harlem, 1880–1950.* New Haven: Yale University Press, 1985.

Pacetti, Dionisio. "La predicazione di S. Bernardino a Perugia e ad Assisi nel 1425," *Collectanea Franciscana* 9–10 (1939–40), 5–28, 494–520, 161–88.

————. "La predicazione di S. Bernardino in Toscana." *AFH* 33 (1940): 268–318 and 34 (1941): 261–83.

————. "S. Bernardino a Belluno nel 1423." *Bulletino di Studi Bernardiniani* 18 (1940): 142–53.

Pacini, Gian P. "Predicazione di minori osservanti a Vicenza: fondazioni, confraternite, devozioni." In *Predicazione Francescana e Società Veneto nel Quattrocento: Committenza, Ascolto, Ricezione* (Atti del II Convegno Internazionale di studi francescani), Padoca, 26–28 Marzo, 1987, 253–64. (2nd edition, Padua: Centro studi antoniani, 1995).

Papi, Anna Benvenuti. *"In Castro Poenitentiae": Santità e società femminile nell'Italia medievale*. Rome: Herder, 1990.

Partridge, Loren and Randolph Starn. *Arts of Power: Three Halls of State in Italy, 1300–1600*. Berkeley and Los Angeles: University of California Press, 1992.

Paton, Bernadette. *Preaching Friars and the Civic Ethos: Siena, 1380–1480*. London: University of London, 1992.

————. "'To the Fire! Let Us Burn a Little Incense to God': Bernardino, Preaching Friars, and Maleficio in Late Medieval Siena." In *No Gods Except Me: Orthodoxy and Religious Practice in Europe*, edited by Charles Zika, 7–36. Melbourne: History Department, University of Melbourne, 1991.

————. "'Una Città Faticosa': Dominican Preaching and the Defense of the Republic in Late Medieval Siena." In *City and Countryside in Late Medieval and Renaissance Italy: Essays Presented to Philip Jones*, edited by Trevor Dean and Chris Wickham, 109–23. London and Ronceverte, WV: Hambledon Press, 1990.

Peristiany, J. G., and Julian Pitt-Rivers, ed. *Honor and Grace in Anthropology*. Cambridge: Cambridge University Press, 1992.

————. *Honour and Shame: The Values of Mediterranean Society*. London: Weidenfeld and Nicholson, 1966.

Peters, Edward. "Pars, Parte: Dante and an Urban Contribution to Political Thought." In *The Medieval City*, edited by Harry A. Miskimin, David Herlihy, and A. L. Udovitch, 113–40. New Haven and London: Yale University Press, 1977.

Piana, Celestino. "Un processo svolto a Milano nel 1441 a favore del mag. Amadeo de Landis e contro frate Bernardino da Siena." In *Cateriniano-Bernardiniano*, 753–92.

Pitkin, Hanna Fenichel. *Fortune Is a Woman: Gender and Politics in the Thought of Niccolò Machiavelli*. Berkeley and Los Angeles: University of California Press, 1984.

Pitt-Rivers, Julian. *The Fate of Shechem*. Cambridge: Cambridge University Press, 1977.

Polecritti, Cynthia. "Watchful Eyes: Gossip, Retribution, and the Devil in Filippo degli Agazzari's *Moral Tales*." In *Self and Society in Renaissance Europe*, edited by William Connell. Berkeley and Los Angeles: University of California Press, forthcoming.

Powell, James M. *Albertanus of Brescia: The Pursuit of Happiness in the Early Thirteenth Century*. Philadelphia: University of Pennsylvania Press, 1992.

Raggio, Osvaldo. *Faide e parentele: Lo stato genovese visto dalla Fontanabuona.* Turin: Einaudi, 1990.

Rocke, Michael. *Forbidden Friendships: Homosexuality and Male Culture in Renaissance Florence.* New York and Oxford: Oxford University Press, 1996.

Roper, Lyndal. "Blood and Codpieces: Masculinity in the Early Modern German Town." In *Oedipus and the Devil: Witchcraft, Sexuality, and Religion in Early Modern Europe,* 107–24. London and New York: Routledge, 1994.

Rubinstein, Nicolai. "Political Ideas in Sienese Art: The Frescoes by Ambrogio Lorenzetti and Taddeo di Bartolo in the Palazzo Pubblico." *Journal of the Warburg and Courtauld Institutes* 21, no. 1–2 (1958): 179–207.

Ruggiero, Guido. *The Boundaries of Eros: Sex Crime and Sexuality in Renaissance Venice.* New York: Oxford University Press, 1985.

———. *Violence in Early Renaissance Venice.* New Brunswick, NJ: Rutgers University Press, 1980.

Rusconi, Roberto. *L'attesa della fine: Crisi della società, profezia ed Apocalisse in Italia al tempo del grande scisma d'Occidente, 1378–1417.* Rome: Istituto Storico Italiano per il Medio Evo, 1979.

———. "Fonti e documenti su Manfred da Vercelli, O.P., e il suo movimento penitenziale." *Archivum Fratrum Praedicatorum* 47 (1977): 51–107.

———. *Predicazione e vita religiosa nella società Italiana.* Turin: Loescher, 1981.

———. "St. Bernardino, the Wife, and Possessions." In *Women and Religion in Medieval and Renaissance Italy,* edited by Daniel Bornstein and Roberto Rusconi, 182–96. Chicago: University of Chicago Press, 1996.

Sassetti, Angelo Sacchetti. "Giacomo della Marca paciere a Rieti." *AFH* 50 (January 1957): 75–82.

Schevill, Ferdinand. *Siena: The Story of a Mediaeval Commune.* New York: C. Scribner, 1909.

Schmitt, Jean-Claude. *La Raison des gestes dans l'occident médiéval.* Paris: Gallimard, 1990.

Schneider, Jane. "Of Vigilance and Virgins." *Ethnology* 10, no. 1 (January 1971): 1–24.

Scott, Karen. "Not Only With Words But With Deeds: The Role of Speech in Catherine of Siena's Understanding of Her Mission." Ph.D. dissertation, University of California, Berkeley, 1989.

Scribner, Robert W. *Popular Culture and Popular Movements in Reformation Germany.* London: Hambledon Press, 1987.

Selwyn, Jennifer. "Planting Many Virtues There: Jesuit Popular Missions in the Viceroyalty of Naples, 1550–1700." Ph.D. dissertation, University of California, Davis, 1997.

Sensi, Mario. "Predicazione itinerante a Foligno nel secolo XV." *Picenum Seraphicum* 10 (1973): 139–95.

Silverman, Sydel. *Three Bells of Civilization: The Life of an Italian Hilltown.* New York and London: Columbia University Press, 1975.

Simeti, Mary Taylor. *On Persephone's Island: A Sicilian Journal.* New York: Knopf, 1986.

Skinner, Quentin. "Ambrogio Lorenzetti: The Artist as Political Philosopher." *Proceedings of the British Academy* 72 (1986): 1–56.

Slater, Candace. *City Steeple, City Streets: Saints' Tales from Granada and a Changing Spain.* Berkeley and Los Angeles: University of California Press, 1990.

Smoller, Laura A. "Miracle, Memory, and Meaning in the Canonization of Vincent Ferrer, 1453–1454." *Speculum* 73, no. 2 (April 1998): 429–54.

Spencer, H. Leith. *English Preaching in the Late Middle Ages.* Oxford: Oxford University Press, 1993.

Starn, Randolph. *Contrary Commonwealth: The Theme of Exile in Medieval and Renaissance Italy.* Berkeley and Los Angeles: University of California Press, 1982.

Stirling, Paul. *Turkish Village.* New York: Wiley, 1965.

Strocchia, Sharon. *Death and Ritual in Renaissance Florence.* Baltimore: Johns Hopkins University Press, 1992.

———. "Gender and the Rites of Honor in Italian Renaissance Cities." In *Gender and Society in Renaissance Italy*, edited by Judith C. Brown and Robert C. Davis, 39–60. London and New York: Addison Wesley Longman Limited, 1998.

Sutherland, Jon N. "The Idea of Revenge in Lombard Society in the Eighth and Tenth Centuries: The Cases of Paul the Deacon and Liuprand of Cremona." *Speculum* 50, no. 3 (July 1975): 391–410.

Swartz, Marc J. *The Way the World Is: Cultural Processes and Social Relations among the Mombasa Swahili.* Berkeley and Los Angeles: University of California Press, 1991.

Taylor, Larissa. *Soldiers of Christ: Preaching in Late Medieval and Reformation France.* New York and Oxford: Oxford University Press, 1992.

Terzani, T. "Siena della morte di Gian Galeazzo Visconti alla morte di Ladislao d'Angiò Durazzo." *Bullettino sanese di storia patria* 66 (1959): 3–84.

Thompson, Augustine. *Revival Preachers and Politics in Thirteenth-Century Italy: The Great Devotion of 1233.* Oxford: Oxford University Press, 1992.

Torre, Angelo. "Feuding, Faction, and Parties: The Redefinition of Politics in the Imperial Fiefs of Langhe in the Seventeenth and Eighteenth Centuries." In *History from Crime: Selections from Quaderni Storici*, edited by Edward Muir and Guido Ruggiero, 135–69. Baltimore: Johns Hopkins University Press, 1994.

Trexler, Richard. "Correre la Terra: Collective Insults in the Late Middle Ages." *Mélange de L'École Francaise de Rome, Moyen Age / Temps Modernes* 96, no. 2 (1984): 845–902.

———. "The Florentine Religious Experience: The Sacred Image." *Studies in the Renaissance* 19 (1972): 7–41.

———. *Public Life in Renaissance Florence.* New York: Academic Press, 1980.

———. "A Widow's Asylum of the Renaissance: The Orbatello of Florence." In *Old Age in Preindustrial Society*, edited by Peter Stearns, 119–49. New York: Holmes & Meier, 1982.

Tubach, Frederic S. *Index Exemplorum: A Handbook of Medieval Religious Tales.* Helsinki: Suomalainen Tiedeakatemia (Academia Scientiarum Fennica), 1969.

Turner, Victor. *The Ritual Process: Structure and Anti-Structure.* Chicago: Aldine Publishing Co., 1969.

———— and Edith Turner. *Image and Pilgrimage in Christian Culture: Anthropological Perspectives.* New York: Columbia University Press, 1978.

Verdon, Timothy and John Henderson, eds. *Christianity and the Renaissance: Image and Religious Imagination in the Quattrocento.* Syracuse, NY: Syracuse University Press, 1990.

Visani, Oriana. "Pubblico e temi del quaresimale padovano del 1455 di Roberto Caracciolo da Lecce." *Giornale Storico della Letteratura Italiana* 157 (1980): 541–56.

————. "Roberto Caracciolo, un imitatore de Bernardino da Siena." In *Caterini-ano-Bernardiniano,* 845–861.

Wainwright, Valerie. "Conflict and Popular Government in Fourteenth-Century Siena: Il Monte dei Dodici, 1355–1368." In *I ceti dirigenti nella Toscana tardo comunale: atti de III convegno, Firenze, 5–7 December, 1980.* Comitato di studi sulla storia dei ceti dirigenti in Toscana, 57–80. Monte Oriolo, Florence: Francesco Papafava, 1983.

————. "The Testing of a Popular Sienese Regime: The Riformatori and the Insurrections of 1371." In *I Tatti Studies: Essays in the Renaissance,* vol. 2, 107–70. Villa I Tatti: The Harvard University Center for Italian Renaissance Studies, 1987.

Waley, Daniel. "A Blood-Feud with a Happy Ending: Siena, 1285–1304." In *City and Countryside in Late Medieval and Renaissance Italy: Essays Presented to Philip Jones,* edited by Trevor Dean and Chris Wickham, 45–53. London and Ronceverte, WV: Hambledon Press, 1990.

————. *Siena and the Sienese in the Thirteenth Century.* Cambridge: Cambridge University Press, 1991.

Wallace-Hadrill, J. M. "The Blood-Feud of the Franks." In *The Long-Haired Kings, and Other Studies in Frankish History,* 121–47. New York: Barnes and Noble, 1962.

Waller, Altina L. *Feud: Hatfields, McCoys, and Social Change in Appalachia, 1860–1900.* Chapel Hill: University of North Carolina Press, 1988.

Webb, Diana. "Eloquence and Education: A Humanist Approach to Hagiography." *Journal of Ecclesiastical History* 31, no. 1 (January 1980): 19–39.

————. *Patrons and Defenders: The Saints in the Italian City States.* London and New York: Tauris Academic Studies, 1996.

————. "Penitence and Peacemaking in City and Contado: The Bianchi of 1399." In *Studies in Church History: The Church in Town and Countryside.* Papers read at the Seventeenth Summer Meeting and the Eighteenth Winter Meeting of the Ecclesiastical History Society, edited by Derek Baker, 243–56. Oxford: Published for the Ecclesiastical History Society by Basil Blackwell, 1979.

Weissman, Ronald. "The Importance of Being Ambiguous: Social Relations, Individualism, and Identity in the Renaissance." In *Urban Life in the Renaissance,* edited by Susan Zimmerman and Ronald F. E. Weissman, 269–80. Newark, NJ: Associated University Press, 1988.

Whitaker, Ian. " 'A Sack for Carrying Things': The Traditional Role of Women in Northern Albanian Society." *Anthropological Quarterly* 54, no. 3 (July 1981): 146–56.

White, Hayden. "The Value of Narrativity in the Representation of Reality." In *On Narrative*, edited by W. J. T. Mitchell, 1–23. Chicago: University of Chicago Press, 1981.

White, Stephen. "Feuding and Peacemaking in the Touraine Around the Year 1100." *Traditio* 42 (1986): 195–263.

Wikan, Unni. "Shame and Honor: A Contestable Pair." *Man* 19, no. 4 (December 1984): 632–52.

Wilson, Stephen. *Feuding, Conflict, and Banditry in Nineteenth-Century Corsica.* Cambridge and New York: Cambridge University Press, 1988.

Wormald, Jenny. "Bloodfeud, Kindred, and Government in Early Modern Scotland." *Past and Present* 87 (May 1980): 54–97.

Zafarana, Zelina. "Bernardino nella Storia della Predicazione." In *Bernardino predicatore nella società del suo tempo*: 9–12 ottobre 1975. Todi: l'Accademia Tudertina, 1976.

Zanelli, Agostino. "Predicatori a Brescia nel Quattrocento." *Archivio Storico Lombardo* 15 (1901): 83–144.

Zika, Charles. "Hosts, Processions, and Pilgrimages: Controlling the Sacred in Fifteenth-Century Germany." *Past and Present* 118 (February 1988): 25–64.

Index